The *Callaloo* African Diaspora Series focuses on literary and cultural productions in the contexts of the history and cultural politics of peoples of African descent in the Americas, the Caribbean, and Europe. Like the quarterly journal *Callaloo*, the *Callaloo* African Diaspora Series is a forum for artists and intellectuals producing challenging and seminal books that help illuminate the African Diaspora as a multidimensional site of evolving complexity, a location speaking, in part, through its literary and cultural productions that are informed by a number of indigenous traditions, which in turn inform and shape cultural productions across the globe.

# black soundscapes white st

# black soundscapes white stages

The Meaning of
Francophone Sound
in the Black Atlantic

**EDWIN C. HILL JR.**

The Johns Hopkins University Press
*Baltimore*

The Johns Hopkins University Press
2715 North Charles Street
Baltimore, Maryland 21218-4363
www.press.jhu.edu

Hill, Edwin C., 1971–
Black soundscapes white stages : the meaning of Francophone sound in the
black Atlantic / Edwin C. Hill Jr.
pages cm. — (The Callaloo African Diaspora Series)
Includes bibliographical references and index.
ISBN 978-1-4214-1059-3 (hardcover : acid-free paper) —
ISBN 978-1-4214-1060-9 (electronic) — ISBN 1-4214-1059-1
(hardcover : acid-free paper) — ISBN 1-4214-1060-5 (electronic)
1. West Indian literature (French)—History and criticism.   2. Sound
(Philosophy)   3. African diaspora in literature.   4. Blacks—West
Indies, French—Music—History.   5. Beguines (Music)—West Indies,
French—History.   6. Negritude (Literary movement)   7. Soundscapes
(Music)—West Indies, French.   8. Poetics—Language.   9. West Indies,
French—Colonization.   I. Title.
PQ3940.5.H55 2013
840.9'9729—dc23      2012048652

A catalog record for this book is available from the British Library.

Photos from *Princesse Tam-Tam* are courtesy Kino Video.
*The Blue Lotus* image courtesy Moulinsart.

*Special discounts are available for bulk purchases of this book.*
*For more information, please contact Special Sales at 410-516-6936 or*
*specialsales@press.jhu.edu.*

The Johns Hopkins University Press uses environmentally friendly book
materials, including recycled text paper that is composed of at least 30
percent post-consumer waste, whenever possible.

*l'oreille collée au sol, j'entendis*
*passer Demain*

Aimé Césaire

# Contents

*Acknowledgments*   ix

**introduction**
*Le Tumulte Noir* (Part 1)
French Imperial Soundscapes and the New World   1

**1**
"Adieu Madras, Adieu Foulard"
The *Doudou*'s Colonial Complaint   20

**2**
"To Begin the Biguine"
Re-membering Antillean Musical Time   47

**3**
La Baker
*Princesse Tam Tam* and the *Doudou*'s
Signature Dilemma   74

**4**
Negritude Drum Circles
The *Tam-Tam* and the Beat   97

**5**
Le Poste Colonial
Short-Wave Colonial Radio and Negritude's
Poetic Technologies   123

**conclusion**
Notes from the Sound Field   146

*Notes*   155
*Bibliography*   161
*Index*   171

# Acknowledgments

I have had the privilege of watching my parents pursue degrees and advanced studies in my adolescent and adult life. Their perseverance and curiosity have been a constant source of inspiration, their encouragement and support have made all I do possible, and their love has made it all worthwhile. I would also like to thank my professors and fellow graduate student colleagues at UCLA in the departments of French and Francophone Studies, Comparative Literature, and Musicology for the years of lively discussions and insightful feedback I've received from them since the beginning of this project. I especially thank Françoise Lionnet: I could not have asked for a more amazing academic advisor, professional role model, and intellectual mentor.

I also want to especially thank colleagues and friends Christopher Shaw, Charleton Payne, Loren Kajikawa, David Fieni, Erin von Hofe, Nicholas Kramer, Seth Jameson, Zara Bennett, Dominic Thomas, Robert Walser, Susan McClary, Natania Meeker, Peggy Kamuf, David Roman, John Rowe, and many others.

Special thanks to Jessica Ng for love and support!

A research grant from the Center for Modern Studies at UCLA and the pensionnaire étranger program at the Ecole Normale Supérieure allowed me to conduct research at the Bibliothèque nationale de France and to occasionally audit classes at the Ecole des Hautes Etudes en Sciences Sociales. A Hamel travel grant allowed me to spend time in Guadeloupe. The Roy and Dorothy John Doctoral Fellowship in International Studies at UCLA provided me funding while completing the dissertation.

I thank Dominique Tauliaut and the students and teachers in his modern *ka* group for welcoming me into their performing ensemble during my stay in Paris. Dominique, a percussionist and unbelievable *gwo ka* soloist who performs professionally with the group, Balkouta, exudes a passion for music and for Antillean culture that is truly inspirational. I thank him and the renowned percussionist and dancer Guem for group and private lessons in Paris. I am deeply grateful for the hospitality of the Dahomés and especially of Annick and Staci Tauliaut in Point-à-Pitre. Without their generosity and kindness and Annick's naturally proud use of Creole at home with her daughter, Staci, my stay in Guadeloupe would not have been possible.

# black soundscapes white stages

# introduction

*Le Tumulte Noir* (Part 1)

French Imperial Soundscapes and the New World

From cabaret stages and colonial expositions to negritude screams and dou-douist polemics the black African diaspora literally cries out. The walls that fix identity, whether conceptual or architectural, are not soundproof; rather, they are shot through with proximities of sonic presence that interrogate faith in structural integrity. The *tumulte noir*—that joyfully raucous sound of black vernacular cultural practices in Jazz Age France and beyond—is, simply put, the sound of black people on the move. The *Trésor de la Langue Française infor-matisé* defines *tumulte* as a "grand mouvement de foule accompagné de désor-dre et souvent de bruit" [great movement of crowds accompanied by disorder and often by noise]. "A list of possible translations of the word *tumulte* includes: uproar, commotion, tumult, turmoil, hubbub, storm, hullabaloo, turbulence, frenzy, sensation, rage, brouhaha, and craze" (Dalton and Gates 903). This noisy movement comes from groups, crowds, not an individual. As the *Oxford English Dictionary* defines the word, it represents the sound of the "multitude, usually with confused speech or uproar; public disturbance; disorderly or riot-ous proceeding" and, by extension, "a riot, an insurrection." It raucously signals motion and commotion, rattling the social machine with an unexpected jolt of perturbation. The *tumulte noir* overwhelms; its turbulent storm of sound threat-ens to drown out its hearing subjects and to carry them away...

In the years between the two world wars the term evokes a combustible com-bination of negrophobia and negrophilia. A sublime wave of colonial mythology flashes through the mind of the French spectator at the sight and sound of black Atlantic performance in France.

> We don't understand their language, we can't find a way to tie the scenes together, but everything we've ever read flashes across our enchanted minds: adventure nov-els, glimpses of enormous steamboats swallowing up clusters of Negroes who carry rich burdens, a caterwauling woman in an unknown port, ... stories of missionaries

and travelers, Stanley, the Tharaud brothers, Batouala, sacred dances, the Sudan, . . .
plantation landscapes, the melancholy songs of Creole nurses, the Negro soul with
its animal energy, its childish joys, the sad bygone time of slavery, *we had all that* listening to the singer with the jungle voice, admiring Louis Douglas's hectic skill, the
frenetic virtuosity of that dancer with rubber legs, and the pretty coffee-colored
ragamuffin who is the star of the troupe, Josephine Baker. (A review of *La Revue
nègre*, qtd in Phyllis Rose, *Jazz Cleopatra: Josephine Baker in Her Time*; my emphasis)

Adventure and travel narratives dating from before the Enlightenment, philosophical musings on the origins of language and music, romantic landscape
paintings, contemporary popular novels of the early twentieth century—the
sublime black tumult that disrupts and carries away the enraptured French
critic above had been built up over hundreds of years. Only deep mythologies
of sound in text could explain why, on hearing and seeing the *Revue nègre* for
the first time in the 1920s, Parisian reviewers "had all that" striking them with
an uncanny familiarity. What are these familiar flash-images? Pulled from "the
sad bygone time," these are not the reviewer's own memories and experiences
of things; rather they are memories of previous inscriptions of colonial siting,
fact and fantasy, realities and fictions, authored by, yet signaling from beyond,
the French imperial imagination. The subject's experience with the *tumulte noir*
highlights the way the spread of black Atlantic popular musical culture and life
to Paris was heard through the framework of imperial fantasies about a history
of discovery and possession in the New World. The *tumulte noir* submerges the
hearing-man in sound, disorienting his sense of place yet situating him within
an imperial history of mapping and valuing black sound begun long ago.

## IMPERIAL EARS AND THE HEARING-MAN

The screaming rhythms of black poetry and performance in France during the
1920s and 1930s resonate with the history of a much louder and longer cry over
the possession and dispossession of black bodies and New World spaces. Just
as "early attempts to write the New World into existence," as Michael Dash contends, "must be central to any analysis of the literatures of the Americas" (23),
early travel narratives constitute primordial texts for the deep mythologies of
New World sound and experience described in the theater critic's review of
performance culture from the Americas. Poets and performers navigate these
mythologies of sound and text, mythologies whose imperial depth was dug in
large part by French ethnographers and colonial missionaries dating back to
slavery and Enlightenment. Writers like Jean Baptiste Du Tertre in the seven-

teenth century, Jean-Baptiste Labat and Jean Baptiste Thibault de Chanvalon in the eighteenth, Médéric Louis Élie Moreau de Saint-Méry and Lafcadio Hearn in the nineteenth and early twentieth centuries—all explore and site the value and meaning of New World sound while they map it into the French imperial and national imagination.

Mary Louise Pratt's groundbreaking study *Imperial Eyes: Travel Writing and Transculturation* shows how early travel texts produce a Eurocentric planetary consciousness that domesticates the site of the other and figures it into economies of imperial consumption. The Enlightened project of modernity involving the cataloguing and classifying of "the visible" world was dominated by what Pratt famously calls "the seeing-man," "an admittedly unfriendly label for the white male subject of European landscape discourse—he whose imperial eyes passively look out and possess" (Pratt 9). Pratt demonstrates the ways travel texts and ethnographies do more than simply describe the world; they inscribe and prescribe its meanings. The "imperial gaze" sees the spaces of others and otherness within Eurocentric systems of knowledge, value, and beauty. The imperial inscription of the world makes possible the efficient dispossession of New World territories for capitalist consumption.

But what of the *imperial ear* and the "hearing-man" of early travel texts? How do representations of sound inscribed in travel chronicles, ethnographies, and adventure narratives produce an imperial order for the valuable and meaning-ful mapping of the New World? How do written soundscapes lay the foundation for mythologies of black sound solidified in the twentieth century? Based on epistemologies and methodologies that rely on sight, natural histories and bo-tanical descriptions of New World space tend to "overlook"—or distance them-selves from—the sonic dimensions of the environment. But the marginalization of sound as a function of both the overt scientific and "covert" imperial objectives of these texts does not mean that soundscapes were absent or irrelevant.

While "natural history conceived of the world as a chaos out of which the scientist *produced* an order" (Pratt 30, her emphasis), the soundscape repre-sents all that the imperial gaze was ill-equipped or unprepared to orderly reg-ister. Pratt's study points toward (and stops at) the blind visions of sound that emerge where the imperial gaze comes up against its own epistemological lim-its and ethical contradictions. Pratt explains: "when it comes to entering the contact zone and confronting the object of extermination [or slave labor], the visual code and seeing-man's imperial authority *break down into sound, blindness, confusion*" (Pratt 180, my emphasis). For example, "[w]hen it comes to concrete relations of labor and property, the seeing-man's powers seem to dissolve into *confused noise, distant sounds*, a tree cut down by unseen hands" (Pratt 177, my emphasis). In fact, Pratt's analysis of the "seeing-man" risks reinscribing her own study within the epistemological limitations of the gaze that she so insightfully critiques. "Confused noise, distant sounds," "blindness, confusion," from beyond the disavowed limits of the imperial gaze, the *tumulte noir* harks to a contact zone whose meaning is full of ambiguity and ambivalence. It is here that the current study listens for crucial slippages and solderings of imperial and anti-imperial systems of order, knowledge, sentiment, and experience.

European and colonial writers inscribe their New World trips in sound from the moment of departure from the Old World to that of the arrival in the New World and all the way back again. If at times subtle or disavowed, travel writers often found soundscapes one of the "newest"—that is, "strangest," most "foreign," most "other"—aspects of the New World. Soundscapes play a crucial role in what Pratt calls anticonquest discourse: a set of rhetorical and discursive mechanisms that underwrites European global hegemony and imperial planetary consciousness while staging the innocence of the writing subject. Because the indefinite and fluid nature of sonic phenomena in New World environment did not lend itself well to the Enlightenment's catalog of the visible, travelers and travel writers often had to supplement scientific method with sentimental or openly subjective assessments and practices of sound description that alternately jeopardized and facilitated both the literal and mythological mapping. Recourse to sounds and soundscapes often served to grasp qualities and characteristics that proved elusive to the visual paradigms of its dominant modes of inquiry, comprehension, and inscription. In other words, techniques and practices of sound, both skilled and amateur, supplement the imperial gaze as they represent distances and forces felt and imagined but unseen or immeasurable in the New World.

Jean Baptiste Du Tertre, the seventeenth-century Dominican missionary and botanist, one of the earliest European travelers to author major French West Indian natural historiographies, exemplifies the way European travel texts naturalize and facilitate imperial expansion all the while coming up against the limits of the imperial gaze. Du Tertre's multivolume *Histoire générale des Antilles habitées par les François* is organized into sections that compartmentalize and catalog his description, while the narrative itinerary moves from island to island in the Antilles in the same order of their imperial possession by French conquest. With the travel experience reorganized, Du Tertre's text disarticulates the traveling writing subject, abstracting him from the scene of scientific observation, while simultaneously naturalizing the French imperial perspective. This imposition of imperial boundaries of space, culture, and social life does not concern itself with the fact that, as Du Tertre commented, residents of the islands often ignore the administrative mapping and official naming of local sites. His detailed descriptions overwrite this local map, converting them into prospects for European knowledge and utility.

Du Tertre, who had served in the Dutch army and navy before becoming a missionary priest, brings all his skills to bear as he goes along describing the layout of the land for each island he travels to on his "civilizing" mission: the terrain suitable for housing, the access to water, the existing and potential agricultural production, especially focusing on the non-mountainous regions. Chapters on minerals, rock formations, plants, temperature, details on manioc, indigo, and most of all sugarcane, provide crucial speculative information paving the way for capitalist investment. But when it comes to the mountainous regions that seem to promise little in the way of potential agricultural investment or settlement, Du Tertre seems less interested in completing his visual catalog. Rather dismissively, referring to what he has not described, Du Tertre sums up a series of trips taken and not taken.

> The entire heart of the Island which I have not described is made up of very high and imposing mountains, of terrible rocks, and of very frightening precipices. I've only seen the least of them, I noticed one especially where a man screaming at the top of his lungs from the bottom of the precipice couldn't be heard by those who were at the top. (Du Tertre 14)

While Du Tertre treats the mountainous heart of the island as unimportant, his scene depicting its immeasurability ("a man screaming at the top of his lungs" from the bottom of the cliff who is seen but unheard by those standing above) registers an intense and terribly sublime sonic non-measurement of the New World island landscape. If "visual descriptions presuppose—naturalize—a transformative project embodied in the Europeans [. . .] in visions of 'improvement' whose value is often expressed as esthetic," as Pratt has shown (59), then no doubt part of the "frightful" (*affreux, épouvantable*) nature of these mountain ranges comes from the way they lay beyond means of imperial measurement, use, and value. In such situations, the "seeing-man" of imperial conquest is pulled from the obstinate inscription of possession that dominates his gaze, and falls into the "immeasurable" pleasures and terrors that are present and proximate yet unregistered or ignored within his imperial mapping.

A similar recourse to sound occurs when he maps the flowing creeks, waterfalls, and rivers of Guadeloupe. At pains to emphasize their beauty, bounty, and awesome force, yet dismissing the importance of all the latter, he again measures his experience of them more so than he measures the waters themselves.

> I won't speak here of the thousand beautiful fountains that flow from the rocks, or spring from the ground, and that, after having pleasantly wound through a thousand places, lose themselves in the biggest rivers. Since this island is extremely elevated in the middle, most of these rivers properly speaking are torrents that violently rush into the sea; and it is a terrifying thing to see them overflow, when there is heavy water fall, for you can hear them coming down from a good league away, rumbling like thunder. As for the rest, this rumbling and knocking against the rocks make a din and a noise so strange that even though it's thundering horribly you cannot hear the claps of thunder. I confess that I haven't partaken in more pleasant delights in Guadeloupe than resting in the coolness under the trees along these beautiful rivers: for after their overflows they leave millions of rocks in disorder, and you can hear, in addition to the agreeable murmuring of the grand canal, a thousand different little babblings which in truth charm more agreeably the ear than the most excellent musics (Du Tertre 19–20).

As was the case when facing the immeasurable distances of the mountains and cliffs, Du Tertre opens the passage with caveat-like distance. The failure to speak, Du Tertre's "I won't speak of," does not fail to speak, but it does fail to remain faithful to the scientific and utilitarian objectives and visualist paradigm of his botanical and colonial inscription of the island's natural history. Sound has no place, as it were, in the purview of the imperial gaze, yet the recourse to sound points up the limitations of the imperial gaze, supplementing it with another means of fully rendering the pleasure-value of colonial inscription. In the move from the imperial gaze to the imperial ear, there is less an absolute break than an alternately subtle and jarring shift: from the imperial *quantification* to the imperial *qualification* of New World space and value.

The shift from science to sentiment points toward the limits of the imperial gaze, but it also suggests the way sentiment crucially supplements the scientific gaze even as it complicates the latter's claims of neutrality and distance. This is the paradox of the natural historian's claim to authority and truth; the seeing-man's power rides a fraught line between his "real world" knowledge, in other words his experience on location, and his "scientific" knowledge premised on distance and detached objectivity. In the switch from imperial eyes to imperial ears, Du Tertre moves from a discourse of science to discourse of pleasure. "In a word, these rivers are so many little paradises where all the senses innocently partake the most delicious pleasure they're capable of, in their purity"

(Du Tertre 20). The "purity" of island sound pleasure contrasts sharply with the condemnation Du Tertre reserves for the materialism of colonial society, especially its women. At the same time as this purity suggests its "untouched" status, a signal for imperial conquest, it also suggests the innocence of the one gaining the pleasure, the imperial inscriber. In this vein, soundscapes mark the desirous and menacing implications of New World sites lying within and beyond the purview of the imperial gaze and the pragmatic and ideological limits of its cartography. Soundscapes mark the physical, psychological, and moral borders that the traveler ventures beyond at his own risk.

Silence functions in tandem with the profusion of confused sounds, commotion, and disorder within the imperial mapping of soundscapes. At the forest's edge, Chanvalon, the eighteenth-century colonial administrator for Martinique, inscribes the romantic imperial symbol of the wilderness into his ethnography of France's New World possessions. "The slightest noises resonate in these dense forests like in an underground cave; there rules a profound silence usually. The birds only live on the borders, and the majority don't sing. Everything inspires in these woods a secret horror; their solitude, their darkness, their silence, and the continual worry one has to have about snakes which always take refuge in these dark places and whose bite is venomous" (Chanvalon 29). The imperial ear sounds out that which lies beyond the forest's bordering trees to record the terrifying sound of silence. A classic trope in the romantic portrayals of New World landscape since René de Châteaubriand, the forest's "secret horrors" symbolize a time before civilization that is itself haunted, crystallizing a potential for life gained and lost.

Lafcadio Hearn's account in the early twentieth century takes this obscure sounding of the wilderness further, even while filling the chilling silence with frenzied and buzzing dark vibrations:

> But the sense of awe inspired by a tropic forest is certainly greater than the mystic fear which any wooded wilderness of the North could ever have created. The brilliancy of colors that seem almost preternatural; the vastness of the ocean of frondage, and the violet blackness of rare gaps revealing its inconceived [*sic*] profundity; and the million mysterious sounds which make up its perpetual murmur, —compel the idea of a creative force that almost terrifies. Man feels here like an insect, —fears like an insect on the alert for merciless enemies; and the fear is not unfounded (Hearn 196–197).

In Hearn's description above, instead of absolute silence, the island forest's thousands of sounds represent its immense productive force. In fact the whole soundscape crystallizes a cycle of life that points up the limitations of human existence while mythologizing about the regenerative power of the New World. The "awe" of natural history is inside and outside of the gaze. While the latter locates nature's norms and laws, the imperial ear registers exceptionality, the "preter"—more than, beyond—emanating from the natural world. The "rare gaps" of "violet blackness" full of a "million mysterious sounds" compel ideas rather than effacing them, paradoxically "revealing" in the darkness an "inconceived profundity."

Amplifying the haunting silence of Chanvalon's prelapsarian romantic sublime, Hearn sites the *tumulte noir* universe under the cover of darkness. A deep and profuse hidden life provokes an intense experience of "the tropics" that cannot be written out:

> One of the greatest terrors of darkness in other lands does not exist here after the setting of the sun, —the terror of *Silence.* . . . Tropical night is full of voices; —extraordinary populations of crickets are trilling; nations of tree-frogs are chanting; the *Cabri-des-bois*, or *cra-cra*, almost deafens you with the wheezy bleating sound by which it earned its creole name; birds pipe: everything that bells, ululates, drones, clacks, guggles, joins the enormous chorus; and you fancy you see all the shadows vibrating to the force of this vocal storm. The true life of Nature in the tropics begins with the darkness, ends with the light. (325)

In this passage "truth" comes not in inscribing visions but in registering sound. His conclusion is striking: "The true life of Nature in the tropics begins with the darkness, ends with the light." What a terrifying statement for the imperial gaze; Hearn flirts with the margins of the imperial mapping project. The "vocal storm" points toward the human boundaries of the black tumult. Often characterized or possibly translated as a storm, the *tumulte* resonates with the trope of "the stormy Caribbean," a designation that naturalizes the Caribbean's violent histories and playfully extends their relation to symbolize romance and sexual mores. Hearn's soundscape captures a visceral vibration in the air, in the ground, in the dark. It testifies to the overwhelming if absent presence of distinctly Creole and New World "populations" and "nations" that so fascinated him.

## *LE DOUX PARLER DES ÎLES*

Birds and birdsong receive special attention in the gendered inscription of French West Indian sonic cultures, and their representation functions prominently in discursive formations that mythologize New World beauty, colonial mimicry, Creole speech, and human subjection. Whether simply observed, kept as pets, or hunted and eaten, the unparalleled beauty and diversity of bird species fascinated canonical travel writers, even as imperial conquest and colonial settlement decimated bird populations, sometimes to extinction. But in this discourse of imperial loss, extinction only functions to further cement the New World as the testament of an ancient world (collapsed imperial civilizations, whether *ancien régime* or Caribbean Mediterranean, whose mythical relics form the resonant chambers for New World soundings). A palimpsest of mythological loss—extinct species, genocidal massacres of indigenous populations, Eldorados and Biblical paradises lost—forms the cadre to be filled by the imperial voice.

Du Tertre, for example, writes that many birds "learn very easily to sing, to speak, to whistle, and to imitate all sorts of animals. They're more lively, and more entertaining, than all the other parrots. All the parrots, big and small, continually *cancannent*; this word signifies a certain nasal murmuring that the inhabitants [*habitans*] couldn't express any other way. I've seen some however speak distinctly before leaving the *Cancanage*" (252, emphases in the original). Even as the sound practices of birdsong serve the imperial mapping project, helping classify the natural world, they also push the linguistic and visual limits of that project's paradigms. Like the deafening *cra-cra* that Lafcadio Hearn would mention much later, Du Tertre's classification of parrots ends up relying on the linguistic structures generated from the soundscape of island life. In today's French the spelling is *cancaner* with one *n*, and the word has two definitions: the first referring to Du Tertre's usage, more commonly employed in figurative speech to signify for example the gossiping *commère* (not unlike the whispering woman Hearn would mention hundreds of years later). The other more popular meaning for *cancaner* dating since Du Tertre is "*danser le cancan*" (to dance the cancan). If "[t]he (lettered, male, European) eye that held the system could familiarize ('naturalize') new sites/sights immediately upon contact, by incorporating them into the language of the system" (Pratt 31), soundscapes and the sonic cultures of life in the New World challenged the linguistic classificatory schemes of botany while pointing up the limitations European practices for the complete mapping of the world.

Father Jean Baptiste Labat's relationship with birds at the turn of the eighteenth century is legendary and mostly culinary (Labat 153–154). As Hearn writes, Father Labat "does not appear to care much for them as pets: if they could not talk well, he condemned them forthwith to the pot" (Hearn). Hearn's discussion of Labat's inhumane treatment of birds leads directly to a discussion of his treatment of slave populations, a subject of some notoriety, so much so that it has entered into local vernacular culture and expression as Hearn notes. Hearn continues: "Labat seems to have possessed but a very small quantity of altruism; his cynicism on the subject of animal suffering is not offset by any visible sympathy with human pain;—he never compassionates: you may seek in vain through all his pages for one gleam of the goodness of gentle Père Du Tertre, who, filled with intense pity for the condition of blacks, prays masters to be merciful and just to their slaves for the love of God" (Hearn 309). (As Pratt notes, the voice and visions of previous travel narratives past haunt twentieth-century ethnographies, and one can add that these voices echo through French West Indian poetics as well.)

On his way to the islands for the first time, Hearn anticipates the soundscapes ahead. "Through the open ports, as we lie down to sleep, comes a great whispering,—the whispering of the seas: sounds as of articulate speech under the breath,—as, of women telling secrets" (Hearn 164). Stereotypes of sound concerning the *doux parler des îles*—the "soft" or "sweet" speech of the islands, work in relation with the gendered inscription of the anti-conquest in New World travel and island landscapes. Hearn uses stereotypes of sound to provocatively hint at the romantic conquests that lie ahead, while subtly figuring the Creole woman as holder and teller of dark island secrets. Soundscape scholars typically consider the sonic life of people as taking place against the backdrop of the soundscape, rather than as being part of that backdrop. (This is due in part to the work of Murray Schafer, the musicologist who first coined and theorized the concept, and whose work I critique at length in the section below.) Yet the meaning of human sounds emerges from and is enmeshed with an imperial history that categorizes some people as less than human, and that figures them as part of the landscape, if it figures them in the environment at all. The inscription of island speech and musical practices occupies an important role in travel narratives, combining the imperial imperative to civilize through language with the exoticized charm and appeal of the unfamiliar linguistic practices and musical styles of France's "oldest colonies." Just as Hearn personifies the sonic trip to the New Word to represent the whispers of a woman cloaked in the rumors of nightfall, the *doux parler des îles* is the exotic stuff of masculinist dreams of conquest and possession.

Just as Hearn connects the song, speech, and treatment of bird populations to that of black slave and other human populations, speech practices serve the ethnographic classification of colonial society. Hearn more than the others inscribed speech and musical cultures into his descriptions of New World soundscapes. Part of this fascination comes from Hearn's particular interest in Creole cultures and populations, an area of specialization he had sharpened while writing his sketches of life in New Orleans. While others brought back botanical drawings and samples, Hearn brought back transcriptions of folksong and vernacular culture. "Half the women are smoking. All chatter loudly, speaking their English jargon with a pitch voice totally unlike the English timbre: it sometimes sounds as if they were trying to pronounce English rapidly according to French pronunciation and pitch of voice" (Hearn 169). While, for the missionary Labat, creolized linguistic practices block inquiry, for Hearn the misunderstandings of language and culture increase the pleasureful discovery of the New World's intimate secrets. While Labat complained that when he first arrived he couldn't ask the slaves born on the island his questions because they could only speak a "corrupted language," Hearn delighted in the diversity of speech and musical cultures. In such soundscape discourse, more than local color, voice is as much a part of the *milieu* as the birds in the trees and the clapping waves on ocean sand. Whether he understood them or not, whether he found them in harmony or in discordance with the sites from which they come and resonate, Creole speech and sound is fetishized and soldered together with the scenic gaze.

## LE NOIR S'AFFICHE COMME SON

Ethnographic soundscapes represent the encounters with the sounds of an environment but also encounters between different modes of siting the New World. Soundtexts crystallize fraught encounters between meanings and institutions of writing and sounding, resonating with the struggle over New World space. A sample frozen in time and space for future (continued) specularization, the soundtext is itself a physical slice, examined on a slide even if on a page. Which sounds constitute background and which foreground? Which are meaningless or otherwise without reason and which form the conditions for the possibility of meaning? The "scape" itself represents the integration of these encountering sounds into an ordering perspective, a structure for registering and distinguishing sounds, with all its ensuing institutions of knowledge, its economies of metaphysical and physical value, and its architectures of hierarchy.

In this way the "scape" is a "scrape," a frictious encounter rhythmically marking the epistemological and sentimental limits of embodiment, a bumping up against boundaries of understanding and feeling that strike the imperial hearing-man with a haunting presence. The "scape" is itself something other than the sound parts that constitute it. That something other results from a "friction" that is not merely metaphorical; it registers the violent context of imperial expansion, what Lindon Barrett would call "the other side of value." These scrapes of sound testify to a violent culmination of encounters whose simultaneity and multiplicity ends up mapped on a matrix of Western intelligibility and textuality like an instructive and inscriptive coming to blows. *Black Soundscapes White Stages* locates this field of sonic blows and scrapes as an anti/colonial struggle over the meaning of black sound in the New World.

My critical usage of the term "soundscape" differs from that of Murray Schafer, who coined the term in the late 1960s and early 1970s and elaborated his concept in *The Soundscape: Our Sonic Environment and the Tuning of the World.* My work responds to Schafer's set of basic research questions: "what is the relationship between man and the sounds of his environment and what happens when those sounds change?" (Schafer 3–4). Yet my feminist and anti-imperial perspective deconstructs the claims of ownership and patriarchal social ordering inherent in Schafer's conceptual model. Schafer's World Soundscape Project, a group composed of intellectuals from several disciplines, grew out of this concern over noise pollution and the transformation of the sonic environment, especially with regard to the industrialization and hyper-urbanization of everyday life. For Schafer the modern world has noisily encroached upon natural beauty of the sonic environment. The group is concerned with "collecting sounds threatened with extinction" and gathering musicians, sociologists, acousticians, psychologists, and others who might study the new soundscapes of postmodernity to "make intelligent recommendations for its improvement" (Schafer 4). The project seeks to prescribe corrective measures to re-create harmony where "original" or "naturally beautiful" sounds are lost or disturbed by the advances of postindustrialization and the advent of global cities.

Schafer's preference for "original" soundscapes over "these new sounds," which he calls "lo fi" as opposed to the "hi fi" quality of nature's sound in the past, rehearses mythologies of origin that curiously resonate with the imperial inscriptions critiqued above. As Ari Kelman puts it:

> His notion of "the soundscape" is far from the broad, descriptive term that it has since become. Instead, his soundscape is lined with ideological and ecological messages about which sounds "matter" and which do not; it is suffused with instructions about how people ought to listen; and, it traces a long dystopian history that descends from harmonious sounds of nature to the cacophonies of modern life. (214)

But where does Schafer find these "harmonious sounds of nature" that are being lost? He generates his conception of the ideal soundscape through readings in the Western literary canon and engagement with its aesthetic norms. Schafer finds his ultimate model "[i]n Robert Fludd's *Ultruisque Cosmi Historia* [where] there is an illustration entitled 'the Tuning of the World' in which the earth forms the body of an instrument across which strings are stretched and are tuned by divine hand." According to Schafer, "[w]e must try once again to find the secret of that tuning" (6). But Schafer is more specific and arbitrary than this: for the authentic sound and natural beauty of the ocean one is to read the maritime poet Ezra Pound. For the haunting silence of the American forest, one need look no further than the aforementioned Chateaubriand. Poetic works in particular provide Schafer with the earwitness accounts of sound from other places and time. Through the latter he gages the loss of sound by, as Kelman puts it, "the cacophonies of modern life," a term whose percussive connotations serve to contrast with the "harmony" of pure original soundscapes.

At the same time as his ideal soundscape comes from literature, his theory of the latter turns on that of the former. After noting different meanings for different types of bird sounds—pleasure calls, distress calls, territorial-defense calls, alarm calls, flight calls, flock calls, nest calls, feeding calls—Schafer dismisses them all in preference to poetic vision. Turning to accounts of birdsong written by poets and novelists, Schafer declares (rather imperiously): "Birds, like poems, should not mean, but be" (31). Schafer conceives of the soundscape as a way to distinguish between which sounds are in place and which are out of place, but he goes on to also decide which accounts count and which can be discounted.

The technological and mechanical transformation of modern life constitutes imperialistic advances to Schafer. "These new sounds, which differ in quality and intensity from those of the past, have alerted many researchers to the dangers of an indiscriminate and imperialistic spread of more and larger sounds into every corner of man's life" (3). Anticipating problems with his unintuitive usage of the term, he explains first (via Oswald Spengler) that "imperialism" has been "the word used to refer to the extension of an empire or ideology to parts of the world remote from the source" (77). Then Schafer moves on his own definition of imperialism for the context of soundscapes: "When sound power is sufficient to create a large acoustic profile, we may speak of it, too, as imperialistic" (77). This imperial profile has to do not just with sound volume but with its dispersion, movement, and transmission.

For this reason, Schafer lists the telephone, the phonograph, and the radio as the three crucial phenomena changing sonic profile of modernity with "imperialist" advances fueled by the electronic revolution. "Two new techniques were introduced: the discovery of packaging and storing techniques for sound and the splitting of sounds from their original contexts—which I call schizophonia" (Schafer 88). Schafer cites modern machines as the cause in some respects of the demise of the soundscape, but he cheers on and employs new technologies of sound inscription for their "more accurate" means of *grasping* the profile of nature's sounds, capturing them and preserving them before they can be lost. Beyond the mobilization of various methods and technologies of writing sound, the soundscape's inscription constitutes a critical and epistemological gesture of inclusion and exclusion, marking the valued from the valueless, meaningful from meaningless.

While Schafer, and even Kelman, insist that the term *soundscape* designates sounds of the natural environment and not human sounds, my use of the term amplifies the importance of these sounds, locating precisely the site of the cut, where the "matter" and value of the human versus inhuman sound in the New World comes to bear on bodies and populations of color. The embodied matter of black sound crucially testifies to the violence of imperial mapping and value. To build from Fred Moten's brilliant formulation, the soundscape constitutes the framework within which resonates "[t]he commodity whose speech sounds embodies the critique of value, of private property, of the sign" (12). The matter of soundscapes must then include the sonorous black bodies and cultures written into, and out of, European systems of value and meaning. The very materiality of the drums and of the hands beating them bespeak sonic otherness, making proximate and manifest specularized erotics of hearing and touch that create black and colonial value. The soundsc(r)ape represents the striking, percussive nature, the skin produced and lost in such encounters, and their sound-text crystallizations in representation and subjectivity.

The imperial valuation of black sound matter constitutes what one might call, following Lindon Barrett, an act of *hearing double* that I contend is not at all unrelated to the "schizophonia" (Schafer) articulated in how the French received Josephine Baker and *La Revue nègre* described at the beginning of this chapter. In *Blackness and Value: Seeing Double* (2009), Barrett's critique of disrupted senses adopts a critical view that "implies a state of impaired, unreliable, or faulty perception" of the violent binarisms within constructs of value (Barrett 1). Rather than focusing on the seeing, and dreading the "out of socketness" of the *tumulte noir*, the current study tunes itself to the "impaired" or "faulty" inscription of black sound matter and value. In so doing I appropriate a Fanonist term for this disorderly sounding: *ratés*—sonically charged backfires and failures "in the sense in which one speaks of engine *failures*" (23, my empha-

sis). *Ratés* are sonic breakdowns at the border between sound and text, the mythologies of Creole and black colonial speech as off script, the shocking sound
of the colonial machine at work in black vernacular culture. The *raté* is a failure
in time, a sonic symbol of slippage, excess, waste in the colonial machine and
what Sartre calls its mental apparatus.

These lost or losing sounds threaten modernity's mapping schemas even as
they are threatened by them. They defy modernity's tools of scription even as
the latter lean on them to push beyond its own limitations. "Writers of Europe's
colonies, ex-colonies, and neo-colonies find they must grapple with European
travel literature as they develop ways of representing themselves" (Pratt 8).
While the imperialist gaze relies on the type of scientific knowledge that, in
Aimé Césaire's words, "enumerates, measures, classifies, and kills;" the "poetic cognition" called the black scream is "born in the great silence of scientific
knowledge. Through reflection, observation, experiment, man bewildered by
the data confronting him, finally dominated them. Henceforth he knows how to
guide himself through the forest of phenomena" ("Poetry and Knowledge" 134).
While *le cri noir* rips through the soundscapes of imperial ethnography, regional
poetry, and a certain legacy of French intellectual and Enlightenment thought,
the screams of negritude, sweet song and speech of the Creole woman, and
mythological inscriptions function on the same terrains of sound during the
first half of the twentieth century. In this context, representations of encounters between sound and text in black diasporic cultural production hark back to
these early encounters and have a stake in their inscriptions of imperial modernity and colonial loss.

## BLACK SOUNDSCAPES WHITE STAGES

With this tension animating its core, this book examines the gendered and racialized construction of musicality and textuality in a wide range of historic
twentieth-century soundtexts: from historic descriptions of New World sound
in travel narratives and ethnographies, to musical folklore and popular early
twentieth-century dance genres and performers, to the construction of the
black scream in the negritude movement, to the impact of sound on colonial
cinema and the launch of the official French colonial radio station and the advent of shortwave radio technologies. In the process, I explore the dreams and
realizations of black Atlantic mobility and separation as represented by some of
its most powerful soundtexts and cultural practitioners and I then pose questions about their legacies for us today.

In tracing the inscription of sound into cartographies of meaning and value, this book pinpoints and deconstructs the imperial meaning of sound and text while it explores their sites of encounter, conversion, and conflict. The Francophone focus of this book's content articulates the special way French West Indian cultural practitioners bear these historic soundtext ruptures. *Black Soundscapes White Stages* sites the imperialist specularity of black sound and the ways poets and other practitioners negotiate the soldering dynamics of desire within such specularization. At the same time, my analysis critiques the ways imperial and anti-imperial discourses gender the designations of authentic sound and text under patriarchal systems of power and authority that seek to regulate racial and gender boundaries.

The method will theorize the gender divide and relation in black radical thought and poetics through the twin concepts I call "negritude in the major" and "negritude in the minor." While "negritude in the major" creates a masculinist hero who intervenes at the mythical crossroads of History, "negritude in the minor" concerns itself with alternate and everyday management of the condition of pain characterizing histories of black Atlantic subject formation. Negritude's screams in the major and the minor resonate with one another in their sounding of black Atlantic grievance and grief, whether in the New World or the Old. This approach (developed especially in chapter 2) revises the poetic genealogy of the negritude scream and beat, articulating their relation to the torn gender dynamics of black Atlantic colonial musicality, speech, and performance. Traditional accounts of the emergence of black avant-garde poetry in the Antilles posit it as a radical break from the so-called doudouist poetics of a previous generation of poets and cultural practitioners. I offer a new critical account of this emergence by investigating the *doudou* on the other side of negritude's black radical break.

A recurrent character in colonial song, fiction, and even ethnography, *doudou* ("sweetie") was the Creolophone pet name given to the stereotypical—and often musical—tragic mulatta in the French Antilles. She represents a Creole woman in love with a white man but who is unable to fulfill her dream of complete union with him due to her color and colonial condition. This study offers a thick critical description of the *doudou* and the black soundscapes and white stages that she has historically navigated. Locating the resonance of "her" voice with the *le cri nègre* creates a provocative genealogy of negritude that extends back into the doudouist poetics it disavows and that contemporary scholarship turns away from as well. At the same time, I adopt a transnational approach that traces the trip between the New World and France, displacing the dominant Anglophone and Afrocentric based notions of traditional academic work in this area while underlining the vibrant cultural dynamics taking place across national and colonial boundaries. By tuning in to the shared and mutually resonant histories of blacks from the Americas in the City of Light, *Black Soundscapes White Stages* highlights the tropes of travel, conditions of voyage, and dreams of possibility on "the other side."

The first chapter, "Adieu Madras, Adieu Foulard: The *Doudou*'s Colonial Complaint" examines an iconic Antillean folk song (circa eighteenth century) and its ambivalent representations of the boundaries of French-Antillean sentimental attachment. The song is the lament of a Creole island girl who sings goodbye to the white sailor of her dreams as his ship prepares to return to France forever. The song's colonial family drama inscribes the figure of the *doudou*, the Creole woman of color desperate to be *aimée comme une blanche*—loved like a white woman.

The chapter traces the musico-textual history of "Adieu" and its relation to the mythological tragic mulatta of the French New World in the first half of the twentieth century—from its ethnographic imperialist inscriptions in the work of Lafcadio Hearn and others, to its acoustic inscription on French record labels in the 1930s by musicians of the popular Antillean dance, the *biguine*, and finally to its anti-imperial poetic inscriptions in Fanon's *Peau noire, masques blancs*. While "Adieu" is traditionally attributed to the Marquis de Bouillé, an eighteenth-century governor of Guadeloupe, my analysis will consider the ways its relation to the *chanson de cocotte* tradition can lead to an analytical interrogation of the patriarchal order inscribed in its musical narrative.

Despite its international success in France during the interwar years, few scholars have turned their attention to the biguine genre. Perhaps since the biguine was born at and across borders of race and colony, it lives its cultural lives and afterlives in liminality, at the margins of New World cultural criticism and French West Indian historiography. Chapter 2, "To Begin the Biguine: Re-membering Antillean Musical Time," investigates the dynamic cultural struggles over the possession, dispossession, and disavowal of biguine music, focusing on accusations that the genre and its musical practices were "doudouist." Brenda Berrian suggests not confusing the *doudou* with doudouism, yet my analysis will flesh out this relation in order to consider the gender dynamics at work in the ambivalent inscription of biguine music in Antillean and French cultural history. My goal is to highlight the discursive economies that mobilize and fuel the doudouist allegation.

The emotional rending, separation, and loss surrounding biguine meaning-making includes—but extends beyond—the lyrics of its melancholy classics such as "Maladie d'amour" (Love sick) and "A si pare" (So it seems). At its core, the ambivalent inscription of the biguine in French West Indian history points up a struggle in critical and popular thought over the aesthetic and ethical problematics of hybridity in Antillean performance, a tradition of critique latent in negritude discourse and that remains unresolved today.

Chapter 3, "La Baker: *Princesse Tam Tam* and the *Doudou*'s Signature Dilemma," focuses on Josephine Baker and the Josephine Baker phenomenon with respect to mythologies of the *doudou*. Baker has historically gotten shortchanged in black Atlantic scholarship and historiographies, yet she crucially transformed the history of Antillean, American, and European popular culture and performance. Focusing on Josephine Baker's star role in the feature-length film *Princesse Tam Tam*, this chapter deconstructs the colonial, gendered, musico-textual dynamics of power in the commodification of contemporary black sound at work in Bakermania. Building from theoretical work by Jacques Derrida, Fred Moten, and Lindon Barrett, I contend that discovering *la Baker*'s value means understanding how our critique of her is rhythmically stuck in a violent anti/colonial cycle of masculinist projection and fantasy, colonial misrecognition, and patriarchal erasure, that dispossess Baker of her historical worth. Full of deconstructive *détours* in a Derridian-Glissantian sense, my methodology and stylistic tactical moves attempt to critique "her" without reproducing the colonial, gender, and racial violence of her commodification. My style is an effort to deflect the masculinist gestures of exclusion and erasure that Josephine Baker dealt with by exploring dreams of her as dreams of our own.

Chapter 4, "Negritude Drum Circles: The *Tam-Tam* and the Beat," examines the curious imperial trajectory of the "tam-tam," a term I contend operates as a "new vocable" (Brent Edwards) in black transnationalism in interwar years. After an extensive investigation into the ambivalent history of the word and its split usage in musicological discourse and travel narratives, I consider the way negritude poets tap into its mythology. The chapter's close reading of Frantz Fanon, Aimé Césaire, and Léon-Gontran Damas suggests the way negritude discourse delivers decisive blows in the "percussive field" (John Mowitt) of black imperial modernity. Analyzing Aimé Césaire's figurations of *le cri nègre* ("the black scream") and *le tam tam* ("the drum") within these debates, I read his "poetic rhythm" as the articulation of a history of sociological, psychoanalytic, and musicological violence *beaten* into the black body. This bulk of the chapter then develops an extended exploration of Léon-Gontran Damas's work, focusing on his neglected 1956 epic poem, *Black-Label*. I hear Damas's poetic refrain as an ambivalently pleasureful negotiation of the dynamics of modernity and the consumption of black sound.

Chapter 5, "Le Poste Colonial: Short-Wave Colonial Radio and Negritude's Poetic Technologies," explores the advent of shortwave radio and French imperialism. Launched at the Exposition Internationale Coloniale, le Poste Colonial, France's first official colonial radio station, sought to take advantage of emerging shortwave radio technology to bring the "authentic voice of France" to the entire world. This chapter assembles the scattered accounts put forth in interviews, articles, opinion pieces, and submitted letters to journals in support of the station's creation, and it critiques the imperialist agenda of this radio initiative through engagement with discourse on technology in Francophone black Atlantic thought, poetry, and musical practices. After a critique of the construction of the French voice in France and in the colonies, this chapter builds from Fanon's take on radio technology and transnational discourse to conduct a close reading of the representation of technology in work by Aimé Césaire, focusing especially on his surrealist poem "Le cristal automatique" ("Automatic Crystal"). This critique builds from the work of contemporary scholarship on technologies of writing and sound to suggest the way the radio constituted a new terrain of struggle over the colonization of black sound.

# one

# "Adieu Madras, Adieu Foulard"

## The *Doudou*'s Colonial Complaint

On departure, the amputation of his being vanishes as the ocean liner comes into view. He can read the authority and mutation he has acquired in the eyes of those accompanying him to the ship: "*Adieu madras, adieu foulard . . .*"

—Frantz Fanon, *Black Skin, White Masks*

If "to speak," as Frantz Fanon argues, "means above all assuming a culture and bearing the weight of a civilization" (1–2), his reference to "Adieu madras, adieu foulard" quoted in the epigraph suggests the way "to sing" does the same.[1] "Adieu" (in)famously inscribed the *doudou*, and critical ideas about "doudouism," into Antillean folklore, the French imperial imagination, and ultimately the emergence of anticolonial discourse. As a character in the repertoire of French colonial mythology, the *doudou* represents the Creole woman of color desperately in love with a French man but carrying the weight of French imperial civilization in the New World. Caged in by geography, culture, and color, she melancholically sings, in the "*doux parler des îles*" ("the sweet language of the islands," i.e., Creole), her hopeless plight of seduction, love, and abandonment.

Bonjour! Monsieur le Gouverneur!
Moin ka mandé ou en tit pétition
Pou Doudou moin qui ka pati
Hélas! Hélas! cé pou toujour (bis).

[Good morning Mister Governor!
I've come to make a request
For my Sweetie who is leaving
Alas! Alas! It's forever (repeat).]

Mademoiselle! Il est trop tard
Les connaissements sont déjà signés
Le bâtiment est à la rade
Il va bientôt appareiller (bis).

[*Mademoiselle*! It's too late
The registry is already signed
The ship is at the port
It will soon set sail (repeat).]

Bel bateau' a qui dans la rade' là
Ou prend Doudou moin ou minnin' i allé
Chè Doudou moin qui ka pati
Hélas! Hélas! cé pou toujour (bis).

[Great ship at the port
You took my Sweetie away
Dear Sweetie who is leaving
Alas! Alas! It's forever (repeat).]

(Refrain)
Adieu! foulard, Adieu! madras
Adieu! graines d'or . . . Adieu! collier choux
Chè doudou moin qui ka pati
Hélas! Hélas! cé pou toujour (bis).

[Goodbye scarves, goodbye madras
Goodbye grains of gold, goodbye necklace
My sweetie is leaving
Alas! Alas! It's forever (repeat).][2]

The designation of the interlocutor as a captain, lieutenant, or another rank in other versions of the lyrics, suggests the *doudou* has fallen in love with a French officer, but it also posits this interlocutor as paternal figure of authority.[3] His (French language) denial of her (Creole language) "petition" enacts a colonial sentencing, a patriarchal "non" of the imperial father that marks her subject status. Her voice resonates as the site of an imperial injunction, a cut that inscribes her originary loss and lack. In this way, rather than a scene of final endings as its lyrics would suggest, "Adieu" serves as a primal scene of colonial subject formation as well as a mythical narrative staging this oedipal scene as the origins of French-Antillean imperial relations.

Called by Martinican composer and singer Léona Gabriel-Soïme "the national song known throughout the world" (31), "Adieu" begins with a patient ascending melodic line made up of a major tonic arpeggio, musically hitting on the *doudou*'s farewell cry out. Rising up, the melody briefly stretches beyond the major triad chord to reach the sixth, the height of its determined aspiration, but its high musical resting place on the dominant tone cannot be maintained. While the melody's steady climb up lasts for the first four bars, the musical fall back down happens in half the time, repeating once to complete the opening eight bar phrase. This repeated melodic descent that closes each verse suggests the sadness of the fall, through its relation with the relative minor, and a sweetness of the fall, through the interlaced thirds and the regular eighth note rhythmic frame to soften the landing.

Just as there are many textual variants handed down and referenced through travel narratives and Antillean letters, musicians have recorded many versions of "Adieu" with French record labels taking interest in "exotic" and "colonial" music in the interwar years. Mademoiselle Armelin recorded the song for Odéon in 1930, followed in 1932 by Nelly Lungla (a performer in Paris at the legendary Bal Nègre on rue Blomet as well as the Boule Blanche and La Canne à Sucre) for Parlophone, and, also in 1932, Léona Gabriel along with the Orchestre de la Boule Blanche for Polydor. In all, the 1920s to the late 1950s offers some dozen recordings of "Adieu" in France by various artists, including biguine leading men like Sam Castendet (under the title "Les Adieux d'une Créole") and Henri Salvador (nephew to Léona Gabriel through marriage).[4]

But while biguine artists embraced the song, dominant negritude discourse, what I will call "negritude in the major," rejected it as an icon of French Antillean imperial rhetoric and a crystallization of the regionalist poetics they abhorred, and which they called "doudouist." The term *doudou* referred to in "Adieu" began as a Creole term of endearment, only later becoming a blank name for French colonial fantasy. Critical discourse has designated "doudou*ism*" as a poetic performance practice that reproduces colonialist portrayals of Martinique and Guadeloupe. René Ménil, Etienne Léro, et al. employed the term *doudouiste* to denounce the sentimentalist ideology that formed the relationship between colonial discourse and the aesthetic conformity of mainstream Antillean poetry. "We hate pity. We don't give a damn about feelings" (1). Fanon's merciless critique of the *doudou* also constitutes a disavowal of doudouist sentimentalism, which he hears as psychically untenable and socially unethical. The appropriation of "Adieu" and its representation of the *doudou* for the official 1935 Tricentennial Celebration of the "attachment" ("*rattachement*") of Martinique, Guadeloupe, and French Guiana to France demonstrated their critique. The song became inscribed in a symbolic economy of colonial and imperial meaning to illustrate that the Antilles belonged to France sentimentally as much as politically. Staging the *doudou* as the embodiment of France's New World colonies plays into the colonial family rhetoric that negritude poets reject as doudouism. In sum, while the French imperial ear hears her song and beauty as fruits of the island landscape ripe for masculinist possession and consumption, the negritude anticolonial ear hears her song as the voice of alienation and betrayal, locating her as intimately involved in the imperial project of "whitening" the Antilles.

Doubly barred in the black Atlantic, marginalized within the colonial family and within the anticolonial one as well, the *doudou* figures the New World *métisse* as a francophone tragic mulatta.[5] In many respects literary criticism and postcolonial studies cosign on this doubled down rejection of the *doudou*'s representational authenticity and value. The early academic history of negritude discourse, as Jennifer Wilks explains in *Race, Gender, and Comparative Black Modernism: Suzanne Lacascade, Marita Bonner, Suzanne Césaire, Dorothy West*, was similarly marked by exclusion. Lilyan Kesteloot's conclusion that "il n'y avait effectivement aucune littérature originale aux Antilles" ("there was effectively no original West Indian literature") prior to the 1932 publication of *Légitime Défense* is to black Francophone literary history in general what Frantz Fanon's commentary about Mayotte Capécia is to Francophone Caribbean women's literature in particular: a defining moment, a line of demarcation between imitation and innovation, self-hatred and self-acceptance" (Wilks 35).

Just as the *doudou* is denied access to recognition, text, or title in "Adieu," negritude discourse (scholarship included) classifies her doudouist voice somewhere between what it deems the exotic creations of white European men (i.e., regionalist poets like Daniel Thaly and Emmanuel Flavia-Léopold) and the sentimental affairs of apolitical Creole women (i.e., Suzanne Lacascade and Mayotte Capécia). Her erasure, part of the suppression of what the present study calls discourse of "negritude in the minor," is a prerequisite for a reconnection with "Mother Africa" and the rebirth of an authentic black subject and voice in negritude's "major mode."

This chapter revisits "Adieu" as an originary soundtext of the French West Indies. The discussion seeks to reinscribe this primal soundtext by suggesting the ways it relates a key imperial struggle over the authentic representation of New World sound and Old World relations. The analysis below moves in reverse chronological order, starting with Fanon's vilification of "Adieu" in *Black Skin* and moving back to the song's earliest inscriptions in eighteenth-century French travel narratives, to retrace the torn discursive genealogy of Antillean voice and to analyze the gendered dynamics of its loss and erasure. Among the many writers and texts that served to construct the "Adieu" *doudou* mythology, Frantz Fanon's staging of the song as a failure in Antillean subjectivity in *Black*

*Skin, White Masks*, and Lafcadio Hearn's description of the song as an ethnographic and musical example of Antillean subjectivity, particularly mark the song's inscription in twentieth-century modernity. The discussion below deconstructs the tensions between two opposing modes of hearing the *doudou*'s song. On one hand, one reading (à la Fanon) hears the voice of "Adieu" as always alienated and inauthentic if not a completely fictitious text written by a white man. On the other hand, ethnographic travel accounts of the song (like Hearn's) insist that "Adieu" represents authentic Antillean voice and that a woman was its original creator. Through close readings of the texts that inscribe her voice into and out of the Antillean soundscape, this chapter locates the *doudou* as the convergence of ideologies and institutions of textuality that deny recognition, authenticity, and value to Antillean cultural expression. But first, how does Fanon critically hear sound, speech, and musicality in black Atlantic culture?

## FANONIAN *RATÉS* AND COLONIAL ENDINGS

As a script of colonial relations and performance, "Adieu" symbolically speaks to many of the major themes of Fanon's work: the dynamics of language and speech given the cultural dictates of French imperialism, the meaning of black diasporic displacement and of Antillean transnational and colonial relations with the *métropole*, and the way economies of desire position the subject to take on, incarnate, and invest in sociocultural mythologies of race and imperial value. Perhaps most of all, the *doudou* sounds out the possibility of black and white love, a taboo topic in dominant French and militant Antillean discourse. Since the time of "Adieu," as Régis Antoine explains, "racism exteriorized and interiorized continued for a long time to establish the impossibility of loving. The beginning is the refrain *Adieu foulard adieu madras*" (*Rayonnants* 145). The song's representations of sentimental attachment crystallize a dynamic of attraction and rejection simultaneously animating French-Antillean relations. "Adieu" interrogates the possibility of authentic love versus colonial order by imagining the climactic colonial *dénouement* (un-doing) of the *doudou* as the ultimate consequence of blurring cultural and racial boundaries. In the end, patriarchal imperialist and anti-imperialist discourse simply cannot allow her to occupy that special position she so longs for in the heart. Yet, while the lyrics instantiate an "adieu" rather than an "au revoir," staging an eventful dénouement and final detachment rather than an iterative, continuing connection, "Adieu" musically and performatively functions as a sonic emblem of French-Antillean sentimental beginnings and attachment.

Sung as a song of departure, "Adieu" marks a physical movement toward France, but for Fanon it signals a cultural and subjective movement of alienation there as well. Such (symbolic, affective, and physical) movement to France creates a "nouveau mode d'être" ("new way of being," 19), he writes, involving practices of speech and text. In its critical performance of Antillean subjectivity, Fanon's hybrid writing voice—full of fragmented and incomplete dialogs, dramatically agonistic performances of colonial and black subjectivity, and antagonistic scenes of race relations—stages the colonial subject as a series of dramatic encounters and relationships with textuality and speech. His opening describes the colonized subject's self-representational voice as succumbing to mountains of pages filled with colonial representation and knowledge: "I'm bombarded from all sides with hundreds of lines that try to foist themselves on me" (xii). Fanon often depicts the internalization of the colonial gaze, the reification of colonial subjectivity, as a specularization from sound to text—or from sound to another type of materiality: skin. The visceral, authentic, immediate sound of "the usually raucous voice" disappears and in its place "un mouvement interne fait de bruissements" (15), "a hushed murmur" as Philcox translates it (4), or "a gentle inner stirring as of rustling breezes" as Markmann has it (20), manifests itself. "In France they say: 'to speak like a book.' In Martinique they say 'to speak like a whiteman'" (Philcox translation 5). Fanonian analysis relates the autobiographical to the otobiographical, interrogating the textual and sonic embodiment of black Antillean subjectivity.[6]

In these moments of encounter and conversion, visual and sonic dynamics come together to fix and racialize the colonial subject: "Je promenai sur moi un regard objectif, découvris ma noirceur, mes caractères ethniques,—et me défoncèrent le tympan l'anthropophagie, l'arriération mentale, le fétichisme, les tares raciales, les négriers, et surtout, et surtout: 'Y a bon banania'" (90). Philcox translates: "I cast an objective gaze over myself, discovered my blackness, my ethnic features; deafened by cannibalism, backwardness, fetishism, racial stigmas, slave traders, and above all, yes, above all, the grinning *Y a bon Banania*" (92). Markmann's translation slips here: "I subjected myself to an objective examination, I discovered my blackness, my ethnic characteristics; and I was *battered down by tom-toms*, cannibalism, intellectual deficiency, fetishism [*sic*], racial defects, slave-ships, and above all else, above all: 'Sho good eatin'" (112, my emphasis).

"*Tympan*" here means "eardrum," not "tom-tom" (the punctuation also suggests "*tympan*" is not part of the list of agents, but part of the body as a direct object of violence). The "*tympan*" constitutes an intimate barrier between self and other, one that naturally remains open. "*Défoncer*," denotes not just a beating but a puncturing or penetration of this membrane or inner skin.[7] "Y a bon banania" (the advertising campaign for a breakfast drink featuring a smiling black "Senegalese" French soldier saying "Banania is good" in "broken" French) breaks down the subject's self-vision and self-hearing to replace it with the imperial gaze and ear. At the same time as it interpellates the black subject through stereotyped speech, it positions all black Antillean or African Francophone speech to resonate with myths of French imperialism and capitalist consumption. In Fanon's scenario, colonial speech overtakes the body, revealing its blackness and coloniality in a modern scene of imperial interpellation and subjection.

Fanon will later refer to the technical term *eretheism*—"an abnormal sensitivity or responsiveness in some part of the body and, by extension, an abnormal emotional sensitivity" (Macey 539, note 125)—pointing up the hypersensitivity of the "ear," its fetishization. The fact that the ear cannot close itself off, that it can't *not* hear, makes it an opportune site for the colonial possession and subjection of the body and psyche. "Since listening remains one of the only physical activities of the human body that occurs simultaneously inside and outside the body," Anne Cheng argues, "we might understand listening here to be *initiating* a boundary contestation. [ . . . ] Coming to listening and then speech condition coming-to-being. The speaking subject serves as, and is conditioned by, the dictaphonic structure, a voice-relay" (162).

Building on Cheng's work through Fanon's scene, one might say the black colonial subject encounters (hears, sees, and sounds) its self as a dictaphonic structure, sees black speech projected onto its body. In this moment, a sonic penetration and possession violently empty the subject out and fill it up with the other. The colonial voice-relay and its dictaphonic structure represent part of a process of subjection where a sonic-visual loop inextricably intertwines desire and surveillance. This bind bars the subject's demand to remain "young and slick" (92) in its relation to the other. Fanon describes the porous rather than protective nature of the black body and specifically of the skin. Rather than a clean slate open to self-designation and inscription (autobiography), the self's black body has already been worn, already constructed with age-old impositions and written out, from within and without. "Where do I fit in? Or, if you like, which should I stick myself?" "Where should I hide?" (93) the subject laments, reeling from this relentless confrontation with the sound scene of its own alienation.

These sound scenes relate the meaning and ontology of blackness to notions of sound and fungibility. Fanon first begins imagining the propagation of race and the fungibility of the subject via an American study arguing that "there is a biochemical modification in a married couple, and apparently they have discovered in the husband certain hormones of his pregnant wife" (6). His (half) ironic suggestion that a similar study be undertaken to discover changes in Antilleans who "relate" with France can be extended to think through the ways language practices and musical culture serve as crucial sites "perpetuating a conflictual situation where the white man infects the black man with extremely toxic foreign bodies" (19). Self-expression, rather than consisting of *parler, dire, entendre* (speaking, telling, and listening), become acts of colonial prosopopoeia, *le faire parler* and *s'entendre dire* (making speak and hearing oneself speak/spoken).

The reification of the black voice in the dictaphonic structure of colonial subjectivity prepares black expression for commodification by rerouting the value of its exchanges. "The relation between pleasure and the possession of slave property, in both the figurative and literal senses," African-American Studies scholar Saidiya Hartman argues,

> can be explained in part by the fungibility of the slave—that is, the joy made possible by virtue of the replaceability and interchangeability endemic to the commodity—and by the extensive capacities of property—that is, the augmentation of the master subject through his embodiment in external objects and persons. Put differently, the fungibility of the commodity makes the captive body an abstract and empty vessel vulnerable to the projection of others' feelings, ideas, desires, and values; and, as property, the dispossessed body of the enslaved is the surrogate for the master's body since it guarantees his disembodied universality and acts as the sign of his power and domination. (21)

Fanon's (and negritude poets') repeated references to "Y a bon banania," suggest the way commodification not only empties the black colonial subject out for exchange, it comes back to confront that subject with its self as an empty commodity, an open signifier, or more specifically, as a space opened up for the other's signification. Borrowing from this francophone linguistic context, we might say that *"Y a bon banania" s'affiche comme son*; its posterized speech operates a specular seizure of the aural subject, while the marketing machinery of postindustrial capitalism relentlessly confronts the subject with sound-scenes of its loss and alienation.

For Fanon, both "Adieu" and "Y a bon banania" emerge from within "a host [*constellation*] of information and a series of propositions." He explains that they "slowly and stealthily work their way into an individual through books, newspapers, school texts, advertisements, movies, and radio and shape his community's vision of the world" (131). Fanon's notion of constellation reflects the industrial mechanization of culture (and advertisement) realizing and reinforcing alienation, and his work interrogates its consequences for black and colonial people in the early and mid-twentieth century. Within this system of sound, the subject's own speech and singing signal the ideological functioning of imperial machination.

Fanon adopts the idea of colonial culture and the subject as machines, using sound as his main metaphorical agent, to characterize the need for a psychoanalytic method to address the epistemological dilemmas of race and colonialism. "If the debate cannot be opened up on a philosophical level—i.e., the fundamental demands of human reality—I agree to place it on a psychoanalytical level, in other words, the 'misfires,' just as we talk about an engine misfiring" (6–7). Fanon's term, *raté*, translated above by Philcox as "misfires" and by Markmann as "failures" (23), plays on several connotations in French. The *raté* is a percussive misfire or backfire of an engine, referring to a person, or to a person's psyche, as a failure or a loser in popular connotation. In addition to meaning to backfire or to fail to function, the verb *rater* means to miss something in space or time and to fail to pass something (like a test). This book will build on these various connotative facets to posit the Fanonist *raté* as a theoretical concept for hearing the sounding of the black body and of colonial subjectivity. Fanon's *raté* functions like a *lapsus révélateur*, but the terminology suggests the (percussive, mechanical, and desirous) ideological violence of this "other kind of talk." Unlike the Freudian and Lacanian discrete slip of the tongue, whose telling mistakes testify to the other's flickering, if profound, presence on the scene of the subject's psyche, Fanon situates the black colonial subject even at the conscious level as the stage for the aggressive outburst of the other. The loud shock of the *raté*, rather than serving as a guarantor of authenticity and life in the present, echoes a repressed past, an elsewhere, an otherness, or, as Aimé Césaire puts it in *Discourse on Colonialism*, a process of "thingification."

Can the misfiring black subject be struck into an explosive black truth (perhaps not unlike the way one beats the side of a malfunctioning machine)? Fanon's opaque performance throws cold water on the notion from the opening of *Black Skin*: "Don't expect to see any explosion today. It's too early . . . or too late. I'm not the bearer of absolute truths. No fundamental inspiration has flashed across my mind. I honestly think, however, it's time some things were said. Things I'm going to say, not shout. I've given up shouting. A long time ago." (xi). The tone and reference are slightly modified in Philcox's translation here. Rather than not "being *seen*," a more accurate expression of the explosive *raté* in this passage might put "will not take place," thus accessing the implications of sound and percussivity, but also the dynamics of mythology, in Fanon's critical figure. The original French for "shout," *le cri*, evokes *le cri nègre*: negritude discourse and ideology. But Fanon's critical voice renounces the explosion, the cry, and later enthusiasm or "zealousness," as *ratés* that, rather than revealing truth or change as promised, only expose the subject as an effect and affect of the colonial machine.

Essentially, Fanon's writing performance suggests colonial culture turns the black subject into a hysteric. The bodily disturbances of colonial subject formation echo the type of conversion disorder psychoanalysis has historically associated with this neurosis. Having consumed charged anxieties, phobias, and desires, the subject physically takes them on, manifesting a new embodied form. His "only solution: to make [himself] known" ("me faire connaître") completes in its theatricality the alienated expression of this new corporeal form, and his tone performs its violent sensitivity and excessive excitability. The sound of the *raté*, in relation to the *tympan* as the site of an erotic aural penetration, signals an ambivalently desirous outburst. Here, racial "passing" relates to an affective and psychic passage, an erotic en route toward the other as self-fulfillment. "Her love," Fanon writes in the person of an alienated black man in love with the white woman "opens the illustrious path [*couloir*] that leads to total fulfillment" (45). While still resonating with discourse on hysteria, Fanon's critique has to do with the fungibility of the colonial subject. This mode of subjective embodiment engenders a mode of situation with respect to the symbolic, where the (black) man's relations with the (white) woman leave *him* the illusion of being "full" of *her* (white) self. This passage, or passing, signaling somehow *his* birth through identifying relations with *her*, "stresses" the racial subject's coherence with the dynamics of colonial emasculation. Fanon suggests that our relationship to and performance of the symbolic, constituted as it is by the dynamics of desire that form the core of subjective identification, is an emotional posture relating colonial gender and race.

The dictaphonics of colonial discourse and its soundtext conversions involve the perpetual construction, breaking up (cutting up, blowing up), and dispersal of its subjects. Transformations and disturbances of sound and text simultaneously signal the disruption of the individual body, the dismemberment and disbursement of the subject's corporeal schema, the disruption of the collective body, and the dispersal and impoverishment of Antillean culture in transatlantic exchange. Fanon's *raté*, at the level of the subject, shouts out a failed attempt to repress, to disavow, or to escape from the machine. Fanon uses similar language to consider this dynamic at the level of sociality and cultural production. "In every society, in every community, there exists, must exist, a channel, an outlet whereby the energy accumulated in the form of aggressiveness can be released" (124). At the level of sociality, the *raté* announces the failure of culture, not only because culture generally does nothing revolutionary with the aggression built up in modernity, but because it fails even to mask this failure.

Close attention to Fanon's intense intertextual dialogs helps crucially in tracing the *raté* within social productions of knowledge and culture. The hybrid nature of *Black Skin, White Masks* comes in part from this multi-disciplinary dialog, a polyvocality that aptly represents the imperial struggle over authentic voice. Fanon's dialog with negritude poets illustrates the *raté*, capturing the way the voice-relay functions in text but also staging the dynamic relations between the black reading subject and the text. Damas's "Hoquet" (Hiccups) is a key example, resonating with Fanon's analytical depiction of the colonial speech as *raté*, and resonating with the black colonial reading subject.[8] Damas's classic renders the Antillean child's subjection to the symbolic law of "le français français," French French as opposed to Antillean French. "Yes I must watch my diction," echoes Fanon's performance voice from Damas's poem, "because that's how they'll judge me" (4). Long before departure from the island, the colonial subject assumes an intense and mythological relationship to the French language and his own speech. Arriving in France brings the complications of the subject's embodied sounds and its lack to a climax. Fanon writes:

> The black man entering France reacts against the myth of the Martinican who swallows his r's. He'll go to work on it and enter into open conflict with it. He'll make every effort not only to roll [*rouler*] his r's, but to make them stand out [*les ourler*]. On the lookout for the slightest reaction of others, listening to himself speak and not trusting his own tongue, an unfortunately lazy organ, he will lock himself in his room and read for hours—desperately working on his diction [*s'acharnant à se faire diction*] (5).

In the expression "*s'acharnant*" ("desperately working"), the use of italics, and the turn of phrase, Fanon's language implies we imagine something stronger than someone "working on" language; this subject wants *to be* diction, wants to embody French speech (as against the black body's own speech and tongue). Especially given the musical context of the current project, the common usage of "diction," the "quality of articulation, of pronunciation" must relate to the performative sense of "diction," "the quality of interpretation, of performance."[9] Portraying the black Antillean in France "locked away in his room," Fanon's scene shows diction as a type of textual performance as much as clear articulation. Indeed, the hard work of mimicry requires constant *répétitions*, an intense *shedding* of the "lazy organ" that is reified colonial speech. In other words mimicry is a performance, but it is the practice (practice, practice) of loss and alienation.

The *r*'s transition from *"roulé"* to *"ourlé,"* signals this shift from "free" expression to an iterative linguistic and mimetic hemming in of Martinican subjectivity. Anchoring the subject in relation to speech sound, his description harks back to the doudouist poetic description of Creole as a "roucoulement divin" (15), a divine birdsong. Linguists refer to this phenomenon as hypercorrection; the speaker's attempts to demonstrate stylistic, grammatical, or pronunciation mastery only end up revealing linguistic (and often thereby socio-cultural) insecurity and marginal status. Fanon's analysis takes this much further in the West Indian context. His language's descriptive dyslexia (ourler/ rouler) represents the inability of the subject to speak its way into the symbolic field in a smooth way. Instead just as with "ourler," to hem a fringe onto something, it indicates materiality and linguistic excess as the terms of black Antillean self-expression. Indeed, Fanon's choice of language suggests, in the context of "Adieu," a consideration of the associative qualities between the fabric *in* the song (madras and foulard) and the fabric *of* the song (music and the Creole language), and the way they correlate to transatlantic and imperial dynamics of desire for the French West Indies.

"Adieu" musically plays out this *raté* of colonial subjectivity, loudly announcing a power-laden slippage in, if not outright violent failure of, the subject's speech within dominant paradigms of cultural value and recognition. Fanon's description leading up to his quote of "Adieu" appropriately harks back to early ethnographic accounts and travel narratives where the trope of the appearing/ disappearing island stages in scenes of arrival the slow specular striptease of nature for fantasies of conquest. His critical performance begins to situate "Adieu" in its most common musicking context, yet his contextualization reworks the positions of enunciation and reception such that, rather than identifying with the singing *doudou*, this Fanonian subject identifies with the departing subject, formerly the white French sailor. The subject effectively hears himself affectionately sung to "comme un blanc," as a white Frenchman.

As seen in the epigraph that opens the current chapter, Fanon marks the impending departure with a provocative paradox; his expression "the *amputation* of his being *vanishes*" (my emphasis) crystallizes the ambivalent presence of the black colonial subject who arrives at the moment of departure. While in practice and lyrics "Adieu" bids *farewell*, Fanon's critical listening perspective situates it as a cultural production that also signals an *arrival*. In one sense the metaphor suggests that the subject arrives "as the profile of the ocean liner becomes clearer." Here, the disappearance of amputation, the departure of lack, leaves the (false) potential of what Fanon calls being "full of oneself." The subject arrives, just as the ship does, and his lack (amputation) disappears. Yet in concert with this subject/ship relation, the metaphor also prepares the subject for a direct, rather than inverse, relationship to amputation, since the latter disappears just as he too will soon depart. In this reading, the metaphor's subject/amputation conflation constitutes the *realization* rather than an absence of lack. Something (amputation) that was (missing) there is now gone (disappears), leaving an empty space, a deep mythological cut, to be filled up by the desire of the other (lack).

He arrives at the port to disappear: sound and vision, literacy and musicality come to bear at this climactic moment. "Adieu" instantiates this torn structure, constructing desirous and dynamic mythologies of fullness and lack. "He can read the authority and mutation he has acquired in the eyes of those accompanying him to the ship: 'Adieu madras, adieu foulard'" (7).

## LISTENING BACK: RELOCATING
## THE *DOUDOU*'S SIGNATURE SONG

The *doudou*'s bid farewell to the sociocultural fabric of her being constitutes a Fanonian "raté," a prosopopoeia slippage signaling the colonial conditions of the song's authorship and whose structures allegorize the *doudou*'s ambivalent, stuck condition. But Fanon does not interrogate the important gender designations and slippages taking place in his scene of departure. Recovering her loss, which Fanon's text signs off on, means deconstructing the reified relationships between gender, musicality, and textuality that seal her representational overdetermination.

While "Adieu" uses the term *doudoux* ("sweetheart") to refer to the departing French male lover, the *doudou* mythology designates *her* as the *doudou* and leaves *him* unnamed. *Doudou* in Creole can refer to men or women, in a romantic or platonic sense, but "*doudou*" in French discourse carries imperial resonance by employing the term exclusively to refer to women and romance. Even today, following imperial mythology more than linguistic etymology, French dictionaries continue to imperiously gender the term. For example, see this listing in the 2006 edition of *Le Petit Larousse illustré*: "2. DOUDOU n.f. Antilles.

*Fam.* Jeune femme aimée." It is important to situate this gendered gesture of naming (as well as its dynamics of address and the topography of its positions of enunciation) within a constellation of tropes of female otherness that fuel the longing in the French imperial imaginary. While the latter deploys the dream of "the French colonial family," we might more accurately call this constellation of colonial women others "the French imperial harem" as Fatima Mernissi does.[10] The terminology indicates the way French imperial discourse creates mythologies of women of color as part of its mission of global conquest, possession, and collection.

To trace the dominant figures in this imperial iconography of colonial women of color—spanning from the representation of Sarah Baartmann, "the Hottentot Venus" given in cartoon caricatures and live shows, to the phantasm of the Algerian harem played out in postcard culture and on the silver screen— is to "map out," as Malek Alloula puts it in the case of the latter, "from under the plethora of images, the obsessive scheme that regulates the totality of the output of this enterprise and endows it with meaning" (4). In all of these cases, the colonial woman's body is literally and figuratively put on display, scientifically and morally interrogated, and ultimately incorporated and consumed in patriarchal economies of imperial knowledge and capitalist value.

Perhaps more than France's other colonial women, the *doudou* represents the delicate negotiation of the intimate racial, gender, and geographic relations implicated in the colonial family dream (harem) of *la France des 100 millions.* "Adieu" constitutes a key soundtext in the early history of colonial family mythology in part because the latter "played a greater role in the *Vieilles Colonies* than in other parts of the empire" as Françoise Vergès explains, "because there the battle between the *Ancien Régime* and French Revolution continued late into the twentieth century" (6). The lullaby musicality of the "Adieu" melody plays a crucial role here in that it prominently evokes the *doudou*'s maternity. At the same time as it weaves the figure of maternity into associations between blackness and sexual promiscuity that have been around since the Middle Ages, it simultaneously intimates the expansion of the imperial family.[11] The association between the *doudou* and the Antillean *da* (nursemaid), and the systematic sexual exploitation of *das* in slave and colonial culture, further suggests that the sonic and specular iconography of Antillean women relates to ideas of colonial maternity and promiscuity.

Unlike the myths of African women, the tragic *mulatta* sexual and maternal phantasms involved in representing the *doudou* symbolize her as a site of race-mixing. Inscribed into her environment, her tropical "hot blood" comes from the sun but also from the volatile mix of her origins. She is a torn creature of nature and culture, making her as volatile and treacherous as she is beautiful and serene. Suzanne Bost's study *Mulattas and Mestizas: Representing Mixed Identities in the Americas 1850–2000* can help situate the *doudou* with respect to ideologies and practices of racial mixture that often come down on the bodies of women. As Bost shows, the uneven patchwork of New World *métissage* discourse reflects the uneven historic terrain of European imperial policies and American colonial practices regarding interracial relations. The *mulatta*, the *mestiza*, and the *métisse* face differing conditions between and within the imperialist juridical and cultural regimes of the United States, Latin America, and the Caribbean. While the *doudou*'s stuck position at the port symbolically relates to the (im)possibility of her mobility within the social stratifications of race and coloniality, women of color moved across cultural and national boundaries, calling attention to the contingency of race and gender while providing points of contact (and tension) between different systems of stratification. These women may be part of large families or entire communities that set up shop across national borders (for example the Creoles in Louisiana). Whether slaves, free, or somewhere in between, they bring with them alternate ways of understanding race and the unspoken rules of race-mixing and thus blur imperial mapping projects.

The mixed message in "Adieu," where musicality signals attraction while textuality signals separation, resonates with the contradictions of colonial and imperial policies regarding interracial unions. On one side, crossing colonial and racial boundaries could lead to the dissolution of criteria for difference, without which the logic and justification of the imperial enterprise collapses. On the other, the possession of the material and symbolic means in the colonies largely created and relied on forms of sexual domination that produce interracial mixtures. In other words, the paradox of the *doudou*'s *raté* represents both the breakdown in the regulatory systems of colonial stratification and the reinforcement of white patriarchal supremacy through the fetishization of women of color and the reproduction of colonial labor.

But while *doudou*'s iconographic sound as a tragic colonial mulatta has been planted deep in the critical heart of colonial and postcolonial New World discourse as loss, the sociocultural context of *métissage* in which "Adieu" and songs like it were composed and performed paints a more complicated picture. As Deborah Jenson explains in her analysis of the earliest known publication of a book of French Antillean Creolophone poetry, *Idylles, ou essais de poésie créole* published in New York in 1804 by an anonymous "Colon de Saint-Domingue," the domestic promiscuities of the French New World slave cultures mean it's possible that *she* composed the text even if *he* wrote it down and received credit for it. Jenson carefully notes that the wording of the anonymous "Settler from Santo Domingo" who signed the poetry collection only claims to "offer" this "collection" [*recueil*]; he never claims to have authored it (Jenson 83). The inclusion of the well-known folkloric *chanson* "Lisette quitte la plaine" in the second edition of this collection of poetry further suggests that the colonial agent was a signer and a collector more than a composer and author.[12]

Lisette quitté la plaine
Mon perdi bonher à moue
Gié à moin semblé fontaine
Dipi mon pas miré toué
Le jour quand mon coupé canne
Mon songé zamour à moué
La nuit quand mon dans cabane
Dans dromi mon quimbé toué [. . .]

[Lisette has left the plains
My happiness is gone
My eyes have turned into fountains
Since I can no longer see you
During the day when I'm cutting cane
I'm thinking about my love
Night, when I'm in my cabin
I dream you come back to me]

Dipi mon perdi Lisette
Mon pas touchié Calinda
Mon quitté Bram-bram sonnette
Mon pas batté Bamboula
Quand mon contré l'aut'négresse
Mon pas gagné gié pour li
Mon pas sonchié travail pièce
Tout'qui chose a moin mourri

[Since I lost Lisette
I haven't touched the Calinda
I left behind my *Bram-bram bells*
I haven't beaten a Bamboula

When I met other *négresses*
I have no eyes for them
I can't work at all
Nothing matters to me anymore]

Jenson's work crucially breaks through the assumed erasure of populations color in early French Antillean literature. Following her lead, how can one hear the heart of the soundtext tradition in "Adieu," like its counterpart, as something more than the expression of white European men?

Often referred to as *chansons de cocotte* or *chansons galantes*, the Creole lyrics and borrowed European melodies of these songs represent the intimate domestic and cultural relations of plantation cultures. Citing research on Médéric Louis Elie Moreau de Saint-Méry's unpublished *Notes historiques*, Jenson explains *cocottes* as "female 'mulatto entertainers' to their mistresses in colonial Saint-Domingue" (94). Interestingly, and perhaps uncoincidentally, the second edition of *Idylles* (1811) was published in Philadelphia, where Moreau had settled to finish his *Description topographique, physique, civile, politique et historique de la partie française de l'isle Saint-Domingue* (1797) after fleeing the events of the French Revolution. Moreau deplored the familial relationships between domestic women of color and young white Creoles with whom they often lived in the master's house. He describes a daily life so close that the white women married to colonists and *cocottes* often even slept together in the mistress's bed. "In this interracial domestic environment," Jenson explains, "women from radically different positions in the socio-racial hierarchy shared 'the songs that they lisped in the sweet and nonchalant Creole tongue.' And much more: the 'cocotte,' who according to Moreau might be mulatto or black, was sometimes the mistress of the husband of the mistress" (94). Despite her social reality, Jensen explains, "the 'cocotte' is in a position of extreme social hybridity, almost too liminal to imagine" (95). Her special place in these imperial and transnational economies of material and symbolic exchange correlates to a "special hybridity" imperial and anti-imperial discourse struggled to grasp.

Lafcadio Hearn includes a transcription of the song in his *Two Years in the French West Indies* and uses it as an authentic document testifying to the special hybridity and allure of women in Martinique. With his experience in Creole cultures gained through time spent writing about and living in New Orleans, Hearn provides a much more thorough and studied documentation of *doudou*, and the term *doudou*, in his ethnography. Noting the many different meanings of *doux*, he writes: "The word *sucre* [sugar] is rarely used in Martinique,—considering

that sugar is still the chief product;—the word *doux* 'sweet,' is commonly sub-
stituted for it. *Doux* has, however, a larger range of meaning: it may signify
syrup, or any sort of sweets,—duplicated into *doudoux*, it means the corossole
fruit as well as a sweetheart. *Ça qui lè doudoux?* is the cry of the corossole-seller"
(Hearn 470). Whether inside the context of colonial tropes or that of Creole
local practices, the Creole woman's sweet stuff in early ethnographies correlates language, sexuality, and the sugar trade, locating the *doudou* in the middle
of imperial economies of French-Antillean exchange.

Most accounts locate "Adieu" in Guadeloupe, but the *doudou* mythology goes
back to the legendary Saint-Pierre, Martinique—the cultural and economic
"little Paris" of the Lesser Antilles destroyed in the 1902 volcanic eruption of
Mount Pelée. In his chronicle of "the lost city" just before the disaster, Hearn
describes "[a] population fantastic, astonishing,—a population of the Arabian
Nights. It is many-colored; but the general dominant tint is yellow, like that
of the town itself—yellow in the interblending of all the hues characterizing
*mulâtresse, capresse, griffe, quarteronne, métisse, chabine*—a general effect of rich
brownish yellow. You are among a people of the half-breeds,—the finest mixed
race of the West Indies" (Hearn 180–181). Note that Hearn's description of this
racial panorama of *métissage* gives all examples in the feminine form. This spec-
trum of racial hybridity in the feminine resonates with Moreau de Saint-Méry's
gendered chartings of racial combination a century before. Doris Garraway explains that "[a]t its origin, Moreau's classificatory system presupposes a fantasy: that of a white male coupling with a black female, whose offspring begins a
chain of successive couplings, always with the same white male factor crossing
with the mixed-race female product of his prior union, to the *nth* degree. Such is
the incestuous logic of the first six categories of color between white and black,
on which Moreau founds his racial organization of colonial humanity" (230).

Hearn undoubtedly was very familiar with Moreau's work given his numerous studied references to previous French ethnographies of the region. He
combines this old taxonomy with his interest in modernity's modes of affecting change, creolization, and continuity in "new" and "old" practices and productions of culture. One of the reasons Hearn fascinates as writer is his way of
operating a discursive turning point and juncture between Enlightenment and
twentieth-century discourse and sensibilities concerning the other. Such junc-
tures and turns take place through Hearn's unique transnational trajectory, of
which the New World and its Creole culture were crucial sites.

The *métisse* figure also crucially represents concepts in temporality and historicity, as does colonial family romance more generally. While Moreau's fanta-

sies engaged in scientific theories of race at the turn of the eighteenth century in the context of anxieties about the historic consequences of the French and later Haitian revolutions, Hearn's accounts modernize the imperial charting of cultural contact zones at the turn of the twentieth century often fetishizing the Creole cultures as temporally heteroclite. Hearn's thick descriptions of the traditional dress and jewelry of *doudou* iconography as a "novelty" lies somewhere between the fetishism of ethnography and that of tourist discourse. His descriptive portrait of the *doudou* classically touching on these themes merits extended citation:

> Perhaps the most novel impression of all is that produced by the singularity and brilliancy of certain of the women's costumes. These were developed, at least a hundred years ago, by some curious sumptuary law regulating the dress of slaves and colored people of free condition,—a law which allowed considerable liberty as to material and tint, prescribing chiefly form. But some of these fashions suggest the Orient: they offer beautiful audacities of color contrast; and the full-dress coiffure, above all, is so strikingly Eastern that one might be tempted to believe it was first introduced into the colony by some Mohammedan slave. It is merely an immense Madras handkerchief, which is folded about the head with admirable art, like a turban;—one bright end pushed through at the top in front, being left sticking up like a plume. Then this turban, always full of bright canary-color, is fastened with golden brooches,—one in front and one at either side. As for the remainder of the dress, it is simple enough: an embroidered low-cut chemise with sleeves; a skirt or *jupe*, very long behind, but caught up and fastened in front below the breasts so as to bring the hem everywhere to level with the end of the long chemise; and finally a *foulard*, or silken kerchief, thrown over the shoulders. These *jupes* and *foulards*, however, are exquisite in pattern and color: bright crimson, bright yellow bright blue, bright green—lilac, violet, rose,—sometimes mingled in plaidings or checkerings or stripings [*sic*] [. . .]. To this display add the effect of costly and curious jewellery: immense earrings, each pendant being formed of five gold cylinders joined together (cylinders sometimes two inches long, and an inch at least in circumference);—a necklace of double, triple, quadruple, or quintuple rows of large hollow gold beads (sometimes smooth, but generally graven)—the wonderful *collier-choux*. Now, this glowing jewellery is not mere imitation of pure metal: the ear-rings are worth one hundred and seventy-five francs a pair; the necklace of a Martinique quadroon may cost five hundred or even one thousand francs . . . It may be the gift of her lover, her *doudoux*, but such articles are usually purchased either on time by small payments, or bead by bead

singly until the requisite number is made up. But few are thus richly attired, the greater number of the women carrying burdens on their heads,—peddling vegetables, cakes, fruit, ready-cooked food, from door to door,—are very simply dressed (Hearn 181–182).

Hearn reproduces the *doudou* myth even as he debunks much of it, commenting on the rarity of such rich attire and the likelihood of the expensive jewelry being slowly earned through hard work rather than given as a gift in exchange for sexual relations. His account relates the tradition of colonial dress to the history of slavery and French imperial oppression then relates that history through to the contemporary context through the *doudou* mythology. Choosing a "quadroon" for his example, Hearn considers the *doudou*'s socio-cultural and musical practices and performances as the *compromissions* of everyday modern colonial life for women of color. At the same time, his orientalist framing of this "Arabian Nights" population that he finds "so strikingly Eastern" adds discursive depth and breadth to his portrait of New World "novelty."

But as important as this visual iconography of the *doudou*, Hearn offers a linguistic and musical depiction of her by inserting his transcription of "Adieu." In Hearn's text the song attests to the sociological and cultural phenomenon of interracial relations described above. Along with the *madras*, the *foulard*, and the *collier-choux*, Hearn's transcription sketches a panoramic portrait of these torn interracial relations, relations that often end with the woman of color being left behind. But "whatever comes," Hearn writes of the Creole tragic mulatta,

> she does not die for grief, this daughter of the sun: she pours out her pain in song, like a bird. Here is one of her little improvisations,—a song very popular in both Martinique and Guadeloupe, though originally composed in the latter colony:—
>
> —'Good-bye Madras! Good-bye foulard! Good-bye pretty calicoes! Good-bye collier-choux! That ship Which is there on the buoy, It is taking My doudoux away.
>
> —'Adiéu Madras! Adiéu foulard! Adiéu dézinde! Adiéu collier-choux! Batiment-là Qui sou labouà-là, Li ka mennein Doudoux-à-moin allé.
>
> —Very good-day,—Monsieur the Consignée. I come To make one little petition. My doudoux Is going away. Alas! I pray you Delay his going'
>
> —'Bien le-bonjou,' Missié le Consignataire. Moin ka vini Fai yon ti pétition; Doudoux-à-moin Y ka pati,—T'enprie, hélas! Rétàdé li.'

(He answers kindly in French: the *békés* are always kind to these gentle children.)

—'My dear child, It is too late. The bills of lading Are already signed; The ship Is already on the buoy. In an hour from now They will be getting her under way.'

—'Ma chère enfant Il est trop tard, Les connaissements Sont déjà signés, Est déjà sur la bouée; Dans une heure d'ici, Ils vont appareiller.'

—'When the foulards came ... I always had some; When the Madras-kerchiefs came, I always had some. . . . That second officer—Is such a kind man!

—'Foulard rivé, Moin té toujou tini; Madras rivé, Moin té toujou tini; Déz-indes rivé, Moin té toujou tini.—Capitaine sougonde C'est yon bon gàçon!

—'Everybody has' Somebody to love; Everybody has Somebody to pet; Everybody has A sweetheart of her own. I am the only one Who cannot have that,—I!'

—'Toutt moune tini Yon moune yo aimé; Toutt moune tini Yon moune you chéri; Toutt moune tini Yon doudoux à yo. Jusse moin tou sèle Pa tini ça—moin!' (Hearn 458–459, his translation)

Significantly, while Hearn calls the song "one of *her* little improvisations" (my emphasis), "Adieu" contains two distinct voices (unlike "Lisette"): that of the Creole woman and the white French colonial agent, which in Hearn's text is called *Monsieur le Consignataire*, translated in English as "Monsieur the Con-signé." The latter represents the captain and the ship's company at the port. One of this post's main duties is to take account of the people and merchandise allowed on and off the ship. This includes the official registry with the names of passengers, like that of the Creole sweetheart's *doudou*. The song's narrative itself turns on the question of the authority of the text, its official record of names, and its signatures. Although left out of the cultural typology the song has been heard to represent, this holder of official texts and names to whom *doudou* must sing her plea before is central rather than peripheral. Even within the fiction of the scene, the presence of the co-signature calls into question the authority of the singing subject, the latter whom requires him to gain recognition and legitimation.

Further, the presence of the "cosignatory" problematizes the notion that the song emerged from improvisation. Unless one imagines the two characters as breaking into song together spontaneously, at least a portion of the music of this scene comes later in a moment of composition, a moment cleanly erased from the historical consciousness of this key French-Antillean mythical scene. Even if improvised, the song in its dialogic and bilingual entirety would not have been completely improvised at the scene of departure. The refrain constitutes the only possible place of musical improvisation within this staged performance (most of which represents spoken dialog set to music). In other words, either the song and its dialog with the *consignataire* emerged in improvised fashion in a scene of departure that someone later put together and composed as one musical utterance, or "Adieu" was inspired by these scenes but composed and performed (whether in improvised or scripted manner) outside of the moment of the port scene. This line of critique puts pressure on the dual mechanisms of authenticity flowing through the text: one which posits its truth as ethnographic— the documentation of a type done by an outsider—and as autobiographic—the pure expression of deep loss and despair for the tragic mulatta. The temporal, narrative, and performative inconsistencies that saturate the song on the slightest close examination have failed to break up the power its mythology has held for centuries. Simply put, the obliteration of the song's "authentic" scene disrupts the monolithic inscription of its performative context as a scene of her loss, and it turns the tables on her presumed erased, marginalized, and ephemeral historic presence on the scene of Antillean cultural origins.

Separating out and even apposing the song's staged scene at the port, to its many other possible scenes of inspiration, composition, and performance, provides the conditions to open up the song to other postures of meaning including seduction, sentiment, and satire. Such contexts point up the instability of the boundaries of authority and authorship on the song's surface, and suggest a path toward restitution of the *doudou*'s musical worth and the value of her song. It suggests an interrogation of authorship that destabilizes the gendered and imperial paradigms with which "she" is cast and staged. At the same time, it suggests the central place of "improvisation," musicality, and textuality in the *doudou* mythology.

More than a decade before Hearn's work appeared, Armand Corre published a transcribed a copy of the text of "Adieu" under the title "Chanson du consignataire" in his work *Nos Créoles* in 1890. Corre's study of French colonial society in the New World contains many songs (including once again "Lisette quitté la pleine") and contains a chapter of transcriptions of local songs. But, testifying to the song's unique emblematic usage, Corre refers to "Adieu" in a chapter called "Les Moeurs privées" and in the context of dance culture and romantic intrigue across racial and colonial boundaries—something he specifically writes his book to warn against. Speaking on the Martinican *bélé* dance and drum traditions, Corre explains the distinct way "*doudoux*" women of color flirt with the boundaries of African and European cultural practices and traditions in Antillean colonial society:

> The *mulâtresses*, who have frequented diverse strata of society, do not give them-selves over to these dances, or they let themselves go only furtively. But they are crazy about song and dance. They show in these activities a delicate charm that is theirs alone. I do not know anything as sweet and tender as the complaint of a poor girl who has just attended the departure of her traveling lover, some long dis-tance captain no doubt. I cannot resist reproducing at this moment the little Cre-ole language song that everyone knows in the Antilles under the title "Chanson du consignataire." (The couplets in Creole are sung in a languorous sad rhythm; the couplet in French, without rhyme, is spoken or sung in a quick rhythm to express the polite regret mixed with the impatience of a man who has other things to do than to listen to the sad story of a woman in love.) (195)

As Hearn does, Corre treats this musical scene as a study in colonial sociol-ogy and language as well as ethnography. In their discourse "Adieu" represents a sound sample, collected through techniques in ethnographic and linguistic study, whose authenticity corresponds to a sociocultural phenomenon. The notion of "improvisation" importantly posits the *doudou*'s complaint as both authentic and typological. Corre finds the fantasy of the helpless and tragic mu-latta "doux" and "caressant"—even the song is irresistible—and he suggests the especially musical nature of their "charme délicat." "Adieu," resonating as it does with the romantic plots and colonial love stories of *récits d'aventure* dis-cussed in this book's introduction, allows the ethnographer to subtly insert nar-ratives of colonial romance into this typology.

It is interesting that Corre gives strophic form to his transcription and trans-lation. The verses are distinguishable on the page but also rhythmically distinct, unlike Hearn's more narrative transcription. The poetic format and versifica-tion, and the subtle insistence in transcriptions that the departing Frenchman be a sailor or other imperial military agent (Corre proposes a "capitaine long-courrier" as the *doudou*'s likely departing love) represents "Adieu" in a highly textual and literary form. But like Hearn would do, Corre overlooks the bilin-gualism of the song to treat it as an authentic *tranche de vie*, as itself a testifying document, of Creole colonial culture.

Corre's transcription and translation unpacks the *Créolisme* "collier-choux" normally found in lyrics, with "collier-sous" and translates it as "pièces de monnaie." The coin necklace associates island pleasure and imperial value and harks back to the coins thrown from ships arriving at port. Corre identifies musical practices as spheres of social and cultural hierarchies as well as occasions to threaten them. The lyrics differ only slightly from Hearn's later version, but the emphasis on the cosignatory in the title highlights the question of writing, signing, and transcribing her and the boundaries of her sound and presence.

Notions of textuality and musicality are necessary in this typology precisely because imperial boundaries of race and paradigms of color insufficiently identify and designate her to assigned places in colonial hierarchies of social order. The linguistic dimension of the song, juxtaposing French and Creole, helps crystallize stereotypes about the sound of Creole language. Corre elaborates in fascinating detail the imperial discourse on the sound and meaning of Creole, and he seems to be articulating in his own way the relationships between language, desire, musical culture, and the proper administration of France's New World colonies. "This strange language, with its simple mechanisms and very visual imagery, lends itself admirably to the expression of elementary feelings, to the painting of things in nature. It is spicy and affectionate [*piquant et caressant*] in the mouth of women, picturesque and at times biting, under the appearance of good-natured naïveté, in the mouths of *nègres*" (261). You can't fault Corre for his bluntness; at least he picks up on the bite behind the already then mythologized "picturesque" sweet talk of Creole sound. But Corre casts that double nature as a mixed binary of gender and color. Referring to the language's seductive sound in the mouth of "femmes," and its biting quality in the mouth of "*nègres*," Corre leads one to understand this to mean women "de couleur," that is, of mixed parentage rather than the less pleasant sound of men. Again, through "Adieu" and its mythologies of the text and the voice, the construction of typologies of race in the New World correlates tightly to constructed typologies of gender.

Before Corre, Sahib, in *La frégate l'Incomprise: Voyage autour du monde à la plume* has a version of "Adieu" with lyrics that relate to a specific story. Titled "Le Départ du Jean Bart," the latter being the name of a transatlantic ship, this version of "Adieu" still serves as a farewell song, mixing in names of Creole lovers left behind in the second verse before taking up the blank names *doudou* and *cocotte* by the end. Sahib gives much more creative credit to women as the clever and skillful composers of these songs. "These *mulâtresses* are very ingenious at adapting the latest melody to words related to whatever occupies them at that moment. Witness the song with which they accompanied the *Jean Bart* leaving for France with all the young shipmen of its crew" (202).[13] Indeed more than a song, "Adieu" became a folkloric icon relating anxieties of relation and separation as constitutive of the *doudou*'s ontological and social being.

"Adieu" seems to symbolically instantiate time and space limits for transatlantic, transcolonial relations. Yet, as Alain Ruscio notes in general regarding *chanson coloniale*, "[t]he most curious thing is that certain songs were in total contradiction with the reality lived by the French" (*Que la France* 298). Often, "*chanson coloniale* acts [. . .] like a veil [. . .] between reality and fantasms" (298). In other words, the myth of ephemeral relations dreamed of by colonial discourse comes up against historical, sociological, and cultural phenomena that prove by their very existence the contrary. Archival research shows that marriage after a long period of *concubinage* constituted a demographic particularity of unions between free people of color and between whites and women of color (Régent). Rather than ephemeral relations, the long history of the *doudou* and the advent of the *métisse* as a sociocultural phenomenon proves the song's mythology of time and space often remains just that.

## CONCLUSION

The "true" or "original" author of "Adieu" may always remain unknown, but the notion of authorship remains crucial, not in the sense of discovering the "truth" of its origins or the "truth" of her representation, but rather because of the way fictions of text and writing have been inscribed onto her in this originary scene of French New World relations.[14] Ultimately, assigning sole authorship and meaning of "Adieu" to the European white male further reifies the *doudou*'s voice. It plays into the binary construct of race by assuming the cultural authenticity of her expression to be an impossibility. Caught between the law of the master/love and that of the state, between the past and the future, between authenticity and affectation, orality and textuality, the *doudou*'s in-between status, her "*mitoyenneté*," both expands and limits her choices. Her aesthetic expands her social mobility yet limits its ethical outlook and appearance, positioning her as the intimate antagonism between old and new orders of socialization, cultural production, and legitimacy in the French Antilles.

How can we then define the situation of the *doudou* in these performative and poetic economies of desire? The *doudou* strives to become diction, but the ear of the other usurps her *jouissance*, making her lost and losing voice itself the performative sign of her being. Her song locates a linguistico-symbolic economy of colonial desire as failed diction. The *doudou* is not a woman; "*she*" is rather a structural, temporal subject position in the intimate psychosocial microphysics of colonial power—stuck, in other words, in the struggle of power in the minor. The *doudou*'s cry geographically fixes her but also signals her emotionally stuck situation and her stuckness in time. It attempts to categorize key connections between race and gender as not political, by occluding the flow of desire as a function of colonial culture and its designation of race. The *doudou*'s precarious position at the frontier between the aural and the textual, between action and acting, singing and scripting, evoke the ethical and aesthetic dilemmas posed by transnational relations while simultaneously constituting for centuries the dominant legal and emotional structure of social life and mobility.

David Macey argues that "Fanon's version of the song ["Adieu"] can also be read as a farewell to the *doudouiste* literature" (Macey 113). My analysis suggests the ways in which musico-textual relations relay, rather than rupture, the desirous poetic dynamics at work in the *doudou*'s literary relationships.[15] But more than a story of final goodbyes, this chapter situates "Adieu" as a—romantic for imperial discourse and traumatic for negritude discourse—story of origins. More specifically, "Adieu" narrates important "new beginnings," an oxymoron translating the retroactive nature of colonial and racial subject formation as well as colonial discourse. But Fanon's gender bias redirects his critical contribution: instead of a clear deconstruction of the binary white/black colonial opposition, his critique of the structures of desire framing this binary can end up reading like a critique of cultural and racial mixing. His analytical stance, where "the question" is either white or black (*Blanc ou noir, telle est la question*), strategically mirrors the demands of imperial and colonial regimes; but its ideological one drop rule structure resonates with politics of purity and authenticity that are paradoxical to the histories of *métissage* that characterize New World cultural production. Fanon's critical model, unless pushed against the grain, leaves little to work with for understanding the dynamics of recognition within Creole culture, nor does it offer much room for the expression of *voix métisses*.

This chapter has sought to unpack the sexual, material, and symbolic economies of violence within this culture of absolute belonging or exclusion that falls on the bodies and voices of woman of color. The discussion here has attempted to locate and implicate the resonance between imperial discourse and anti-imperial discourse at the site of the woman's body. Both the imperial and anti-imperial ears hear the *doudou*'s torn situation as a demand for categorization, line-drawing, and ethico-juridical judgment more than an expression of authentic creation or a petition for a just hearing. The *doudou*'s stereophonic exclusion comes from ideologies of gender and soundtext that block ears on the right and the left.

As a cultural statement about origins, "Adieu" makes claims on the very nature of coloniality and of the Antilles. Despite its position at the cusp of the 1789 French Revolution, and despite its supposed authorship by a staunch representative of *ancien régime* colonial power, "Adieu," rather than clearly singing the swan song of feudal colonialism and the transition into modern imperialism, instead claims that the essence of French/Antillean colonial relations fundamentally transcends the vagaries of politics and History.

This myth stages a break in relations that its song belies, turning an apparent moment of pain into the lingering refrain of melancholic lament. The materially and temporally finite needs of colonialism having been met, "Adieu" stages a relation of mutual desire, where emotional (familial and romantic) attachment continues to resonate beyond the spatiotemporal and textual limits of *l'Exclusif*.[16] The representation of desire therefore becomes a representation of representation, a (fixed) testimony of willing submission, whereby the colonial subject has always already elected the endlessly ambivalent trajectory of difference mapped out by French imperialism. But if the *doudou*'s performance elicits "the desire of the other," it attaches to the latter "the pity of the other" in order to stage the debate about the consequences and realities of French colonialism. The *doudou*'s beauty is her passion, but her performance of lament—which the colonizer cannot *not* hear—sets the stage for ethical demands.

# two

## "To Begin the Biguine"
### Re-membering Antillean Musical Time

How it was beautiful ... my Martinique!

—Léona Gabriel

While twentieth-century Antillean regionalist poet Emmanuel Flavia-Léopold affectionately names his nostalgic collection of poems after the folkloric song "Adieu madras, Adieu foulard," negritude poet Guy Tirolien's "Adieu 'Adieu Foulards,'" in *Balles d'or* aligns himself with the poetic camp of a certain Antillean black radical musical refusal:

> We will no longer sing the defunct romances
> that the honey sweet hearts used to sing long ago
> unfurling handkerchiefs on beaches of sugar
> waving goodbye to the setting sails of winged ships.
>
> We will no longer pluck on our plaintive guitars,
> to celebrate Ninon or pretty Amélie
> the pure crystal of laughs, the kisses full of spice
> nor the moons reflection on the golden brown skin
> [ ... ]
> We will raise our voices in a bouquet of screams
> to rupture the eardrums of our sleeping brothers
> and on the ardent bow of our island
> the fires of our anger
> in the night will rage our raucous bonfires of hope.[1]

Tirolien's poetic scream breaks up the colonial romance between the *doudou* and departing French sailor so fondly represented in French colonial and Antillean folkloric song and poetry. *Le cri nègre* drowns out the *doudou*'s romantic sweet talk and her somnolent lullabies; but at the same time, it ignores the plight of the women of color inscribed in the imperial poetic economies it mockingly disparages. Instead the black scream intends to awaken "sleeping brothers" and to rally them for the coming revolution, and a coming new black *fraternité*.

In a similar vein, Guyanese poet Léon-Gontran Damas, like other negritude poets, expresses frustration with black Atlantic popular musical culture in the imperial metropolis during the interwar years. In his poem "Nuit Blanche" (Sleepless Night) from the collection *Pigments—Névralages* (1937), Damas alludes to the imperial violence haunting the depths of contemporary black Atlantic musical practices. He darkly writes,

> I've waltzed my friends
> madly
> waltzed
> to such a point that often
> I thought I had an arm about the waist of
> Uncle Gobineau
> or cousin Hitler
> or that good Aryan gumming out his years
> on some park bench[2]

Damas represents popular dance culture as a site of historic complicity and of (homosexual-incestuous) colonial family romance. His double play on the French expression *nuit blanche*—"sleepless night," literally "white night"—poetically relates a late-night musical culture to the loss of black time and the whitewashing of black cultural authenticity.

In "Trêve" (Enough), Damas calls for a break in this musical beating, evoking the violent historic depth fueling the popularity of black New World and colonial musical performances in France.

> Enough with blues
> with hammering pianos
> with muted trumpets
> with tapping feet crazy
> with rhythmic satisfaction
>
> Enough with swing sessions
> around rings
> excited
> from wild screams

Damas's description of the hammering of the piano, the clacking of the feet, and the wild cries of the crowd invert the scene of pleasure into one of violence, suggesting a deep complicity between the beating of black Atlantic musical culture and the beating of black bodies and subjectivities in the imperial metropolis. (Chapter 4 takes up this question more thoroughly in a critical reading of the figure of the *tam-tam* and Damas's modernist epic poem *Black-Label*.)

It should come as no surprise that women Antillean thinkers listened more carefully to the Antillean folkloric and popular musical culture that negritude's male poets wanted to drown out. Much like "Adieu" constitutes an origin myth of French Antillean relations, so too the origins, authorship, and cultural authenticity of the hybrid folkloric dance and musical genre the biguine is a source of contentious debate turning on questions of gender and belonging.[3] While dominant and male-centered negritude discourse operated in the "major mode," creating heroic poetic figures who engage in epic struggles with History and make absolute choices, what the analysis below will call "negritude in the minor" expresses the negotiations of the everyday that take place across colonial and racial lines. Eschewing the mythical return to African roots, "negritude in the minor" instead involves expressing transnational relations of continuity. Traditionally dismissed as "middle ground" or "less radical" within negritude circles and histories, writers Jane and Paulette Nardal along with Andrée Nardal excel in this minor mode. They pinpoint the gendered imperial dynamics of Antillean cultural consumption on both sides of the Atlantic operating within the doudouist accusation.

Just as Tirolien and others virulently denounce in tandem regionalist poetry and a certain musical "vie de bon enfant" (Damas), negritude's critique of regionalist, so-called doudouist, poetics extends to the history of biguine musical culture in the Antilles as well as in France. When asked about accusations of doudouism, mimicry, and lack of black authenticity that still haunt biguine musical culture today, the genre's leading men offer mostly musicological explanations. For example contemporary Antillean musician and historian Édouard Benoit emphasizes the numerous ways in which biguine was "subject" to influence from musical styles coming from outside of Guadeloupe and Martinique. He suggests the improvisatory experiments of jazz artists as well as the rhythmic stylings of Latin artists greatly influenced biguine musicians, detracting from the genre's "authentic" development.

Similarly, legendary Guadeloupean guitarist, trombonist, composer, and bandleader Al Lirvat explains: "We have always tried to imitate Cuban bands as well as South American, African, Argentine, etc. This isn't a criticism, it's a fact" (quoted in Jallier and Lossen 45). Lirvat, who went to school in continental France (where he earned a degree in radio technology) explains: "It comes from the fact that we didn't have music schools, conservatories, or musical fundamentals [ . . . ] We learned from albums coming from elsewhere and tried to reinterpret them as well as we could, and we killed our own sense of creativity [ . . . ] There is therefore the risk of losing our Antillean authenticity" (Jallier and Lossen 45).

At the same time, Lirvat explains that this "mimicry" required a lot of practice, likely done at the expense of the biguine.

> We followed the evolution of Cuban music through records, but the biguine itself always stayed the same in Guadeloupe. When I got my start in music after the war, we rehearsed, orchestras had arrangements for all their pieces except for the biguines, American music, New Orleans, "middle jazz," Cuban music. Along the way, while polishing up our repertoire, we told ourselves "Yeah, we'll slip in a few biguines," but we never rehearsed them. So it was biguines from our folklore that we played. One instrument played the melody, and two others accompanied, that was it. (Uri and Uri 137)

Lirvat seems to suggest that the amount of time required to pick up a large range of musical genres leads to a popular folkorization of the biguine and correlates to its nostalgic and sentimental treatment. (His view likely inspired his musical development of the biguine into a mixed style he called the "biguine-wabap" in the 1950s.)

Choreographer and composer Loulou Boislaville, in contrast, with his *groupe folkorique* performed biguines, mazurkas, waltzes, and rumbas all over the islands by 1935. He recognized the extra-musical political and aesthetic demands implicit within doudouist accusations: "I love singing about my island [*chanter mon pays*] so I end up with the 'doudouist' label. I don't do politics, I sing of my land, that's it. I believe an artist must be free. I'm not selling out to anyone" (Jallier and Lossen 99). Boislaville's remarks pick up on the problematic equivalencies drawn between Antillean cultures of sound and imperial cultures inscribing Antillean soundscapes.

Like the critical double bind the *doudou* must sentimentally and musically negotiate, biguine culture and cultural practitioners are accused of self-exoticism, alienation, and white longing by masculinist black radical discourse, while they are simultaneously inscribed in losing economies of French-Antillean exchange and abandonment in French imperial patriarchal discourse. Brenda Berrian rightly suggests not confusing the *doudou* with *doudouisme* in that such a move risks conflating women of color with the ideologically charged stereotypes of imperial and colonial patriarchy. Yet the following analysis will flesh out the *doudou* and *doudouisme* relation, a relation of the minor, in order to critique the two as part of the anti/colonial gender dialectic at work in cultural economies of Antillean sound and text. Given the deconstruction of the *doudou* in the previous chapter, rather than attempt to prove the biguine is or is not doudouist, this chapter seeks to highlight the discursive economies of gender and race as well as the sociocultural dynamics of diasporic transnationalism and metropolitan imperialism that mobilize and fuel the doudouist allegation.

Simply put, this chapter argues that the biguine, like the *doudou*, is a (musical) genre of New World miscegenation; accordingly gender dynamics play crucial symbolic and material roles in its emergence, circulation, and consumption, as well as in the continued interrogation of its historic worth and cultural authenticity. To come to terms with doudouist accusations levied against the biguine, one must consider the way the latter's politics of mixing disrupt both anticolonial and colonial patriarchy and their gendered encoding of Antillean cultural expression and French-Antillean relations.

This discussion requires a focus on biguine culture and loss on both sides of the Atlantic, from its torn emergence and loss in the Antilles—taken up here in large part through an analysis of the film *Biguine: La fabuleuse histoire d'une ville et de sa musique*—to the ways "Jazz Age" Paris incorporates biguine culture and loss into economies of imperial consumption. In order to critically frame the gender dynamics of this musical historiography concerning the black transnational performance and production of colonial loss and imperial value, the discussion will be framed through prominent women of negritude and biguine cultural discourse. Paulette Nardal's short story "En exil" (1929) and Jane Nardal's critical essay "Pantins exotiques" (1928), both published in the journal *La Dépêche africaine*, as well as Andrée Nardal's "Etude sur la biguine créole" appearing in the December 1931 edition of the bilingual journal *La revue du monde noir / The Review of the Black World* offer crucial commentaries on the gender dynamics of black transnational culture in the metropolis. But this framing begins in the Antilles, with Léona Gabriel-Soïme's collection of Antillean folk songs and biguines published as *Ça! C'est la Martinique!* (1966). While her text appears much later than the Nardals', Gabriel-Soïme, then known by her birth name of Léona Gabriel, was a major performer and player on the Parisian biguine scenes during the interwar years, and her text is a compilation of weekly radio programs she hosted during and after the Second World War in Martinique.

## ÇA! C'EST LA MARTINIQUE!

The Nardal sisters are now beginning to receive more critical attention in the academy, but many other women who were key cultural practitioners of Antil-

lean popular music remain largely absent or in the background of scholarly discussions of black internationalism and black Atlantic musical culture in France
during the interwar years. No absence is more glaring than that of Léona Gabriel's and her monumental *Ça! C'est la Martinique!* A (*métisse* or white) Martinican
Creole whose father managed a sugar plantation, Gabriel grew up listening to
the songs of sugarcane field hands and house workers at the turn of the twentieth century. Following her parents' early death, she spent her adolescence in
Cayenne Guyana with relatives, before moving to Paris. As Brenda Berrian, one
of the few scholars to write about her, notes in *Awakening Spaces*, Gabriel performed and recorded under the stage name Mademoiselle Estrella in France.
Although not pictured in the iconic photo of the group, Gabriel performed with
Alexandre Stellio's group at the Colonial Exposition in 1931. By some accounts,
she served as a key connection for new arrivals from the islands looking to establish themselves in the French capital. Returning to Martinique during the Second World War, Gabriel hosted a program called *Ça! C'est la Martinique!* on Radio
Martinique in a period stretching from the 1940s to the 1960s. In the book by the
same name published in 1966 she compiled a selection of her radio programs.

Her book lies at the crossroads of authentic Creole voice and "exotic" colonial representation. Despite Gabriel's dismissal of any literary aspirations for
her text, *Ça! C'est la Martinique!* dialogs with the regionalist poets and poetics
that negritude poets scorn. From the opening prefaces to the body of text itself,
Gabriel's work is situated with respect to authors like Lafcadio Hearn, Auguste
Joyau, Salavina, and Gilbert Gratiant. In addition, Gabriel incorporated a literary element into her radio programs to go along with her singing. Brenda Berrian explains, "Every Saturday she sang one of her own songs and *recited a historical literary piece about the Martinican landscape to the accompaniment* of either the
trombonist Archange Saint-Hilaire's orchestra or sometimes the clarinet player
Hurard Coppet" (74; my emphasis). The focus on landscape is one of the dominant traits in regionalist poetics. Gabriel's literary narration of the landscape to
music enacts relationships between sound and text that hark back to the imperial soundscape genre discussed in this book's introduction.

In effect, Gabriel's work pulls together a corpus of Antillean sound-text-
image relations, and an ensuing Creole and colonial genealogy for Antillean
letters and popular music, that dominant negritude discourse and criticism ignores. While negritude's scream specifically disavows the sweet songs of tropical women and weather, Gabriel's imperial soundscape directly relates island
beauty and song to Western panoramic art and ethnological portraiture, solidifying the imperial framing of the eyes and ears of her writing and reading

subjects. The studied and aesthetic French narrative voice instantiates the distance between the time and place of the culture presented and the time and place of the person to whom the culture is presented. But—rather than providing further background as to the songs' origins or providing insight into the character types of the song—Gabriel's descriptive and picturesque introductions inscribe the song into the scene, or more precisely the scenery, staging it as part of the island's natural history rather than the expression of a unique voice or the creation of a singular individual. Her text weaves transcriptions of Antillean folk song and popular music together with nostalgic descriptions of Antillean culture and postcard photography, and she plugs them into an imperial discursive economy that consumes images of Antillean women and island landscapes.

But, while Gabriel stages the songs in a problematic way, somewhere between travel narrative and tourist discourse, her text and many of her songs still offer a wealth of perspectives on the torn sociocultural life of the Antilles at a crucial point in modern history. As Berrian notes, some of Gabriel's songs employ the gendered terms of the imperial island relations and consumption, but others challenged the helpless *doudou* stereotype travel writers found so irresistible and typical. Many of the women protagonists in Gabriel's work defy authority or cleverly claim the upper hand in domestic and social situations. It is misleading to consider Gabriel's work doudouist when one considers the ways these songs adopt many different perspectives, positions, and postures in the colonial family romance and Antillean society.

In fact, unlike the regionalist poets accused of doudouism and unlike Gabriel's introductions, the songs in her collection rarely simply describe the beauty of Antillean flora and fauna. Especially given the conditions of cultural promiscuity and colonial *compromission* in which the biguine emerges, anxieties about breakdowns and breakthroughs in ethno-class status structures often manifest themselves. In addition to the overtly political songs like "La Défence ka vini folle" (La Défense is going crazy), romantic songs like "Yaya moin ni l'agent" (Yaya, I've got money) are rife with anxieties about symbols of social status such as work, clothing, speech, and beauty. As Brenda Berrian notes, the "[c]lass distinctions in songs of this period are embedded in gender struggles" (Berrian 75). *Madras* and *foulards* frequently appear, serving in folklore and social life since before the turn of the century as material and symbolic signifiers of wealth and sociocultural status. In this context, the domestic space as well as romantic life represents a crucial site for exploring the contested values of race and ethnicity manifest in Antillean colonial society and culture.

Gabriel's book also offers candid stories of folkloric songs and carnival culture whose representations of gender are distinctly absent in negritude black radical thought. Describing the morning sounds and sites as the city awakens, Gabriel comes to a description of gay culture that Fanon's discourse completely disavows.

> HOW IT WAS BEAUTIFUL . . . MY MARTINIQUE! With its *commères* [*queens*] (in France, these are *tantes*). They are only men because they have a penis. Our *commères*, "COUCOUNE," "CHERUBIN," "FERNAND," "ETIENNE," all work at the market. Kings of good humor. But in a dispute with someone, or when angry, no rapid river was faster or made more of a ruckus than the indiscriminate flow of violent words they threw at people, often punctuated with a kind of humor not just anyone could even grasp. Their specialty was disguising themselves as women during carnival and selling songs. (23)[4]

The expression of queer culture is given as an untamed force of nature. Just as the blurred gender boundaries between women of color and plantation mistresses that Moreau decries was likely a crucial social ingredient in the creation of early Antillean musical culture, Gabriel seems to suggest that Antillean queer culture participated importantly in the dissemination of popular song that has now become folkloric.

Gabriel situates the importance of her work as safeguarding Antillean folklore and local tradition from loss and degradation. At the same time a large part of the nostalgia for a lost time and place within biguine culture has to do with the impact of the city of Saint-Pierre on Martinique and its destruction in the volcanic explosion of 1902. Ultimately, figured simultaneously as the likely birthplace of the genre and the site of its essential loss, the biguine itself is primordially marked with a deep cultural melancholia that goes far beyond the scope of its packaging as simple "doudouist" colonial nostalgia.

## "THE FABULOUS STORY OF A CITY AND ITS MUSIC"

The biguine does memory work for its cultural practitioners as well as its historians. This memory-work is at the origin of the film *Biguine: La fabuleuse histoire d'une ville et de sa musique.* Guy Deslauriers explains that he started the project with the desire of representing Saint-Pierre, the "little Paris" of the Caribbean, at the turn of the twentieth century. While researching he later realized that the biguine provided more insight into the historic cultural life of Saint-Pierre than any other documentation he could find. The film offers an imaginative history of the birth, the life, and the destruction of the biguine in Saint-Pierre. With its screenplay written by Patrick Chamoiseau, the film sketches out the powerful and even mythological associations attached to the genre, designating it as an Antillean sound sign of attachment to a lost place and giving it meaning in ways that extend far beyond its empirical musicology.

*Biguine: La fabuleuse histoire d'une ville et de sa musique* strongly resonates with Gabriel's *Ça! C'est la Martinique!* Both works present biguine musical history as the only way to really understand the cultural life of Saint-Pierre, and by extension the only way to represent and remember the trauma of its destruction. In addition, both works employ radio technology as a means of relaying and safeguarding that history for future generations. While Gabriel hosted a radio show herself, Deslauriers and Chamoiseau situate the narration of this history in the film through the voice of a woman who works as the late-night host of a radio program. Just as the film *Biguine* portrays musicians who had the courage to sacrifice and adapt to the conditions of colonial culture, "Gabriel wrote about women who suffer, regain hope, and move beyond being the easy doudou. [ . . . ] Powerlessness is transposed to an alternative position of autonomy and control" (Berrian 76). Lastly, Gabriel's *Ça! C'est la Martinique!* contains transcriptions of several of the Creole language carnival songs performed in the film and its soundtrack: "Marie-Clémence," "Eti Titin," "Célestin! roi diable dérô," "Agoulou pas calé guiole ou," and "L'estomac en bavaroise." Relating and responding to specific local histories, anecdotes, and events, these songs perform memory-work through their specific relationship to different carnival years preceding the volcanic eruption. More than historical events, these songs represent popular sentiment regarding Antillean modern history and society, freely drawing up brutal stereotypes or cultural myths within their structures of feeling.

As the radio host prepares to tell the story about a lost city and the curious musical genre that acted as its "protecting divinity," the film shows a unique mix of tools scattered about the studio desk—old postcards and photographs, several thick book volumes, ink pens, a thick pad of paper covered in handwritten notes. Once she lights the candles and prepares her notes the producer gives her the thumbs up in the control room signaling the show is "on air." The *speakerine* (played by Nicole Dogué) performs her late night storytelling as part bedtime *conte*, part séance, part archival research. Addressing the radio audience as "mes enfants," she delivers the story of the city and its music like a family history, that of her great-grandparents Hermancia (Micheline Mona) and Tiquitaque (Max Télèphe), when they first made their way, singing and playing along with a small group of others through the wooded hilly terrain, down to the big colonial city.

Both the film and Gabriel's book implicitly foreground the voice of women in the emergence, performance, and guardianship of this important cultural history. In the film, just as the DJ plays an important role in remembering the lost city and its musical genre, Hermancia, the female protagonist, plays a decisive role in the family's arrival at Saint-Pierre and birth of biguine. The film essentially puts the biguine under the sign of a Creole matriarch as much as under the sign of the volcano. It is her musical and lyrical adaptations of European art music and Antillean drum traditions that provide the foundation for the development of the new musical genre. Her determination helps the couple survive economically and culturally. And her encouragement pushes Tiquitaque to adapt to the city's musical taste and to adopt its modern instrument, the clarinet. But Hermancia's musical creation seems to engage in an ambivalent series of colonial *compromissions* in order to survive and eventually thrive given the imperial conditions of the Martinique's cultural capital. Throughout the genre's emergence and success, the film alludes to a primordial if necessary loss of authenticity and moral integrity that provide the conditions of possibility for biguine culture, while simultaneously staging it as an unsustainable form of Antillean colonial decadence.

When Hermancia and Tiquitaque first arrive in the colonial city, they marvel as they wander through the enchanting imperial port's activities and paved roads, its products for sale and textual registries and its laboring dark bodies. Both are musicians, she a *bélé* singer, he a drummer and flutist. They get to know the city and its musical culture, going from one rich home to the next offering their musical talents for compensation. They quickly learn that the conditions of race and class leave no place for their rustic instruments and their African-dominant musical style. "Neither white farm owner [*béké*] nor mulatto wanted drumming." The film's narrative structure underlines the powerful loss involved in this rejection. We rarely hear the film's protagonists speak, and when they do their dialogs consist only of short phrases and short scenes. Instead of their language, the story is told uniquely through the voice of the *speakerine* and through the music and musical practices even as the latter undergo loss and transformation.

The problem is not only their country instruments; it is their country genres, and their country ways more broadly. Forced to drop their musical aspirations, the couple endures grueling work for a time, but Hermancia is thinking ahead. She saves up and surprises Tiquitaque with a new instrument to try: a clarinet. Initially he is stubborn and his feelings are hurt. The musical tension creates relationship tension, and the plaintive melodies that Tiquitaque plays on his bamboo flute cry out to no one. But Tiquitaque recognizes the limitations of his bamboo flute one day when he encounters a mulatto musician playing clarinet on a stoop. For a while Tiquitaque plays along with the gentleman dressed in an all black suit in an improvised jam session. But Tiquitaque is forced to admit he can't keep up with his counterpart's range and chromatic flexibility. Intrigued and challenged in his musician-hood, even if it tears at his cultural and emotional musical roots, he decides to leave his old instrument behind.

Delauriers's film shows the colonial conditions affecting the choice of instrument and the way the latter signaled positions within the cultural field of production relating to class, race, and urban hierarchies of value. Tiquitaque, whose very name sounds out a percussive rhythm akin to the *cinquillo* rhythm sung by Antillean drummers (*"takpitakpitak"*), makes a crucial step away from tradition when he takes up the new clarinet. The instrument was an important one in the emergence of modern colonial music in the Antilles as were the introduction of other modern, urban instruments like the trombone and the piano. There is a strong tradition of lead clarinetists in the French West Indies beginning with Alexandre Kindou, who spread a new sound and vibrato developed by pinching the embouchure (Mavounzy 32), following through Léon Apanon, Alexandre Stellio, Ernest Léardée, Sam Castendet, Eugène Delouche, Honoré Coppet, and many others. The percussive tradition changes as well. The groups incorporate modern drum sets into their ensembles while keeping auxiliary instruments like chacha shakers.

The new genre emerges from an act of musical survival as much as musical choice. While the couple struggles to survive, they put enough aside to go off to the theater and watch operas from the cheap seats. They peak between closed blinds through windows of fancy homes to watch and hear "strange rhythms played by strange instruments," violins and pianos, trombones, banjos and mandolins. The emergence of the genre is not posited as an intentional abandonment per se; but "[w]ithout realizing it," the radio host explains, "Hermancia and Tiquitaque were going down the road of change." The musical style changes its beat to the colonial step as well. The rhythmic syncopations of percussion and dance traditions encounter modern instruments but also European popular musical genres such as the quadrille, the mazurka, the polka. The resulting musical expression seems like the only idiom that speaks to everyone in the colonial city.

The film's music scenes offer a vivid and imaginative sense of the tumultuous dynamics of race, class, nationality, and gender animating biguine practices in New World contact zones. In raucous night club scenes local *beaux* slap one another on the dance floor amid mixed dancing couples, white sailors of varying ranks and uniform negotiate with working girls on the laps of their clients, and older *béké* men happily take the whole thing in while the band plays on.

In the sociocultural and musically fascinating contact zones in which the biguine emerged, *"casinos,"* a type of local music venue, play an especially important role. "The *casinos* were originally places of passage and encounters of freemen and freed slaves who were looking for a moment of rhythmic escape through the local music. Later these same places were preferred places for illicit love, without class distinction. Musicians built up their chops there and used their talents to earn their reputation" (Uri and Uri 109). Martinique had, in addition to the Select Tango, les Folies Bergères, the Dancing Palace, Le Grand Balcon, and le Palais Cristal. Guadeloupe's early *casinos* include le Monte-Carlo, la Voûte Enchantée, le Coq d'Or, and la Boule Verte. The biguine's hybrid musical style, performed along with polkas, mazurkas, and waltzes as well as merengues and rumbas, would be especially adaptable to and popular in this culturally mixed milieu.

In the film *Biguine*, the camera furtively shows the sordid activity taking place in the shadows during the couple's performances at *casinos* and other sites of "ill repute." While the biguine triumphs, its cultural practices provide fertile grounds for continued exploitation. These musical scenes of imperial modernity where the biguine flourished imbricate with other economies of the flesh. At this point, French imperialism no longer enslaved bodies of color in its American colonies, but it continued to consume them, even in transnational zones, through the broader and deeper "skin game" (borrowing Claude McKay's terminology) of imperial modernity. Still within these structures of cultural and corporeal consumption, the genre seems to do more than just hold its own. In the film, the biguine slowly takes over the town from below. Thriving in the transnational margins of French imperial order in the New World, it begins to make its way into dominant culture. Putting everyone in close contact, seeing and telling everything, this border-crossing genre of musical praxis watches over the town, both dirtying and airing the town's collective laundry. In this way the biguine's voice uniquely represents the collective—there where its practices involve the unspoken and taboo—becoming a powerful tool of political satire and biting social ridicule. Hermancia and Tiquitaque are "commandeurs de Saint-Pierre," an ambivalent title, but their music spreads from *bastringues* and *casinos* to the Cercle des Sang-Mêlé and workers lodges. "People danced all over the place," the DJ narrates.

The actors who play the protagonists, Micheline Mona and Max Télèphe, are themselves the musicians performing the songs on the film's soundtrack. Mona's powerful performance of Hermancia on stage importantly gives a lively depth to the performativity of the *doudou*; the power of the *doudou*'s presence in this early history challenges typical anti/imperial receptions of her within biguine discourse and beyond. Eventually the force of her voice and style come to bear in performances of political critique. The film offers musical performances of classic biguines "Celestin Roi Diab," a turn-of-the-century musical intervention on the volatile political events that marked the early 1900s on the island colony, and "La Défense ka vini fol," a critique of the conservative colonial Martinican newspaper *La Défense*. Despite its humble beginnings in the margins of colonial order, the biguine essentially gains a level of recognition that can take on and rival the official discourse of the French text, and that power lies particularly in Hermancia's performative voice.

But as the genre's popularity swells, so does Hermancia's sense of unease about the ominous signs coming from the volcano. Before the volcano's eruption, the last song Hermancia performs in the film, "Marie-Clémence," a carnival folksong from the turn of the century, portends Hermancia's ultimate loss. Léona Gabriel presents the song in her text with the volcano looming in the background in similar fashion. "Saint-Pierre" celebrated its last carnivals, she writes, "as if sensing a premonition, a bad omen! Saint-Pierre, in this carnival of 1900, rushes to live, to dance, while Pelée, majestic and grave like a beautiful woman with the smile of a sphinx, rises up with its tranquil airs and seems to say to Saint-Pierre, laid out at its feet in all its splendor, 'Guess or I will devour you'" (97).[5] In contrast to the song's upbeat tempo and melody, as recorded on the *Biguine* soundtrack, the lyrics to "Marie-Clémence" recount a mythological tale of exclusion and suffering. What starts as a beautiful carnival day for Marie-Clémence will end tragically cursed.

> Marie-Clémence lévé en samedi bon matin
> I dit la journée belle . . . mais au souè ké plus belle
> Samedi de carnaval, moin caille 'Palais Cristal'
> Moin ké fè 'Ciryque' ouè, ça yo dit a pas vrai.

> [Marie-Clémence woke up one beautiful Saturday morning
> She said to herself it's a beautiful day . . . but the
>     night will be even more beautiful
> Carnival Saturday, I'm going to the 'Crystal Palace'
> I'll make Ciryque see that what they've been saying
>     isn't true.]

Les ennemis déclaré moin cé en femme maudit,
Yo prend papillon a, yo brûlé tout' tête li
Le lendemain matin ouélé la rue Dauphine
Marie-Clémence lévé, épi guiol li brûlé

[Enemies declared me a cursed woman
They took a butterfly and burned its head
The next day *voilà* on the rue Dauphine
Marie-Clémence woke up with her face burned.]

Marie-Clémence ma fi, ça ou fè' a pas bien
Ou tounin papillon, pou ou té ça tué soeu' ou
Cyrique té ka veillé, i tiembé ou en volant
Seule chose ou ni pou ou fè, fouté cô ou dans lan mè.

[Marie-Clémence my girl, what you did was bad
You turned into a butterfly, so you could kill your
    sister
Cyrique was watching, he caught you flying
The only thing you can do now is throw yourself in
    the sea.]

Marie-Clémence maudit ... tout' bagage li maudit,
Macadam li maudit ... patate bouilli' i maudit,
Marie-Clémence maudit ... tout' bagage li maudit,
Macadam li maudit ... patate bouilli' i maudit,

[Marie-Clémence is cursed ... all her things are cursed,
Her Creole fish is cursed ... her boiled potatoes are
    cursed
Marie-Clémence is cursed ... all her things are cursed,
Her Creole fish is cursed ... her boiled potatoes are
    cursed]

*Refrain*
Ouaille! lagué moin, lagué moin, lagué moin
Moin caille néyé cô moin
Dans grand lan mè bleu' a
Déyè gros pile roches là (bis).

[Hélas! leave me be, leave me be, leave me be
I'm going to drown myself
In the grand blue sea there
Behind that pile of rocks (repeat).]

The song portrays a young woman who wakes up carnival Saturday with plans of going to dance at the Palais Cristal casino, but whose enemies have put curses on her. The burned face represents a darkening, a tragically atavistic return for the song's presumed *métisse* character. Accused of killing her sister, Marie-Clémence figures a sororicide, betrayal. Her curse resonates with the tragic mulatta mythology inscribed in the *doudou*'s "Adieu." Once again this *doudou* and the value of her word are under patriarchal interrogation and ultimate condemnation in this key Antillean soundtext. Once again she is portrayed as a traitor to the community who must be excommunicated. The figure of the butterfly might be read as a symbol of *doudou*'s fickle character and capricious temperament. Staged by the water, she takes up the *doudou*'s position of ultimate loss by the border. With her person and her "cooking" cursed no one will touch her. Having lost her beauty and her worth, stigmatized socially, spiritually, and physically, it seems suicide is her only way out.

While *Ça! C'est la Martinique!* and *Biguine* stage this song as a premonition to the volcanic eruption, the performance of the song offered in the film likely differed from the way Léona Gabriel performed it. According to Brenda Berrian,

> Gabriel affected and adopted a singing style that originated when mulatto mistresses entertained their French lovers with Creole songs. This method consisted of singing gallicized Creole with a French intonation. Instead of singing in a natural voice, a nasal tone was affected to duplicate a more pronounced French accent. In fear of being identified with the lower class whose Creole was said to be more authentic, Gabriel adopted this singing style by not breathing from her diaphragm and prolonging the final notes. Since then, this affectation became so popular and acceptable that contemporary women singers were judged critically when they punched out a song in the fashion of an African American jazz or gospel singer. (Berrian 72)

While Antillean singing voice traditionally intones a very nasal timbre, suitable for cutting through drum ensembles and carrying a long distance, Gabriel's use of this intonation in performance of "Marie-Clémence" might have especially resonated with *doudou* mythology. (In the context of the biguine cultural staging, outside of the adopted Creole diction for musical performance, a high level

French was a valued asset for band leaders. Speaking "proper" French likely facilitated access to performance venues on both sides of the Atlantic, even while audiences feasted their ears and exotic appetites on Creole speech and sound during the music.)

Going against the gendered, imperial performance timbre that risks reifying Creole women's voices into postures of sexual seduction and submission, Micheline Mona's lively recording on the *Biguine* soundtrack adopts a contemporary singing style, in other words without the pointed nasal affectation that Berrian describes. Mona's superb performance is full of attitude, often highlighting *double entendres* with the meaning of the lyrics or with the apparent pathos of the song's musical dimensions. In addition, Hermancia never "gains" or adopts French voice in the film; musical performance constitutes her sole modes and means of recognition and retort.

Although Hermancia senses the danger within her song, its ultimate meaning escapes her and she ignores her premonitions. Somehow intoxicated by the music, she and Tiquitaque pay no attention to all the signs of impending doom around them. This music's poetic relation and spiritual connection involves a type of continued rupture, loss, and transformation that seems to call for its own end and destruction. The couple still plays away while people flee the town in mass exodus (despite assurances by colonial authorities that the volcano represented no imminent danger). As white ashes fall like snowflakes to coat the city streets, and to white out the finale, Hermancia and Tiquitaque dance like ghosts living amidst and beyond their final erasure.

The film closes with images of the ruins of the city today, and the Antillean *speakerine* blowing out the candles and gathering up all her notes as the radio show comes to a close. Situated at the border between storytelling and literacy, musical séance and textual historiography, with its highlighted shots of the radio studio and the latter's technologies, texts, and scripted performances, the film emphasizes the modern ways of continuing the very biguine-like practice of integrating tradition into new modes and forms of cultural expressivity. At the same time the danger of the compromise and loss are underlined in the story.

At one level, tying the genre's demise to the volcanic eruption and the city's destruction allows for reactionary readings concerning the colonial conditions of the biguine's emergence and practices. In a reactionary negritude reading, for example, the volcanic eruption (a key figure in Césaire's poetic) represents a divine intervention, enforcing apocalyptic retribution and a *tabula rasa* of the earth for an authentic black renaissance. But, the film suggests a more interesting reading of the symbolic connections between the volcano, the genre, and the music. In addition to capturing the way the Martinican collective psyche associates them, the film resonates with the poetics of relation—between the music (culture), the volcano (nature), and the city (urban development)—that Edouard Glissant describes as constituting Creole culture. In this reading, the opacity of the relation goes far beyond the logical grasp of essentialist thought. As the film's framing by modern-day radio culture and the archeological ruins of Saint-Pierre aptly represent, this poetics of relation discovers cultural value by telling this history, invoking it, conjuring it up through the historic rupture. This memory-work, in digging through layers of loss, multiple histories of fragmentation, and sorting through the remains, suggests the temporal dynamics at work in the musical time of biguine cultural practices.

Certainly the eruption of Mount Pelée and the destruction of Saint-Pierre marks the end (and the beginning) of an era in the Antilles. The volcanic disaster sends the entire region into shock, "suddenly putting an end to any desire for entertainment and activities closely or loosely associated with light music and dance," Martinican biguine musician Ernest Léardée explained. "It was a long time before those open wounds would start to heal" (Léardée and Meunier 93). But even as Mount Pelée's eruption dealt a serious blow to Antillean musical life, its disruption of the cultural and economic flow of the region likely provoked an intense period of musical migration, influence, and creative collaboration. Like the musical movement contemporary musicologist Sara Johnson traces from the social turmoil surrounding the Haitian revolution, biguine's historic itinerary echoes from the "lost moments" Johnson locates in pan-Caribbean cultural interactions often occluded in Antillean nationalist discourse. The dynamics of cultural and social mixing that came together to form and perform the biguine's musical practices could only continue to proliferate as the genre's cultural practitioners moved through the islands to Paris.

## BIGUINMANIA IN THE CITY OF LIGHT

In other words, the break, the rupture, the cut constitutes another link in the poetic relation of biguine musical time. As a genre of break and continuity, biguine music and musical practices resonate well for feeling Antillean experiences of exile in the City of Light. Such transnationalism and emigration find their place in the nostalgia for the past and the structures of feeling loss that take a prime position in the matrix of biguine musical meaning since before 1902. While songs such as "Moin descan'n Saint Pierre" and many others inscribe nostalgia and loss into the genre through association with leaving behind the ways of the country in a movement to the city, and then through association with the city's loss and destruction, many other songs like "Ti Paul" and "Paris-Biguine" inscribe nostalgia and loss in the genre by associating it with the experiences of life away from home in Paris.

Just as the negritude women were (more than the men) attentive to musical culture in their critical essays, they also offered important representations and critiques of quotidian life of exile for Antilleans of color in France during the interwar years. In her short story "In Exile," Paulette Nardal depicts a rhythm of alienation and nostalgia as part of the daily experience of an Antillean woman working in Paris away from family and friends. The day-in-the-life story picks up as the protagonist, Elisa, takes the bus across the Left Bank after a long shift. The bus trip highlights the difference between Elisa's life and that of the wealthy Parisians whose home she cleans, but it also maps her proximity to, and marginalization from, the dominant sites of Antillean culture and society that most remember and study. Traveling from rue des Ecoles to boulevard Pasteur, Elisa moves from the seat of educational privilege where the negritude's privileged poets attended courses at some of France's best universities to the seat of exotic entertainment in Montparnasse where the biguine's ardent cultural practitioners made a name for themselves. Nardal has her protagonist arriving home just a few blocks from the Bal Nègre on rue Blomet, but Elisa traverses these spaces of noted Antillean success without regard for them; her reality of exile does not include them.

Instead the rhythm of imperial modernity for Nardal's female protagonist can be counted by the daily insults and misrecognitions she suffers (like the kids who snidely call out "beautiful blond" to her) as well as the regimented and restrained time of her work schedule as a domestic. Nardal portrays Elisa as closed in on herself; memories of home and nostalgic daydreams form a shell that buffers her from the race and gender charged shocks of modernity in the imperial metropolis. Nardal's story situates Elisa's subjectivity as a composite series of beats and strikes, a concept I return to more thoroughly and theoretically in chapter 4.

Buffering herself from the routine knocks of her experience as a black woman in the *métropole*, Elisa's daydreams carry her away, back to the dance and drum cultures, and storytelling traditions of her home island. The first-person voice of interior monologue reinforces the sense of Elisa's isolation and alienation from her social, cultural, and physical environment in France. Nardal's narrative focalization locks the reader into Elisa's mind, as if indicating this interior dream time/space as the only place where Elisa can find her true body and voice.

But when Elisa arrives home at the story's end, and learns that her son, who had left for work in South America, has written to promise her a ticket home, "Briskly, she climbs up her six stories, and the neighbors, who every evening have pitied her upon hearing her painfully clamber up the worn-down steps, wonder who indeed could be humming so that strange refrain with the jerky rhythm and the guttural and sweet syllables" (118). For the first time Elisa claims representational space outside of herself and transcends her stuck position. Nardal shifts the narrative focalization as Elisa comes alive and regains her authentic voice and step. The reader is thrust out of the interior monolog, and placed in the position of a neighbor who hears but does not understand what has happened. Authentic "gutteral" timbre and "sweet syllables" mark her linguistic break from the French neighbors but also the French language reader. Elisa's recovery of voice entails a new relation to her environment, a new dynamic of recognition. Nardal's story suggests modernity in the imperial metropolis for France's black New World subjects meant coping with the way dynamics of transnationalism and imperialism create torn experiences of time and place. In the story, sound and vernacular culture as well as rhythm and percussion come together to make manifest these time changes. Nardal shows that musical expressions in France emerged from a matrix of nostalgia and loss that had to do with the hostility of Parisian life, the rough conditions of employment, and the breaking up of family relations mandated by a lack of work on the island.

Paulette Nardal marks the Colonial Exposition as an event that operates a shift in white attitudes toward Antillean women and the difficult experiences for them sketched out in her short story. In "L'Eveil de la conscience de race chez les étudiants noirs" (The Awakening of Race Consciousness among Black Students), originally published in *La Revue du monde noir* in April 1932, she writes, "the aspirations that were to crystallize around *La Revue du monde noir* asserted themselves among a group of Antillean women students in Paris. The women of color living alone in the metropolis, who until the Colonial Exposition were less favored than their male compatriots, who have enjoyed easy successes, felt long before the latter the need for a racial solidarity that would not be merely material" (Sharpley-Whiting 122). The assertion that the Exposition "improved" women's conditions seems paradoxical. Nardal writes that the Exposition increased women's visibility, but reading her against the grain, one might posit the Exposition as a turning point away from the forms of women's solidarity that she describes as preceding it. The Exposition may have increased the volume and presence of Antillean women's voices (as happens in the film *Biguine*) but it comes with a price. As Anne Décoret-Ahiha notes, the expositions crucially transformed "exotic" cultural practices into products for imperial consumption. "It's in ethnological exhibitions, international, universal, and colonial expositions, that exotic dances first appeared" in France (19). By the 1889 exposition in Paris, the same one for which the Eiffel Tower was built, "exotic dances" and musical performances represent standard fare at these spectacles of European imperial power.

In fact, calling the musical scene flourishing during the interwar years in France "Jazz A Paris" belies the diversity and the long history of "exotic" musical performances and expatriate musical scenes active during the early twentieth century. While French may try on *"la danse du ventre"* and other musical practices and traditions from Africa, the latter musics were commodified in the capital more as spectacle than as practice. Musics from the Americas made a particularly strong impact in that French bands and dancers adopted and practiced them in France more directly. The biguine is only one of many genres of music and dance styles from the Americas that become popular in Europe, ranging from the Charleston and the cakewalk to the Cuban *danzón* and Brazilian *maxixe*. Accordingly, what we call biguine musicians and the clubs boast repertoires complete with rumbas, tangos, merengues, boleros, and *sones*, along with waltzes and Creole mazurkas. These genres and their practices resided within a larger cultural field of exotic musical production and consumption that included *chanson coloniale*. Like the biguine, many of the musical genres and practices too became transformed, lost, or erased given the colonial conditions of their emergence and the imperial conditions of their circulation and spread.

The genre's practices and its field of reception change in the Hexagon as the Colonial Exposition helps connect it to international tourist circuits flowing through Paris. According to Léardée, the 1931 Colonial Exposition in Paris turned the biguine into an "institution," even though several Antillean musicians arrived, launched biguine clubs, and started their recording careers before the gates opened at the Bois de Vincennes. The original group playing the Bal Nègre consisted of Robert Charlery (banjo), Jean Rezard-Devouves (piano), Robert Claisse (clarinet), and Bernard Zelier (drums), but Stellio arrived in France in 1929 to play the Bal Nègre on rue Blomet in 1930. Ernest Léardée, Archange Saint-Hilaire (trombone), Victor Collat (cello), and Crémas Orphélien (drums, vocals, songwriter) came with him. Many other groups followed these musicians before and after the interwar years. Performance venues opened up with the success of the Exposition shows. Créol's Band under Félix Valvert began performing at the Bal Colonial by 1930 with Crémas Orphélien singing. While Stellio opened Tagada-Biguine after Sam Castendet took over for him at the Exposition, Ernest Léardée, who explained he was too busy running the Bal on rue Blomet to play the Exposition, opened up and played at a club called l'Elan Noir in 1931. Nearby, the Boule Blanche featured Léona Gabriel, Eugène Delouche (clarinet), Robert Charlery (guitar), Robert Rock (bass), Finotte Attuly (piano), and Maurice Banguio (drums). The Cabane Cubaine opened in the immediate postwar years.

The musicians and dancers enjoyed the popularity, but as Léardée explains:

after a while, the *bal* had become a curiosity, a tourist site in the capital good for an exotic change of scene [*se dépayser*], and for contemplating the pretty *mulâtresses* shaking their bodies to the rhythm of the biguine, without spending too much money. When it was its busiest, when the Colonial Exposition was in full swing at the Porte Dorée, drawing thousands of French and foreign visitors every day, buses would file down rue Blomet letting loose waves of tourists hungry for sensations, and picking them back up half an hour later as soon as the show was over. Sometimes up to twenty buses would come in the same evening, and when the room was so packed people couldn't get inside, I would strike up a furious biguine and introduce my Antillean ballet dancers in folkloric costume so as to clear out space, and so other guests could get to the gallery overlooking the room reserved for them. I had agreements with several agencies that took tourists to see "Paris by night" and brought them to Blomet just long enough to see the show. [ . . . ] That's how out of control, though a craze for exoticism, this business had become, that was once nothing more than a meet up place where Antilleans in Paris liked to relive among themselves memories from home to the sound of a biguine plucked out on a guitar. (Léardée and Meunier 171–172)

Léardée laments the way the musical "home away from home" becomes itself inscribed in alienating dynamics of an emergent French pleasure industry. Set up by the Colonial Exposition and the tourist industry, the fury of a biguine *forcené* fuels the consuming male gaze, situating the genre as "a tourist site in the capital good for an exotic change of scene [*se dépayser*], and for contemplating the pretty *mulâtresses* shaking their bodies."

But doudouist discourse in literature and travel narratives help set up biguine music for its imperial consumption (as in the reactions of French critics to the Revue nègre discussed in the introduction). Just as Gabriel's *Ça! C'est la Martinique!* writes in the genre of the imperial soundscape, inscribing the biguine within the paradigms of the imperial gaze and ear by relating it to is-land scenery, this long and literary colonial romance helps stage the biguine as a tourist attraction in Paris. While Gabriel's framed representations of the bi-guine focus on the landscape, imperially framed representations of the biguine in the metropolis focus on the bodies on the dance floor.

In other words, the imperial eyes and ears taking in the biguine in the me-tropolis fall squarely on body of the Antillean women of color. The politics of biguine consumption in France mark the biguine musical scene as a special site for cross-cultural relations. As Décoret-Ahiha contends, "It is in the clubs and *bals nègres* that cultural and social mixing was no doubt the most remarkable" (Décoret-Ahiha 76). The tourist circuit's focus on cross-cultural and cross-racial romance receives the biguine's nostalgic farewell to Saint-Pierre, and to island life more generally, as a nostalgic longing for colonial romance and taboo love. This taboo love was not limited to white men longing for women of color. For artists like the caricaturist Georges Coursat, who worked under the name Sem ("Le bal de la rue Blomet," 1929) and the photographer Brassaï ("Couple au bal nègre, rue Blomet," c. 1932), representing the biguine scene meant capturing the sexual charge and close contact between black men and white women.

While estranging biguine musical culture from its island practices, the tour-ist industry especially fueled the fetishization and surveillance of colonial boundaries of race, gender, and culture. Rather than setting up the possibility for authentic contact and exchange, tourists, according to Léardée's descrip-tion, were hustled in and out of seated areas. "In the strictly Parisian dance halls," Andrée Nardal writes, "this dance was presented as the attraction of the evening" (121). Presenting the biguine as an attraction contributes to the "freez-ing" of its development during the interwar years, sealing the commodification and consumption of the genre through dynamics of imperial folklorization. "Contemplating the women," that is, not just watching but casting a gaze that studies and imagines them simultaneously, rather than dancing, becomes the dominant activity, shifting the emphasis from the ears and moving the body to the gaze. As folklore the biguine becomes a mythological document, a fetish of a previous time and place, something one studies, buys, and sells rather than something one practices, improvises, and poetically relates to in the Glissan-tian sense.

Contributing to this transformation, commodification, and ultimate era-sure, other genres and media represented and consumed the biguine genre. *Chanson coloniale* as well as jazz composers signify on it by association with its name, colonial or tropical romance, and the implementation of assorted syncopations and percussive instruments, but they rarely offered an actual biguine at all. Colonial cinema portrayed ideas about African and American dance forms while exploiting the newly available technology of film sound, enhancing its exotic force and sales appeal. At the same time, record industries took interest and further inscribed authentic Antillean music into imperial networks of consumption, creating a corpus of "colonial music" that likely served as a precursor to what is now called "world music." Finally, advertising campaigns posterized the musicality of black expression and embodiment, literally but also symbolically sealing it like a label onto food products, rum, travel deals, colonial brochures, among other things. At the core of this loss of authenticity and incorporation into the imperial pleasure industry lay the imperial dynamics of gender that specularize women's bodies and voices musically while denying them recognition socially, culturally, and legally.

While Paulette Nardal's short story "In Exile" portrays a day in the life of an invisible woman of color in the city before the Exposition, essays by Andrée Nardal and Jane Nardal critique this hypervisibility of Antillean women as black Atlantic musical culture became popular in the *métropole*. In "Study of the Creole Biguine," published in the December 1931 edition of the bilingual journal *La revue du monde noir / The Review of the Black World*, Andrée Nardal insightfully articulates the dynamics of colonial desire operating in the international consumption of Antillean music and culture. Beyond explaining the genre's popularity as a function of the Colonial Exposition, Nardal relates *biguinemania* to the hypersexualization of the dances in the Parisian context. "In the real biguine, as it is danced by the Creoles themselves," Nardal explains, "the performers do not embrace; they mimic the everlasting pursuit of woman by man. The former advances and retreats to the accompaniment of a thousand enticing gestures while her partner artfully approaches or feigns a haughty indifference which he drops quickly in order to catch up to his flippant companion who is running away, borne along by her swishing skirts" (121–122).

Nardal's scene describing the female dancer fleeing with a ruffle of her skirts will hark back to the *doudou* waving her scarves goodbye in the imperial imagination, but for Antilleans it relates to a range of pan-Caribbean dance traditions practiced since slavery. Jacqueline Rosemain signals the resemblance between the way women danced the biguine and the ethnography of Antillean dance given by Moreau de Saint Méry in the seventeenth century: "The art for women dancers holding the ends of a handkerchief or her skirt consisted principally in shaking the lower back while keeping the rest of the body still" (Rosemain *La*

*Musique* 21). In fact Sara Johnson, tracing the "inter-island aesthetic" of Antil-lean rhythmic traditions, highlights a mid-nineteenth century painting called *French-Set Girls* by Jamaican artist Issac Mendes Belisario that depicts the same choreographic posture. "The women," Johnson writes, "are dressed in a fash-ion typical of what has come to be known as the folkloric '*doudou*' in the French islands" (38). This *choreography* scripts the dance steps but also inscribes the Creole woman's *corps* (body) while evoking (for some) a corpus of mythological representations of the Creole tragic mulatta.

But the biguine's doudouist resonance in France takes it away from the deeper forms and meanings of this pan-Caribbean dance style. The Nardals remark the shifting quality of the dance and music practices in Paris, and they critique the discourse of colonial romance animating biguine culture in the me-tropolis. Andrée Nardal laments, "it is to be deplored that the biguine should be presented to Parisians only under an obscene interpretation when it can ex-press both languorous grace and an extreme liveliness" (121). Her discussion insists on the shifting attitudes of the dancers and the dance, the emotional ex-pressivity of clarinet, "by turns coquette, breathless, mocking, lascivious" (123, my translation), and the frequent satire within the biguine's lyrics. Her depic-tion of the playful and artful relating within biguine dance movements conjures up potential alternate readings of the *doudou*'s performances and representa-tions even in reified form. The biguine's ambivalent and specular cultural cho-reography, and its relationship with the *doudou*, does not prove its doudouist tendencies. Rather it demonstrates the genre's torn situation of authenticity, and it points up the musical investment relating the figure of the Creole woman to the cultural politics of mixing and the cultural problematics of black dia-sporic loss.

Jane Nardal, in the essay "Exotic Puppets" ("Pantins exotiques"), offers an even more trenchant critique of the way French writers and artists pick up on the perversion of biguine cultural practices, and the advent of black interna-tionalism, to propagate essentialist ideas about black intellect, social behav-ior, and cultural value. Critiquing Paul Morand's stereotypical representations of black rhythm and atavism, Jane Nardal writes: "Paul Morand did not invent it out of the blue—a few sharp observations bear this out. If the sociologi-cal works of Lévy-Bruhl, as he himself indicates, were his sources for the American Negro; if as I believe, he made extensive use of *The New Negro* by Alain Lock (a man of color) to represent the American black, who gave him the stereotype for the black Antillean? Undoubtedly the Blomet Ball, analogous to our casinos, or worse—his stopovers of a few hours in the Antilles—perhaps some 'quimboiseurs'—and literary stereotypes, like that of the dangerous mulatto" (111). In calling attention to the varied sources of mythical inspiration for Morand, Nardal outlines a network of institutions and discourses—anthropological, literary, anecdotal, and musical—involved in the construction and consumption of ideas about New World blackness. Her reference to the rue Blomet's *bal nègre* as similar to Antillean *casinos* "or worse" suggests the type of sexually charged behavior taking place in the club—likely as shocking to Nardal's critical race consciousness as to her black bourgeois upbringing.

"But above all," she writes, "—and I'm finally lighting my lantern—all the trouble comes from the fact that the vogue for Negroes these last few years has led to their being considered as folk destined to serve as amusement, to see to the pleasure, artistic or sensual, of whites [ . . . ]; but when it is a question of intellectual, or moral, qualities, when it is a question of no longer being their clown but their equal, that disturbs nature's plan and the viewpoints of providence" (111). Nardal highlights the ways musical culture created sites for the exotic consumption of blackness as much as for meaningful encounters and exchanges.

Nardal reserves her most biting criticism and insightful critique for Josephine Baker, whose phenomenal success, as I contend in chapter 3, relies heavily on the *doudou* mythology. One could have hoped, she explains, that colonial nostalgia would fade with the passage of time. "But Josephine came," she writes, "Josephine Baker you understand, and bored a hole through the painted backdrop associated with Bernardin. Here it is that a woman of color leaps onstage with her shellacked hair and sparkling smile. She is certainly still dressed in feathers and banana leaves, but she brings to Parisians the latest Broadway products (the Charleston, jazz, etc.), [ . . . ] the transition between past and present, the soldering between virgin forest and modernism."[6] Nardal picks up on the temporal dynamics operating at the core of Bakermania, biguinemania, and the fascination with métissage. Her work homes in on the important and complex encodings of time within the structure of imperial New World cultural consumption.

By designating the fascination with Josephine Baker as a boring through the picturesque still panoramas of imperial contemplation, Jane Nardal captures the curious skips in time, sudden and uncontrolled jumps back and forth between structural feelings of the past and the future, that animate the imperial consumption of black New World bodies, spaces, and cultural practices. Nardal's insight locates the French feeling for black musical time as less a complete denial of coevalness than a deep consumption of the temporal fantasies haunting imperial and anti-imperial discourse. Rather than relegating the Antilles to the past, it projects them as modernity's anterior future after three hundred years of paradisiacal stasis. Together this discourse figures the Caribbean as an incongruous temporal space, a site that is out-of-time with itself and with the world. La Baker incarnates thus a site for the modern re-consumption of histories of French imperial value.

## CREOLE WOMEN ENDINGS

Léona Gabriel and the Nardals may not have made speaking out against French imperialism part of their work's primary agenda. But when it comes to the history, the value, and the authenticity Creole cultural practices, these women and many others actively engage in heated debates taking place in journals, on the airwaves, and on stage. The Nardal sisters' forceful and insightful critiques do not deny the way Antillean musical culture in France posed problems for achieving black equality and recognition; however their critique differs substantially from that of negritude's and even the biguine's leading men. "Negritude in the major" grandiosely rejects the sweet and sentimental (read: effeminate, feminine, maternal) lullabies and *chansons* that nostalgically express the beauty of islands and island women. It attacks these symbolic musical relations as testimony of doudouist complicity.

The Creole women this chapter foregrounds instead suggest that the biguine can be considered "doudouist" primarily in its failure to follow the patriarchal rules of French imperialism and black radicalism during the interwar years. Biguine's politics of mixing and its gender trouble offers "pictures of individual love and psychological turmoil" and expressions of female sexuality that negritude patriarchal order distinctly banished (Condé, "Order and Disorder," 123). Songs like Guitarist Gérard Laviny's "Neg ni mové mannié" can only be considered "COMIQUE ET LAID" in the logic of Aimé Césaire's *Notebook*. Black radical thought positions the biguine as just a little too "sweet"—that is, apolitical, subservient, and effeminate, in short, too *métisse* and *doudouiste*, to be considered part of the black fraternity. Both black radical thought and imperial discourse exclude the biguine from their histories, marking it as ephemeral, nostalgic, unfaithful, or out of time. Both designate the biguine as a scene in social disorder, sexual deviance, and part of modernity's heteroclite bag of cultural decadence. And both are involved in the regulation and valuation of the voices and bodies of women of color.

In contrast to the critically blunt and aesthetically oblique attacks of the negritude men, the Nardals generate a much more nuanced and sophisticated critique of biguine musical culture in France by locating its dynamics of gender. Indeed, scholars must be careful that the desire to rewrite "negritude women" (back) into the history of negritude discourse does not result in a conflation of their work with dominant negritude discourse, and particularly the latter's gendered erasures of *métissage*. Their work traces the historical and quotidian shifts between the invisibility and specularity that women of color experience in Paris during the interwar years and beyond. In other words, these women show that accusations that biguine culture is "morally suspect," "apolitical," or "inauthentic" have everything to do with the material and symbolic exploitation of Antillean women on both sides of the Atlantic.

Biguine's "song and dance" in critical and popular histories, whether dismissed as the province of the white colonial, or flagged as essentially black African, function to shore up notions of gender and race into the sandy critical and popular boundaries of colonial culture and island histories. Like the *doudou*'s "Adieu," the biguine has been positioned at the temporal, cultural, geographic, and linguistic borders of authenticity and legitimacy for the colonial and anticolonial alike. Like the beautiful *doudou*, biguine's aesthetic of *métissage* expands its social mobility, and the social mobility of its musical practitioners, yet inscriptions of it limit its ethical outlook and appearance.

# three

## La Baker

*Princesse Tam Tam* and the *Doudou*'s Signature Dilemma

Being musicians, we knew she stank.

—William Shack

Why say it under your breath
why say
here
here
here
here he goes again
here he goes again saying
Shit

—Léon-Gontran Damas, *Black-Label*

Josephine Baker has historically gotten shortchanged in black Atlantic schol-arship and historiographies: despite her unheard-of success, many critics write her off as a failure and/or completely erase her altogether. William Shack, in his otherwise quite enjoyable and useful contribution to black American jazz his-tory in France, goes out of his way to disqualify and undercut Baker's status in *Harlem in Montmartre*: "Despite *La Baker*'s phenomenal popularity, she was not one of the missionaries of jazz. Jazz was going strong when the *Revue* troupe arrived in Paris. 'The jazzmen who played in 'la Butte Montmartre,' who knew Bessie Smith, Ethel Waters and Adelaide Hall, did not take Josephine seriously. Being musicians, we knew she stank'" (Shack 37, qtd from Chris Goddard's *Jazz Away from Home* 83). Shack's dis, cosigned by Chris Goddard, seems to turn on Baker's lack of talent as well as her lack of "firstness." And why deny it? A few of the notes she belts out for example in "C'est si facile de vous aimer" (You're So Easy to Love) are not so easy to love; in fact they are as difficult to love as what the songs like "Si j'étais blanche" (If I Were White) represent. Even her fellow chorus girls were shocked by the signature number that made her famous, "la danse sauvage": "We were horrified at how disgusting Josie was behaving in front of this French audience, doing her nigger routine. She had no self-respect, no shame in front of these crackers, and would you believe it, they loved her" (qtd in Jean-Claude Baker 6). This is the dirt on Baker that buries her critical reception and historic importance.

But why say she wasn't *one* and then also say that she wasn't the *first* one? Why double down on this marginalization and erasure of her? The doubled act of exclusion enacts a profound gesture of expulsion, suggesting the condemnation stems from more than musical ability or historical chronology. To anticipate my larger thesis, representations of Baker, whether fictional or nonfictional, imperial or black radical, involve endless fantasies of her failure, her lack of value, her loss in cultural time and space. In other words, this double disqualification (*not* and not *first*) that erases Josephine Baker's contribution and historic importance, replays the very (not quite black enough, not quite white enough) scripts many criticize her for performing both in fiction and in real life in the first place.

If for Shack, Baker made the trip, but wasn't the first, and failed to bring the authentic sound anyway, Kaiama Glover pinpoints the question more probingly by turning it on its head in her introduction to a wonderful special edition of *The Scholar and Feminist Online*, "Josephine Baker: A Century in the Spotlight." Glover simply asks:

> Indeed, why Josephine Baker? Or rather, how? How is it that, of all the half-naked chorus girls to appear on the stages of Montmartre during the Roaring Twenties, Parisians chose to make Josephine Baker into a star without parallel? How was Baker transformed, in what seems a matter of mere moments, into the incarnation of Africa, America, and even Paris itself? How is it that a 19-year-old black girl from St. Louis, Missouri, who was neither the most beautiful nor the most talented entertainer to hit interwar France, was able to captivate *the* European cultural capital in 1925 and then to keep it mesmerized for nearly half a century, until her death in 1975 at age 68? [ ... ] *She is a moment that has yet to be repeated* (my emphasis).

Glover's comments hark back to "the transition between past and present, the soldering between virgin forest and modernism" that Jane Nardal critiques in Bakermania (as discussed in the previous chapter). Despite her utter reproducibility ("of all the half-naked chorus girls") and despite the techniques of mimicry that are the staple of her performing incarnations, *La Baker*, not just Baker but *the* Baker, remains original and perhaps even originary, unparalleled and unrepeatable. Rather than discount Baker's value, Glover asks about that value's formation.

Josephine Baker's real and imaginary life stories are inscribed in *partitions*: soundtexts, musical transcripts, and filmic scripts that function as so many screens for projecting fantasies of the other and the elsewhere, even as they also serve as so many walls of separation and exclusion, papering over histories of border-crossing and the possibility of authentic love across the line. Embodying everything from the most primitive to the most cosmopolitan, from dirty animal to cutting-edge diva (but never African-American), *La Baker* was first everywhere. As Margo Jefferson provocatively compares, "Josephine Baker produced three autobiographies—just like Frederick Douglass." Jefferson's sharp juxtaposition of Baker and Douglass gets at the way Baker's soundtext lives; her prolific career and prolific life stories constitute a primal text of black American modernity even as she remains stigmatized within black Atlantic history. Beyond the autobiographies, biographies, and loose biographical references in her performances, Baker's signature choreography too constitutes another body of writing in her name. These dimensions of embodied textual partitions, in addition to Baker's own torn relationship to writing, reading, contracts, and signatures, sound out the gendered limits of institutions of representation, ownership, and belonging in black Atlantic modernity.

Although scholars praise the way Douglass laced his autobiography with black sound, and ignore her signature song and dance, one could argue that *she* more than *he* incarnated "[t]he commodity whose speech sounds embodies the critique of value, of private property, of the sign" (Moten 12), at least for those who critically listen. *La Baker*'s real life and fictional life stories resonate in the many products sold in her name, from cabaret shows, colonial movies, and record sales to dolls, chocolate, and *garçonnette* hair gels. *Joséphine*'s sound corpus is the "product" and production of French dreams of New World blackness, and black Atlantic freedom dreams of France. But if her signature song and dance made her famous, it also made repeated demands on her, her body, and her name, so many claims on her that violently mark her as a site of imperial and black Atlantic possession, dispossession, and exclusion.

Denunciations of her as being a sellout aren't wrong; she sold out night after night. Problematics of recognition and value, interrogations of authenticity and worth—all are part and parcel of the antinomian dynamics that fuel "her" then and now, whether she is pointedly not counted, subtly discounted, or simply unaccountable. After all, what does it mean to play a savage while everyone knows you're the biggest diva in Paris? What does it mean to play a "ragamuffin in blackface wearing bright cotton smocks and clown shoes," a character "straight out of the racist minstrel tradition," when you're the highest paid chorus girl in the world (Dalton and Gates)? What's the value, and the cost, of being "the (black) shit" in "gay Paree"?

These aporia, with their spatiotemporal ambivalence and their musico-textual tensions are constitutive of the *doudou*'s signature dilemma. Like the *doudou*, Josephine Baker and her signature musical corpus remain haunted by temporal and spatial *décalage* (from within and without) that problematize her value. For many people, calling Baker a "doudou" rings like homophonic poetic justice and musical truth. But it also means that the critique of Baker, and the critical subject doing the critique, both play roles, wittingly or unwittingly, in this anti/imperial, racial, gendered mess. As Antonio Gramsci puts it, "Nobody [wants] to be the 'manure' of history." We all agree in the abstract that the terrain of history requires both ploughmen and manure. "But in practice? Manure for manure, as well draw back, return to the shadows, into obscurity" (qtd in Manning 27). Even critically returning to the site of the *doudou* and her "historical manure" runs the risk of getting oneself and others dirty. Considering her dizzying performances of failed speech, and her endless performances of colonial romance, *Joséphine* must have made Fanon sick, worthy of one of his classic peremptory "la nausée" verdicts.

How can we critique her without rehearsing and reproducing scenes of her marginalization and erasure? How can we not write (about) her without signing off on her failure? This chapter retraces Josephine Baker's *doudouiste* mythology and considers the relations between (black female) sound loss and (white male) textual gain, through a close reading of her performance in the film *Princesse Tam Tam*. It contends that Josephine Baker's sound corpus echoes the *doudou*'s cry, crystallizing the double bind of success and failure within the imperial and transnational consumption of black Atlantic popular culture and the iconicity of black sound. To get at these questions without reproducing her loss, without remarking and signing off on her as the border out of bounds, the marginal line, the methodology adopted here attempts to deflect the masculinist violence of her critique and its gestures of exclusion and erasure by exploring the dream of this special "flash agent" (Glissant), which are dreams of our own.

## PRINCESSE TAM TAM

In the film *Princesse Tam Tam*, Josephine Baker's character, Aouina, though not from the islands, finds herself in the *doudou*'s signature dilemma: love of (African/colonial) "home" versus love of (white/imperial) France. The soundtrack musically symbolizes her hybrid and stuck position while providing an organizing musical structure for the narrative. Her dreamy desire for the white

French male manifests itself in two songs, "Rêves" (Dreams) and "Le Chemin de Bonheur" (The Road to Happiness). Sung before she leaves for Paris, both songs represent a desire for mobility and dream of the possibilities it might afford. On the other hand, two other musical numbers represent Aouina's longing for home once she's in the imperial metropolis. "Sous le Ciel de l'Afrique" (Under the African Sky) represents the nostalgic love and loyalty for colonial home, and "Ahé Conga" portrays the atavistic return of the "true" savage self hiding behind Aouina's move to "civilization." These two songs represent a sentimental and even physiological attachment to home that Aouina cannot hope to escape. Book-ending her songs, she performs two dance numbers, one that situates her at the site of the Dougga ruins, and the other, after the singing portion of "Ahé Conga," that will eventually push her to return to the figurative ruins of the imperial villa in Africa at the film's end.

As a whole the soundtrack's musical numbers and extra-musical sounds locate fantasies of Aouina in space and time. Frequently adopting musical stereotypes of the black and North African diasporas, the soundtrack resonates with French orientalism in its playful variations of the film's theme songs, but it also stages musical scenes resonant with blank Africanist discourse and the French imperial New World imagination. The film juxtaposes this hodge-podge of "exotic" performances and sounds to Western art music in pivotal scenes at the opera or in high society galas. These alternately abrupt and subtle musical overlays represent the types of border-crossing the film takes up as its narrative subject, but they also demonstrate the heteroclite nature of the consumption of the other taking place in French imperialist circuits of "exotic" entertainment.

The musical exoticism begins with the film's opening credits as the bold majestic sound of horns seems to announce a royal entrance before the music cools with timpani playing alternate dominant-tonic eighth-notes. Musically, this opening plays out the break between the nobility of the "princesse," and the primitivism of the "tam tam" hiding underneath. As panoramic shots scan the Tunisian landscape, "Sous le ciel," anticipating the presence of "the Jazz Cleopatra," suggests the "playful" layering of colonialist male fantasy that constitutes the structure and plot of the narrative. First played in its normal tempo, a medium swing, then picking up steam, the song's quick ending stages the first scene of the film that takes place in France. Its snappy tempo and closing is punctuated with a slap delivered during a lovers' quarrel.

Max de Mirecourt (Albert Préjean), a successful popular novelist, is suffering from writer's block. He blames Lucie de Mirecourt (Germaine Aussey), his wife, who is having none of it.

LUCIE: (*slapping Max*) Repeat that!

MAX: I will!

LUCIE: You brute [*Voyou!*]

MAX: You and your dukes and princes! (*He pushes her away and leaves the bedroom.*) I've had it! I'm sleeping in the other room! (*Max slams the door shut.*)

LUCIE: You have no talent whatsoever. I hate being the wife of a failure [*un raté!*]

[...]

MAX: If my talent's gone, it's because of the life you force me into. I'm good for nothing now!

LUCIE: Is that my fault?

MAX: With that bunch of imbeciles you bring around I'll end up turning into a complete idiot [*gâteux*]

LUCIE: You've been an idiot for a long time.

[...]

LUCIE: Failure, failure, failure, you're nothing but a failure [*Raté! Raté! Raté! Tu n'es qu'un raté!*]

(*There's a knock at the door, and Max's assistant Coton enters.*)[1]

The opening slap, the slamming and knocking on the door, and the repetitions and insults percussively sound out the relation between Max's writing failures and his domestic failures while providing the comedic timing of the scene. The film's broader soundscape—full of multiple languages, accents, and broken speech, hurled insults and slaps to the face, clapping hands, slammed and knocked on doors, flashing bulbs and ringing phones, car crashes and other beatings—prefigures the inevitable percussive eruption of the film's finale.

Lucie accuses Max of simply being washed up, a "*gateux*" (ruined or doddering), "*raté*" (failure or loser), "*vidé*" (empty, dried up, read: without his masculine writing juices). Max is a *raté* by Fanon's definition too. *Ratés* are failures of speech and soundtext in imperial and racial technologies of desire. As Fanon suggests in his definition, the *raté* sounds out a failure in speech that reveals ideologies of desire at the intersections of race and coloniality as well as speech and text. Ultimately, the *raté* sounds out the dynamics of alienation taking place within self-representation. Of course Max blames his loss on his wife. She's what has left him *claqué*: literally beat and literally slapped. His wife and her clique of snobby friends, the decadence of the Parisian high society she loves, in short, her cosmopolitan lifestyle, have eroded, if not destroyed, his cultural authority. (Ultimately the film will develop the theme that the "hyper" modern, decadent bourgeois Parisian lifestyle and African primitive savagery might be two sides of the same uncivilized coin.)

How can Max get his writing groove back? His assistant/ghostwriter Coton (Robert Arnoux) has the perfect idea: the writing's on the wall, the living room wallpaper specifically, which figures a large map of Northern Africa with a few palm trees, camels, giraffes, and people scattered here and there. The wallpaper intimates the limits of Max's textual power within the domestic space of the Hexagon (continental France) and the bedroom, and it points the direction for expanding that power beyond the domestic space while solidifying it at home. He decides to escape his wife and her chic clique by heading not for the countryside (where she could easily keep tabs on him) but to Africa, "where the *real* savages are!" Max triumphantly proclaims.

Just as Max looks to Africa for his writing project, French colonial film looked to Africa to inspire French cinematography in the 1930s. Neither would be possible without the French imperial mission. The opening credits offer special thanks to Services de propagande de la résidence générale for footage. As the film moves from the confines and privacy of the domestic to the expansive wide open spaces of the North African landscape, it offers ethnography-like scenes shot on location in Tunisia. As French cinema reinforces and circulates imperial knowledge about the world, the advent of sound in cinema plays a crucial role, naturalizing and testifying to imperial discourse and its ideological frames of reference. "Sous le Ciel d'Afrique" offers the musical mise-en-scène, relocating the action in Tunisia. A *pizzicato* passage in the lower strings gives the rhythmic basis for this African return. While the violins take up the "Sous le Ciel d'Afrique" melody, the woodwinds, especially oboe and clarinet, play orientalized musical ornamentations against and on top of them. Even as the melody moves on it continues to echo and develop fragments from the song. At this moment we see Aouina for the first time in the film (outside of the opening credits) as she peeks through a cactus bush and tends to her sheep while frolicking in the desert sand.

Aouina is neither Tunisian nor French; she is a North African Bedouin peasant. Echoing the structural situation of the *doudou*, a figure of the third in a place of loss in the binary operations of colonial logic and anticolonial critique, her location in the margins of both cultural systems forms part of her appeal. She is untamed yet vulnerable, nomadic but constantly under police, community, and imperial surveillance. When Max runs into Aouina in town, he sees her slipping into and out of one tight spot after another. First she's under the table sneaking fruit off of a vendor's tray. ("She's a riot," Max exclaims.) Then she's being "playfully" attacked by a group of Tunisian children who throw fruit at her to chase her away. (Hilarious! Max bursts into laughter.) Later she's getting some payback for being humiliated by the snobby French tourists. (Max is starting to really appreciate this cheeky imp!) As Saint John Perse might have put it, "Rire savant du mort, qu'on nous pèle ces fruits!" *Anabase* II. He can't resist her blend of naïve charm and mischievous hustle (read: her colonial vulnerability imperiously—and literarily—turn him on).

In contrast, his side-kick Coton sees her as nothing but a waste of time. Picking up on her name when she introduces herself, he translates it from the Arabic for Max as "little spring" or "little source of water," but quickly adds that she's more likely a "little source of [trouble]."

> MAX: (*laughing*) [That's] getting back to nature!!
> COTON: (*scoffing*) If that's getting back to nature I prefer the little Breton girls on rue de la Paix. At least they're perfumed.
> MAX: But nature has a better fragrance than perfume!
> COTON: Manure is natural.
> MAX: So? Isn't that where pretty roses grow?[2]

Coton compares Aouina to manure and locates her within French imperial hierarchies of otherness by comparing her to one of France's interior colonial female others in the metropolis, *les Bretonnes*. For Coton Aouina stinks; she is sexually repulsive, indecent, and untouchable. Jules Rosette astutely points out that "Coton" is one letter from "Colon," French for colonizer. Despite the fact that it was his idea to go to Africa, Coton seems alternately underwhelmed and overwhelmed by what they encounter there. As *colon* he stereotypically holds Tahar, their North African domestic, and Aouina, as well as the heat of the tropics more generally, with much disdain.

But while Coton and the stuffy French tourists think Aouina stinks ("The smell of [wild animals] makes me lose my appetite," one tourist underhandedly remarks), Max sees her as a source of fresh inspiration. If Africa "doesn't speak to him," Max thinks maybe *she* can fill in the blanks of his book project and put him on a path toward domestic redemption as well.

> COTON: Aouina?? (*laughing*) [What do you want us to do with *that*?]
> MAX: A novel.
> COTON:...?
> MAX: Yes. Scrub her off, educate her, and [study] how she reacts!
> COTON: How she reacts? That's easy. High heels will hurt her feet.

MAX: Idiot.

COTON: That's your novel? Your publisher will be delighted . . .

MAX: The more I think of it the more I like it.

COTON: But there's no story!

MAX: I know, but we'll create one. I'll pretend to be in love with her. We'll see what that does to her. She's smart. An interracial story. It could be a modern [hip] novel!

Max calls "race stories," narratives about relations between white French men and colonial color women, the latest thing. By calling it a "study" the film shows the way the cultural production and consumption ideas about the world during the interwar years blurred the discursive and formal boundaries between fiction, visual arts, postcards, and music, on one hand, and fields of scholarship like ethnography, anthropology, and psychology, on the other. This is why, importantly, his plan to bring her to France does not involve trying to get her to pass for white. Instead he wants her to pass for an exotic noble Indian princess, "La Princesse de Parador," in hopes she will garner media attention and drive his wife into a jealous fit of pique. If the civilizing experiment will serve as the pretext of the novel, Max's and Lucie's abilities to manipulate Aouina to teach one another a lesson will be the novel's real story.

When Max proposes that she live and love like him ("comme un blanc" as Fanon writes), she doesn't understand the rules of his game, but she's willing to give it a try.

AOUINA: Why do you say you're in love with me?

MAX: Because I feel something for you.

AOUINA: A feeling?

MAX: I like you? I enjoy being with you. And you?

AOUINA: Me? (*hesitating*) I think you're nice.

MAX: (*chuckles*) Are you nervous around me?

AOUINA: What does "nervous" mean?

MAX: Flustered.

AOUINA: Flustered? Nervous? Flustered? Nervous?

Walking around the room repeating and pondering these words, she comes upon Coton at a desk on the other side of a partition writing down everything they say.

AOUINA: Why is that guy always around here with his pencil?

MAX: He's my slave.

AOUINA: I didn't know you people had slaves!
COTON: [I'm a *nègre* at this very moment my dear.]

Significantly, Aouina encounters and questions the writing of her story in this scene. The colonial *raté* of broken speech encounters the writing apparatus, both stuck in a discourse of colonial desire. Max and Coton joke that Coton is Max's slave, "un *nègre*," punning with the French word for ghostwriter, but their essential articulation of the technologies of possession and dispossession in/forming the French imperial writing project rings true.

When she stumbles upon the scene of her (incomplete) writing, and when Max and Coton jokingly evoke the racial technologies and economies fueling the imperial writing machine, Aouina senses the way her voice may be transformed to her disadvantage due to her relations with Max. As Peggy Kamuf writes in another context, "This fragment of text about a fragment of text is also about the fragmentation of names as arbitrary signifiers that, at any moment, can be cut off from their referent—the bearer of the name—and left to their fate, floating in the currents of chance encounters with readers who are free to associate a meaning with the name" (Kamuf 3). The fragmentation and expropriation of her life story, her name, and her performative corpus prepare the commodification and consumption of her body in a way not unrelated to New World slave histories involving the fragmentation, valuation, and displacement of black people.

Intrigued if confused by Max's offer to love and spoil her (so that she become the *gatée* and *gateuse*), the first singing scene, featuring the song "Rêves," marks Aouina's fantasy of the unknown beyond the confines of her marginalized colonial existence. Aouina sings "Rêves" while taking a boat ride with Tahar, as if in dress rehearsal for the big trip she will (not) take later to Paris. The jazzy music again here functions like a *clin d'oeil*, reminding us of the playfully crossed line between *real* (rich and successful) Baker and the *fictional* (poor and failing) character she performs.[3] The film suggestively cuts between close-up shots of her looking stunning and blissful and close-ups of Tahar's hands rowing the boat. His rowing evokes the rhythmic inscription of the dream of the other, a romantic lullaby, and foreshadow her unraveling in the finale "Ahé Conga," which will end with her relocation *chez elle*.

The broken hesitant French Aouina adopts in her interactions with Max vanishes in the singing numbers as Baker's trained French singing diction comes through. Whether deliberate proof of the success of the assimilation experiment in the film, or proof of the tear in the narrative fabric, musical transformations play a crucial role in the story. The studied nature of her musical voice—attentive to *e caducs* and other points of diction that allow for rhythmic execution and linguistic articulation—and the song's virtuosic climax, a (hold on to your eardrums) dramatic leap up an octave, anticipate a transcendent imperial arrival. In other words, the melodic emphasis of this number represents the types of cultural transformations made possible through the imperial encounter and civilizing mission (although it will prove able cover to the black beat for only so long).

Meanwhile, Max is in a fury; rumors are flying around that his wife is entertaining her own exotic love interest in Paris. This is what really flips his pen into high gear: the society pages and anonymous letters arriving from Europe that spot Lucie scandalously flirting with a rich Indian "Don Juan" (as Lucie calls him), "le Maharajah." Unlike Aouina, Max fully understands he is in the presence of texts that are writing him out of the picture. After pushing Coton off to bed and tossing through his papers in a rage, he sits down contemplatively with his pipe and pen. When we see the pipe and pen going, and the camera slowly following the smoke that rises above his head, we arrive unknowingly at a crucial moment in the narrative. Spoiler alert: from here on out the whole thing is just a fiction. Like Aouina stumbling onto the fragment(ation) of her text and the scene of her writing, so the spectator without realizing it slips into another script.

The smoke fades into roles of fabric: it's the tailor sizing up Aouina and preparing new clothes for her! (She giggles in delight!) She's getting her nails done. (She loves it!) She's learning to play scales on the piano in time and with a metronome, under the careful direction of a piano teacher and with written music! (Not enjoying this one so much, but maybe it's because she's so focused . . .) She's getting formal dance training, learning to point her toes and hold her back straight! (Pretty focused here too . . .) Finally, she's learning math, practicing her multiplication tables being written on the chalkboard. ("Two times two is four" she says with satisfaction; she's happily succeeding! But setting herself up for a mathematical breakdown.) By teaching her to be so civilized that she can pretend to be an Indian princess, or so the story goes, Max will stage his triumphant return with two exotic beauties: a fashionable black princess that will upstage his wife's own experimental tryst with the mysteriously rich Maharajah and a fashionable "race novel" that will reestablish his authority on the French cultural scene.

When Max finally "produces her in society," as the Maharajah puts it, he takes her to a classic venue of Western social spectacle, the opera, to perform her social role as Princesse de Parador for all of high society. The opera scene underlines the organization and order of Western musicality, while suggesting the staged, scripted, and performative dynamics of European social life as well. Repeated views of the musical score from the perspective of the conductor, with the hands and baton directing, emphasize the scripted structure of this musical experience, laying out its order with a clear musical hierarchy of roles, within which one might say the absent composer occupies the top role as the author of the script. But the conductor's hands simulate a writing gesture as much as a reading one. His baton moves observe and enact the form, call the orchestra to attention, mark the opening and closing of the piece, and inscribe performance into experience. The film implicitly juxtaposes the musical form and structures of the opera to Aouina's own singing and dancing outbursts. As Phyllis Rose notes, French and American audiences saw black musicality and textual musicality as antithetical.

Princesse de Parador's presence at the opera practically upstages the performance, foreshadowing her explosive irruption onto the stage itself in the film's musical finale. Rather than focusing on the scripted musical experience, the opera-goers avidly watch the scandalous spectacle unfolding between the popular novelist, his wife, and their respective exotic love interests. Charming sequences highlight the perspective of the opera spectators who zoom in on the balcony lodge with binoculars or hide behind columns to catch the action. Though playful, the scene captures in some senses the increasing scrutiny of black/colonial and white/French intimate relations, as well as the general specularization of blacks and colonials in Paris through entertainment culture and the tourist industry during the interwar years. In the end, the audience takes their cue to clap from the *Princesse* at the acts' closing rather than from the formal structure itself.

In other words, Max's plan works; she's a sensation! *Princesse Tam Tam fait tourner tout Paris!* She's lighting up all the telephone lines and covered in all the papers. The film relates black colonial performance to the technologies of travel and communication in numerous shots of telephones, telegraphs, typewriters, radios, phonographs, as well as ships and automobiles. The speed of modernity and its untraditional and constantly changing modes of communication that presented so many problems for Max before now function to his benefit. Moreover, his creative powers of text and his manipulation of modern technologies of communication have led back to the traditional venues of French artistic value: visual culture and the museum. Once frozen and lost in colonial time, now she's seen, pictured, and painted at all *the* Parisian scenes, she's displayed in salons and immortalized in stone. She's no *ratée* now! Now she has become another colonial post: writing and sounding out imperial space though dynamics of inscription related to new technological means of sound recording and transmitting. She works like a charm (for him); Max has got his groove back.

But while he gets payback, Aouina's success as Princesse de Parador comes at a price for her: the constraints of her role in his script, of living in "civilization" where the beauty is fake and bottled up, and where she has no freedom to be herself, to make herself at home. Alone in her room, the "exotic" music she listens to on the radio takes her back to simpler, freer times—at least until the market report comes on, breaking the spell. "La noire de . . . " has realized her dream of France, she's made it there, yet she's seen nothing, or rather what she has seen and done, she has as and for someone else.

Images of Aouina throughout the film peering and seen through the bars of windows or other types of frames closely resemble the staged portraits of Algerian women that were so popular in the 1930s, and which gained in popularity through the Expositions just as other black Atlantic and non-western performance forms did in France. As Malek Alloula notes, the window frames represent bars imprisoning the women, representing the barbarity of the orientalist, and especially North African, systems of social and domestic order. This postcard phenomenon explicitly represented Algerian women as ethnographic types, often staging them as dancers and musicians. Alloula pinpoints the way the postcard taps into and incarnates the mechanical power of the camera and its networks of distribution. La Baker circulated on postcards in this very same period in much the same way, even though she was neither colonial nor in a distant land.

Deciding she needs to cut loose if just for one night, needing to explore, to be herself and to be with "real" people, Aouina sneaks out with Tahar for a night on the town with the common folk, leading to her second singing number, "Sous le ciel de l'Afrique." While "Rêves" sings of her burgeoning desire for Max and all that he represents, "Sous le ciel de l'Afrique" portrays her nostalgia for home after having made the trip. It thus represents the expression of fidelity to the "other" love, the first one, lost, erased, or otherwise passed over in the two love dilemma. "Rêves" sings of an impossible future elsewhere, "Sous le Ciel" dreams of an impossible recovery of the past. In both cases, the dream is just barely perceptible, whether in sound or space, fleeting yet unmistakable and undeniable, a distance often articulated in Joséphine's work (in "Sous le ciel" it's "a voice rising up," in "Nuit d'Alger" it's "a force calling me," in "Deux amours" she sings "In the distance I make out / a ship sailing way / and I say

*Princesse Tam Tam*, Josephine Baker as Aouina peering out.

'take me'"). The musical situation establishes her structural position as a tragic colonial *mulatta*. While most of her representation in the film turns on a certain resonance with *l'Algérienne*, her performance of "Sous le ciel de l'Afrique" posterizes her in the plaintive sound posture of the *doudou*.

It's not enough that she plays *une bédouine* playing *une princesse*, she's also a North African singing as if she was West Indian. (With Joséphine, there's always an/other side, an elsewhere, just out of reach yet constitutive of the dreams of her [as white] fulfillment.) While "Fatma" danced and was represented under the mark of the plural, the *doudou* sings, and *this doudou* diva was a harem unto herself.

Escaping momentarily the bourgeois constraints of high society, Aouina paints the town red. Hearing a sweet Antillean (sounding) melody, she and Tahar descend into a sailor's dive where they see mixed couples dancing and a small combo playing live music. Once again, this place is not where it seems. The scene itself seems more akin to Marseille than Paris, representing white and black sailors, dockers, and other travelers, mixing with a few high society types slumming it—among them a close friend of Lucie. One can catch a glimpse of what looks distinctly like an ocean port, not the Seine, in the background when they open the bar doors.

This *mise en scène* places her at the border's edge, near the water, and by/on the boat. The music is markedly different from the North African soundscape that locates the film in Aouina's original "home." Instead of the tambourin and recorder, the combo features a saxophone, a piccolo, a guitar, and a piano. The ballad is being "performed" by what seems to be a West Indian ensemble, identifiable by the instrumentation and dress. (In reality, the song was being performed with the Comedian Harmonists, a German all men's singing group popular throughout Europe and with whom Baker would record the song for release.)

Lost in the music, we see Aouina listening while looking off dreamily in

*Princesse Tam Tam*, Josephine Baker, nostalgic gazes.

the distance as she did while singing "Rêves," but this time her image is compared to that of two other presumably colonial woman looking dreamily in the distance. While the song sings of Africa, and North Africa would represent her home, the film juxtaposes her with women whose particularly highlighted skin tones and dress contribute to ethnic ambiguity. The absence of North African women from all of the Tunisian scenes facilitates this pointed boundary-crossing fantasy of "dreamy" women. This sequencing of faces provides the spectator with a larger discursive reading context for Aouina's musically induced melancholia.

From her representation as *bédouine* the film now begins to juxtapose her pointedly with the *doudou*. Structurally echoing "Rêves" in the narrative, her performance of "Sous le ciel" further inscribes her in the ambivalence of her dreams, in her place of duplicity, her position as the third passing in the place of the other. Just as Josephine Baker's hit song "J'ai deux amours" was supposed to represent an African girl in love with (but abandoned by) a white French sailor and ended up symbolizing black Atlantic New World relations, "Sous le ciel de l'Afrique" in this scene tends as much toward the Americas as Africa.

After Aouina has joined in with the group for the second verse the tempo picks up and the tune turns into a modern popular dance routine containing elements of the charleston and other popular dances, in addition to some of La Baker's signature moves, complete with a white sailor that appears from the spectators to dance with her. Now Aouina has *her* groove back! Lucie's friend reports to her the "savage dance" she witnessed at the sailor's dive and the two devise a plan to reveal the Princess's true identity. With the Maharajah's help, they stage an elaborate party that includes an elaborate dance number with African/West Indian/Oriental instrumentation and performance. All she has to do is slip Joséphine an extra drink or two, and when the drums start a beatin' Aouina will come out and come undone in a climatic final musical *dénouement*.

## THE TAM TAM STRIKES BACK

The film's finale pointedly stages and juxtaposes two systems of imperial gender order and cultural value, one of the central themes of the story. Throughout the film, the Maharajah (and the local colonial agent Tahar) increasingly represents Max's other (and his colonial agent Coton), as each one struggles over the woman of the other (Aouina and Lucie) and her placement in their imperial scripts. The Maharajah literally sees Lucie as the missing, crowning specimen in his exotic collection of butterfly beauty. Max sees Aouina as a savage terrain for gardening and flowering a exotic beauty for collection in writing. The Dougga site subtly sets up this competition and overlapping of imperial archaeologies and histories of power and social gender order. The old Roman ruins, "where king's dressed in purple" (as Tahar explains), one of the best preserved sites of Roman imperial expansion in Northern Africa, signals this palimpsest, tracing the loss of previous (western) orders there.

These histories and overlays essentially pose cover for one another, suggesting that forms of empire building, patriarchy, exoticization, forced displacement, cultural domination, and so on, cannot be condemned at a certain level because they simply represent History, the movement of history, change, progress, difference, evolution, and the sad but inevitable loss that comes with it.

The pageantry of the Maharajah's elaborate stage show—which will ultimately feature Baker but includes a large cast of chorus girls, male dancers, and musicians—and its mix of colonial performance styles and traditions, echoes the pomp and glamour of *Paris qui remue*, especially its "Colonial Jazz" sketch in which Joséphine played "L'Impératrice du Jazz." Fireworks exploding against the backdrop set of a city skyline open the show, playfully if obliquely representing a fantastic imperial war. After the striking of a large illuminated *tam-tam*—a large cymbal, not a drum—a powerful ruler appears.[4] The show's orientalist narrative employs film editing tricks to give fantastical proportions

*Princesse Tam Tam,* finale.

to the eastern ruler, whose symbolic spins of a golden globe situate him as a mythical god-like figure. As he spins the globe, innumerable white women, his harem, emerge from the spin, as if products on display, turning on their own axes, ready made for possession and consumption. But it's not enough, the "sultan" makes them spin more furiously; this god's goal seems to be to make the Earth spin out of control, his will seems to be to introduce the disorder, in a word "tumult," into the order of the world. Turning wheels, spinning of a collection of women, spinning plates, and especially a large turning black-and-white swirl that take up the entire screen, represent the order of disorder that reigns in the "sultan's" tumultuous harem. In contrast to and against the sultan's efforts, the women, though momentarily dazed and literally blown over, always end up in intricate geometric shapes and formations. The "sultan" eventually wipes his face exasperated and resigned; growing smaller, now looked down on, he fades from view, and a drum solo takes over the scene that will transform into a performance of "Ahé Conga."

Aouina, as Princesse de Parador, is eating up the show, but she's also drinking up the drinks Lucie's friend keeps handing her. Finally, after being egged on—"Do you hear that music?" "How can you resist?" "Dansez voyons! Comme l'autre soir! Dansez!"—Aouina jumps up and into her own undoing. Kicking off her heels, unraveling her golden dress revealing a black one underneath, Aouina leaps from her balcony lodge onto the top floor of the spiral staircase, pushing others out of the way, she makes her way down to the stage front and center and steals the show.

While the finale is initially dominated by French orientalist harem imagery,

Aouina's eruption onto the stage for the climactic finish to "Ahé Conga" shifts the scene to Caribbean. (Baker says she was most excited about this final number because she thought the dance would catch on in Paris.) The song makes one think of the Spanish-speaking Caribbean, but the performance costumes inscribe the sound within the traditions of the French West Indies. The Creole madras headdresses the chorus girls now wear (looking like today's playboy ears) constitutes the meeting place for the French orientalist elements of the Maharajah's show and the French West Indian and black African elements of the show. Once she's joined by male dancing partners, they too wear traditional Antillean performance attire. Along with the chorus girls, each male dancer holds a scarf, echoing the dance performance styles of the Antilles harking to the *doudou*'s posture at the port. The scene captures this as only cinema can, especially newly powered by sound in the mid-1930s France.

A sequence of images alternately speed through close shots cutting between the percussion instruments being played, Josephine Baker's upper body and face, and the amused, fascinated, and/or alarmed expressions and gazes of the spectators. As the images of maracas, guiro, woodblock, and drum playing flash by, the percussion seems to be taking over rather than merely accompanying her. The focus lands on two competing images: one of Aouina dancing frenetically, the other of a lone black drummer (the only black performer of the percussionists, the only musician whose face we see.) At times it feels as if the footage of the drummer performing for the camera has been taken from some ethnographic document, so isolated and separate is the player/playing from the scene's stage. Then again, we never actually see any of the percussionists on stage, and it's likely that all of these scenes of drummers were recorded separately in studio. The percussion turns Aouina's dance from joyous liberation to savage possession.

Princesse Tam Tam's name always signaled an impending percussive unraveling, an atavistic return to a state of lack, symbolized in the unrolling of her gold evening dress to reveal the black one underneath. Figuring her as a drum, setting up her sonic specularity as desirous and beaten skin, the film stages her as a *raté*. The beaten and struck black colonial subject incarnates and bears the brunt of the minting of French imperial value.

At first Max and Coton turn away, horrified and embarrassed by Aouina's outburst, and Lucie is enjoying the success of her ruse. But at the close of the performance, the audience bursts into applause and all the men storm the stage to carry away the undone princess like a hero on their shoulders. Lucie, seeing her plot has backfired, runs to her car in tears and speeds away; Max chases after her in his own car. After she crashes in her haste to get away, Max rushes up, and

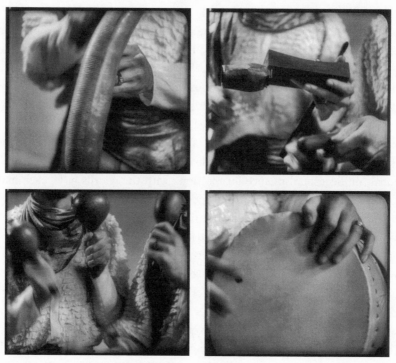

*Princesse Tam Tam*, "Ahé, la Conga" number, percussion.

after a brief spat the two reconcile in passionate embrace. Although successful and cherished in her public life and outburst on stage, Aouina is abandoned, left alone in private life. She realizes (with the Maharajah's help) that there's no place for her here or in Max's heart and chooses to return home. This was and was not change you could believe in. The transformation breaks down, revealing the failure of the civilizing experiment, but it is the writing of the experiment that will trump her successful failure, erasing the metamorphosis, revealing an unchanging present.

## FAILURE, FALSE ENDINGS, AND OTHER *RATÉS*

After all Aouina's dramatic acts in black Atlantic orientalism, and Lucie and Max's intrigue, separation, and reunion, the film uncovers a loop in the narrative, revealing that the whole thing has just been the novel that Max frantically wrote so he could return to the capital and reclaim his wife from the advances of the Maharajah. In the end, Aouina's choice was not one, it was only the textual unwinding of a narrative that never actually took place. After Aouina's faux

*Princesse Tam Tam*, images from the savage dance.

decision the scene fades and we see Max and Coton autographing their (Max's) new successful novel at a book signing event.

In the struggle over worth, Max returns to his position of authority and social prestige; his signature has recovered value. Even Coton gets to co-sign his name. "A signature, however, is not an author or even simply the proper name of an author. It is the mark of an articulation at the border between life and letters, body and language. An articulation both joins and divides; it joins and divides identity with/from difference" (Kamuf 39). In *Princesse Tam Tam*, and what I have been calling "the *doudou*'s signature dilemma" more generally, imperial scripts and performances of race and gender deeply inform this black diasporic "articulation [that] both joins and divides [ . . . ] identity with/from difference." The loop in the narrative represents this split of the writing subject, engagement into institutions of representation, and a disavowal of the other. Max interfaces with symbolic economies of representation and regains cultural capital and social recognition by "interfacing" with colonial desire. His signature recovers its force, but it triggers a "force de rupture" sealing her fate.

| CENTENAIRE | CHRONIQUE LITTÉRAIRE | LES H |
|---|---|---|
| Twain | | Jean |
| 0 novem- | | La p |
| ssait dans | | Jean |
| souri Sa- | Ce soir, à la librairie | dépas |
| anghorne | | le lieu |
| s, dont le | Rysa, Max de Mirecourt | Elle c |
| ne fut pas | | per le |
| té dans la | signera son dernier succès. | l'ento |
| s hommes | | d'art |
| eudonyme | | Que c |
| ait imposé | C'est en Afrique où l'écrivain | Rome |
| ire. | rencontra la petite sauvage Aouina, | dans |
| croire le | que germa l'idée de l'ouvrage. Un | une n |
| te célèbre. | | pas d |
| nvementé | | |

*Princesse Tam Tam*, Newspaper clipping showing the character Max's success with his "little savage Aouina."

*Princesse Tam Tam*, Max's book signing for his book *Civilisation* about Anouina.

The fragmentation of her life story that he textually sets into motion generates the force of his recovery and her erasure. But given the proximity of *her* life story to *his* signature, *she* must always be doubly barred. What else is the narrative loop than a double turn of the lock, excluding her and safely repositioning him back in the center? Why else write her off as a failure in France and then erase even her trip to France? Ultimately, the film's title itself indicates Aouina's

*Princesse Tam Tam,* Aounina's mule eating *Civilisation.*

fate from the beginning. Like a true *doudou,* her name is "a source of problems" for French and black Atlantic modernity. Even her fictitious name and title, the one Max does (and does not) give her, "La Princesse de Parador," will not be the name of the film (or the novel). Instead, the film calls her "Princesse Tam Tam," casting nobility against primitivism, imperial order against rhythmic tumult, linear genealogies against temporal loops and mimicry.

While the fantasy portends origins and blank slates (as Aouina's name suggests), the beginning is really the end. The *doudou,* like the Indian in American films, must "perform a narrative of manifest destiny," as Shohat and Stam write, "in which their role, ultimately, [is] to disappear" (119). This erasure happens as a function of textuality in *Princesse Tam Tam,* as Max, the signing subject, overwrites Aouina's story. At least while she was the Princesse de Parador, Aouina was conscious of playing a role, of pretending and thus at least co-authoring her fictional biography. Max's final act of signature transfers the story, and its profit, to him, and transfers the loss, the failures, back to her. He gets the story, and the profit, and foots it, leaving her to foot the bill, the loser. *Quel raté!* And even though Lucie's plot backfires, Aouina will be the true *raté de l'histoire.*

In the film's final scene, we see Aouina in the villa in Tunisia Max leaves behind for her when he returns to Paris with his new novel. The film portrays her and Tahar as living there the whole time, starting their own family, having a newborn baby. At the same time, the villa is a mess: books strewn about, dirt and grass on the floor, animals all over. Aouina is right at home! Panning across the villa, the camera centers on Max's novel, *Civilisation*, lying on the floor. A mule comes up and rips off and begins eating the cover page as the music signals the film's end. Aouina has moved from the ruins and lost civilization of Dougga to Max's ruins and loss. The mule, a classic symbol of racial mixing and degeneration, and its book-eating gesture suggest that even in Max after all the lessons and love, after being given a place to live, Aouina has a new start yet is still destined for loss.

### POST SCRIPT

And on my tombstone, I trust
Will be written "excuse the dust"
Of a past, but a class cocotte

—Cole Porter

That night, after dining with members of the show, Josephine Baker went to sleep, surrounded by newspapers featuring reviews of her success. She suffered a stroke in her sleep and slipped into a coma, dying the following day at the age of sixty-nine. Her death could not have been more perfectly arranged had it been scripted by Hollywood.
—Tyler Edward Stovall, *Paris Noir: African Americans in the City of Light*

Is the *doudou* aware of herself as a failure to change? Perhaps not, but maybe that's what she wanted. "Can a strategy be unwitting? Of course not fully so" (Spivak 15). Baker's signature dance moves, and especially her performances of atavism, constitute their own type of poetic cry. They point up a chilling experience and flash encounter with lost time and history. In other words, these choreographies constitute in and of themselves historiographies of the New World and its encounters with the Old and the Timeless.

The *doudou* is unofficial, the stuff of rumors and taboo relations. Written out of the official narratives of colonial and anticolonial patriarchal order, the *doudou* is twice barred from "her" dream. But if her signature bears no weight, if it cannot be, her voice disrupts the text's closure. Her performances, however compromised, still incarnate the freedom dreams of the black Atlantic and still offer alternate routes to the materialization of value within the circuits of transnationalism. How can we reauthorize this value? (And to visualize one might imagine Baker performing a furious *danse sauvage* to convince us, like in one of those credit card commercials, that she is the real Josephine Baker.) Discovering her value means coming to terms with the dialectical relations of consumption and repulsion that violently come to bear on her body and her body of work.

# four

## Negritude Drum Circles
### The *Tam-tam* and the Beat

> In leafing through this collection, one will have the impression that the
> *tam-tam* is becoming a genre of black poetry.
>
> —Jean-Paul Sartre

When Jean-Paul Sartre designates the poetics of negritude as a *genre de tam-tam* he picks up on the struggle over a crucial soundpost in black transnational and French imperial thought. The timely critical strike of his essay "Orphée noir" delivers extra force from its position as the preface to the historic negritude collection, *Anthologie de la nouvelle poésie nègre et malgache de langue française*. As Brent Hayes Edwards argues, not only are anthologies in the early and mid-twentieth century an effort "to grapple with *modernity* itself: the form [that] serves to 'mark time.' Most strikingly, the power of the anthology is concentrated in its discursive frame—in its preface, introduction, or opening statement" (44–45). Heard in this framework, Sartre's famous blow does more than identify an emergent aesthetic in black Francophone poetry. It forcefully marks this poetic as a new critical time, and a new critical rhythm, in black diasporic relations.

The transnational dimensions of this soundpost are as important as the temporal ones. As with negritude, Harlem Renaissance discourse takes up the Anglophone corollary to the *tam-tam*, the *tom-tom*, to mark crucial distinctions between opposing poetic practices and schools of thought. This is how Langston Hughes famously sounds out the distance between two styles of poetic production from the Americas:

> We know we are beautiful. And ugly too. The tom-tom cries and the tom-tom
> laughs. If colored people are pleased we are glad. If they are not, their displeasure
> doesn't matter either. We build our temples for tomorrow, strong as we know
> how, and we stand on top of the mountain, free within ourselves (44).

Hughes locates "The Negro Artist and the Racial Mountain" far from Countee Cullen's poetic ideals of beauty and form—and far from Cullen's beloved biguine clubbing. This black subject beats a poetic tom-tom from the mountain top like a literary *nègre marron*. The francophone term *tam-tam* responds in sympathetic vibration with Hughes's rallying call, and considering the importance of Paris as a site where blacks from the Americas took on ideas about Africa, that resonance is a deep one.

This chapter deals with the ambivalent way the *tam-tam* serves as a "black label" in French imperial and black transnational conceptualizations of value, temporality, and poetic expression. In France today, the term *tam-tam* carries an imperial and *petit nègre* resonance heard by many as a problematic (even if still served up and consumed on a regular basis like *tête de nègre* pastries and nostalgic *Y a bon banania* souvenirs and references in advertisements). But the ambivalent imperial provenance of the term does not prevent its reappropriation by the black radical imaginary as a cutting sign of a racial authenticity and anti-imperial resistance. As shown below, "*tam-tam*" and "tom-tom" are old ambivalent words, but together they form a complex "new vocable" (Edwards) in the interwar years, helping create "another register, now transnational" for framing black critical discourse on imperial modernity (Edwards 65).

The first third of this discussion tunes into the curiously split trajectory of the *tam-tam* as a term for what we can call "the percussion of the other" in French musicological and ethnographic discourse from the Enlightenment to interwar years. The remaining two thirds of the chapter focus on the ways Frantz Fanon's *Black Skin, White Masks* and Léon-Gontran Damas's *Black-Label* sketch out and navigate what John Mowitt calls the *percussive field*, "the production (through drumming, beating, and striking) of [a] sense of the skin— hence, not strictly the body, but the embodied subject" (Mowitt 20). Building on Mowitt's work, this discussion maps the historic trajectory of the *tam-tam* as it sounds out the alternately desirous and violent beatings and temporal breaks animating black transnational experiences of imperial modernity.

The history of the *tam-tam* label that I outline below will in many respects corroborate Kofi Agawu's notion that black "'African rhythm,' then, is an invention, a construction, a fiction, a myth, ultimately a lie" (Agawu 387) assembled and propagated largely through imperial discourse. The *tam-tam*'s split nature and ambivalent origins begin with the various versions of the word, with or without space, with or without a hyphen, or lowercased or with capital letters: *tam tam, TamTam, Tam-tam*, and so on, with as many variants for plural. The transferring circuits of European knowledge about music from around the world are full of static and saturated with—on top of the problematics of translation, misrecognition, and cultural bias—the noisy imperial cartography of the world discussed in this book's introduction.

But does the transnational and transcolonial trajectory of the *tam-tam* and black rhythm more generally, does its constructed and historically torn nature diminish and delegitimize its power? Or does it rather opaquely mark the profundity of its subjective vibration and the transnational breadth of its discursive reverberation? The opaque power of the beat strikes us beyond, before, during, and after the "musical event," and its varied aesthetic, behavioral, and material cultures as such. This is one reason why strictly musico-poetic analyses of poetic rhythm and musicality will leave us at a loss. Following Agawu, my goal is not to "contes[t] the pragmatic value of such an invention, but rather [to try] to understand some of its enabling structures and ramifications" (Agawu 395). Such structures and ramifications for negritude writers come from navigating the psychological, social, geographic, and imaginary terrains of French imperialism and black radical thought.

## A STRIKING TERM'S HISTORY

What is a *tam-tam*? The answer depends on whom you ask, where, and when. In French from the eighteenth century into the present the term *tam-tam* designates two distinct types of instruments: one sense refers to a metal Chinese cymbal or gong, the other any Indian, Caribbean, or African membranophone (skin) drum. In English the distinction is plain and the ambivalent imperial histories of the term are muted: the *"tam-tam"* is a type of Chinese cymbal, while "tom-tom" refers to any pair of mounted drums. But the imperial confusion over the name, more pronounced in French, echoes other imperial and New World naming problems. Hence, as much as the *tam-tam* stands for authentic cultural roots, it still marks "the violent penetration of European consciousness into a new world" (Nesbitt "Caribbean Literature in French" 645). To catch the imperial rhythm of the *tam-tam* one must follow a skipping historical groove back—a broken line of difference dug deep into the foundations of ethnomusicology and French popular culture.

Jean Joseph Marie Amiot, a French Jesuit missionary with a passion for Chinese culture, played a key role in the early dissemination of ideas about the *tam-tam* cymbal through his contributions to the influential late eighteenth-century multivolume collection *Mémoires concernant l'histoire, les sciences, les arts, les mœurs, les usages, etc. des Chinois par les missionnaires de Pékin (Memoirs Concerning the History, Sciences, Arts, Mores, Practices, etc. of the Chinese by the Missionar-*

*ies in Peking).* While writing widely about Chinese language, philosophy, and culture, Amiot paid special attention to Chinese musical culture, and he postulated ideas about the nature of musical difference along the way. The question intrigued him from the very beginning of his mission in 1751, when he first tried to impress the Chinese court with the quality of European music, playing works by his contemporary Jean-Philippe Rameau and others; the court's indifference stunned him (Irving). While Amiot immersed himself in Chinese language and thought, he also immersed himself in Chinese music, transcribing it into Western notation, sending scores to Europe for study and safekeeping, and offering other information about Chinese music and instruments in personal correspondence.

Some consider Amiot one of the very earliest pioneers of comparative musicology and ethnomusicology—a claim that speaks to the problematic yet often disavowed imperial genealogy of the field (Barz et al.), as well as the problematic inscription of non-Western instruments and musical practices into the Western art music canon. Amiot's work on the *tam-tam* included efforts to obtain its exact alloy composition from Chinese monks. A letter containing the Amiot's *tam-tam* formula would be published years later by important nineteenth-century Belgian composer and musicologist François-Joseph Fétis in *La Revue musicale*, a foundational journal in the publication of French music history reviews, but its accuracy would become a source of debate. It appears the monks may have fed Amiot faulty information. It is interesting that this percussion of the other first sounded in Western art music in Paris to mark an important event in the early history of the French republic. François-Joseph Gossec employed a *tam-tam* in his composition of the *Marche funèbre* performed during the national funeral procession of French revolutionary figure Honoré Gabriel Comte de Mirabeau on April 4, 1791 (see James Blades, James Holland, and Alan R. Thrasher. "Gong." *Grove Music Online*). Not only was Mirabeau's death an important event in French national history, the funeral procession to the Pantheon particularly marked France's cultural psyche. The context provided a striking occasion for a musical inscription of *tam-tam* sound, one that would orient its meaning in the sensibility of Western art music towards associations with otherness, mourning, and loss.

Gossec's work also marks the site where musical and musicological discourses take over for eighteenth-century ethnographic methods of knowing the *tam-tam* cymbal. After Gossec composers increasingly explored and expanded this *tam-tam*'s musical meaning, organologists struggled to classify it, and acousticians debated its material makeup. While attributing to it a certain power, the musicological field developed and designated its own meaning, value, and aesthetic limitations of the *tam-tam*, all now removed from the Chinese culture. Specialists defined the instrument's sound as "a bit rough and muted, but strong" (Pagès), and its musical qualities for them evoked "terror, fear" (Lichtenthal). This "powerful and lugubrious" (Colomb) musical value meant composers were to "rarely use the *tam tam*, only in certain scenes in dramatic music where one seeks a somber or terrible effect, and in funeral ceremonies" (Colomb 89), or perhaps for expressing "desperate passions, whose effect must be terrible" (Blaise et al.). At the same time, debates over the metallurgic makeup of the cymbal went on designating its precise material value, defining what constituted high quality *tam-tam* instruments, and mapping where they could be purchased and at what cost. This imperial map finds a way around the fact that, according to all accounts, Western music instrument manufacturers fail to produce cymbals of the same quality, a fact merchandising catalogs make this clear in pricing. In short, systems of scientific knowledge, material exchange, and Western musical meaning converge on *this* tam-tam instrument, labeling it and inscribing it in symbolic, material, and temporal economies of value. But whether in music dictionaries, acoustic treatises, or instrument catalogs this musicological discourse continues to refer to the *tam-tam* exclusively as a type of cymbal.

While this first *tam-tam* group of professional musicians and scholars inspired by the Enlightenment continue to label the *tam-tam* a Chinese cymbal, a second group of European natural historians and ethnographers working in the global south and the New World took the label in a different direction. Late eighteenth-century French naturalist Pierre Sonnerat, notorious today for his misrecognitions and misnaming, epitomized the ambivalent way imperial discourse expropriates and effaces the world's percussion traditions under the generic *tam-tam* as drum label. In his *Voyage aux Indes orientales et à la Chine: fait par ordre du roi, depuis 1774 jusqu'en 1781*, Sonnerat systematically and ideologically reifies Indian culture, transforming it into so many demands for imperial intervention. He laments, for example, that "The tyranny of a despotic government, the aggravating hot climate, and the attachment to ancient ways have always been invincible obstacles" to cultural and historical progress (174). Considering his inventory of Indian painting ("Indian painting is and will always be in its infancy" 175), and his summary account of Indian sculpture ("The sculpture is no more advanced than painting, and all the statues one sees in the temples are poorly designed and poorly executed" 177), his take on Indian music will not surprise: "Music is in the same state of imperfection as the other arts"

(178). Sonnerat situates the *tam-tam* as a noisy example of the poor aesthetic tastes and the temporal lag of Indian culture.

Sonnerat at least tries to give original language for his account of percussion instruments: "The Indians have many instruments, but they don't seem to be made to accompany voice. The one that makes the most noise is for them the most beautiful and harmonious. In the Pagodes, to signal the hour of prayer they use a trumpet, the *Bouri*, the *Toutaré*, the *Combou* (*a*), the *Naguar* (*a*), the *Dole* or *Tamtam* (*b*) and the *Talan* (*c*)" (178–179; letters refer to labels in the original drawing). Dismissive but thorough, Sonnerat gives a single word in the original language for each instrument except for the "*Dole ou Tamtam.*" In his footnote he explains: "The *Dole* or *Tamtam* is a long drum one beats on both sides with sticks." He also offers an illustration. The italics for "*Tamtam*," and the formulation's use of "or" as equivalency between two terms, suggest the term comes from the local language, yet the very fact that there are two terms here, as opposed to the previous structure of listing, makes its accuracy dubious.

Despite the fact that the first group, with its Rousseauian discourse, most closely resonated with Enlightenment thought, Diderot and d'Alembert's *Encyclopédie ou dictionnaire raisonné des sciences, des arts et des métiers* tends toward the rather unsystematic way that the second group of natural historians and ethnographers inscribe *tam-tam* drums. As a result much of the ambivalence remains: "A. N. *TAM-TAM*, Type of instrument very commonly used by all the Orientals. It seems to take its name from the noise it makes for its sound is nothing other than what it expresses. It has the shape of a kettledrum with a wooden belly and a tight skin covering the top, which one strikes with a single stick. This instrument is used on the streets to announce auctions or other extraordinary things. Thus, one says to sound [*battre*] the tam-*tam*." Somewhat dismissive in tone, the *tam-tam* makes "noise," not "sound" or "music" (each which term represents an idea musical scholars conceptualized in Enlightenment thought). The definition has the type of vagueness that suggests a second or third hand account as primary source. Using the tentatively suggested etymology for the term as an onomatopoeia to describe the sound of the instrument itself, the *Encyclopédie* is a long way from capitalizing on some of the more precise, "scientific," musicological study available at the time. But scope and authority of the *Encyclopédie* likely helped inscribe this vague designation of the *tam-tam* into the French language, legitimating the loose usage of the term in both technical and popular discourse.

This bifurcation between two systems of ascribing musical value widens as the *tam-tam*'s geo-cultural coverage moves from the south Asian contexts into black African and Caribbean ones. By the nineteenth-century travel narratives and popular culture increasingly use the term as a blank name for any "primitive" drum (where "primitive" describes the instrument, as well as its music and musician). In contrast to the way the *tam-tam* cymbal scholars designate value by the instrument's material makeup, its musical meaning within European art music, and its acoustic qualities, *tam-tam* as "primitive" drum scholars articulate the instrument's value through anthropological discourse, often positioning it as the ultimate symbol of African alterity.

Works such as Pierre Bertrand Bouche's *Seven Years in West Africa: The Slave Coast and Dahomey* (1885) call the *tam-tam* drum "the national instrument" in African cultures. Bouche refers to the other usages of the term, but distinguishes with specificity those he saw and heard in the following fascinating account:

> The *tam-tam des nègres* is not like the Indian or Chinese ones: it's not a simple plate of metal, it's the trunk of a tree or a hallowed out branch, covered with skin on one or both ends. The skin, struck with the help of a stick, produces an almost uniform sound. [. . .] *Ilou*, [a] generic name designating all *tam-tam*s in general, has for its root the verb *lou*, to strike. One strikes on this resonant skin, one strikes, always one strikes: so much and so strong the eardrum is ruptured. Nevertheless, all this noise is not without a certain passionate delirious harmony. Each tribe has its *tam-tam*s of war for which the negro soldier has a cult similar to our soldiers professing their willingness to die for the flag. The war *tam-tam* stolen from an enemy is a glorious trophy that the victor brings back triumphantly. Dahomey's is adorned with human skulls (95).

Bouche's designation of the *tam-tam* as "*nègre*" places it outside of the national/cultural designations allowed for in the Indian or Chinese "*tam-tams*." One might have hoped that an anthropological ethnographic account would provide more cultural fidelity to the instrument's original contexts of meaning than the musicological scientific discourse of the previous group. Bouche's scene (which is not a specific scene but the imaginary "typical" and typifying scene that one finds so often in classic ethnographies), and his discursive move from the ethnic to the racial, belies this hope. It is almost as if Bouche's attempts to faithfully inscribe the *tam-tam* in local structures of meaning end up only further fueling mythologies of blackness, rhythm, and drums in the imperial imagination. Bouche fetishizes the *tam-tam* as a physical as well as cultural and metaphysical value. The drum represents the site of a terrifyingly mysterious and overwhelming force at the service of national belonging. The stakes of this fetishized power can only be high for French imperialism given its own projects of possession and dispossession.

If Bouche's reference in his subtitle to "la Côte des Esclaves" (The Slave Coast) reflects the direct linguistic correspondence between *nègre* and *esclave*, lasting into the late nineteenth century, by 1908, Abel Lahille is able to subtitle *Mes Impressions sur L'Afrique Occidentale Française* (My Impressions on French West Africa) with a new equivalence in parentheses: "Etude documentaire au pays du *Tam-tam*" (Documentary Study in the Land of the Tam-Tam). The juxtaposition between Bouche's "la Côte des Esclaves" and Lahille's "pays du *Tam-tam*" might not be as fortuitous as one would assume. Twenty years after Bouche's study, "*tam-tam*" has strikingly replaced "esclave" as, if not a synonym of "nègre," at least a dominant signifier in twentieth-century discourse on black culture and value. Put differently, if the percussive field, as Mowitt describes it, can be thought of as the place where percussive associations encounter one another, then black bodies figure prominently within this field, forming and informing its genealogies and matrices of naming and value.

## BEATING SYNCOPATIONS

Summing up, the *tam-tam*'s ambivalent value comes from the ambivalence of the colonial machine itself, which fetishized the sonic site of the other in musical culture, creative expression, and natural history since before the Enlightenment. Along the way, slippages both subtle and blatant in this colonial machine mark a curious time, producing their own historical rhythm. This slipping beat, these *ratés* coming from the colonial machine are not simply the noise or silence of imperial mislabeling and erasure; they are complex composite rhythms full of gaps, holes, and breaks that seem off beat but that "come around" again at certain special moments of historical polyrhythmicity.

It is this cross-rhythm that the postcolonial critic must hear to find the position-taking beats of the percussive field in the interwar years. How can we hear this *tam-tam* and critically as well as literally translate its force—and how can we not? Brent Hayes Edwards's study *The Practice of Diaspora* on translation and black transnationalism in the interwar years comes right up to the edge of this problematic and key term in a discussion of Guadeloupean Suzanne Lacascade's *Claire-Solange, âme africaine*. The Lacascade novel, set in Paris, narrates a doudouesque love affair between the young *mulâtresse* protagonist Claire-Solange and a distant cousin. In this key passage on the inarticulate yet still affectively audible history of cultural exchange and loss, Edwards choses to not translate the word *tam-tam*. Edwards writes of *Claire-Solange*:

Over and over, the text performs the edges of Caribbean vernacular culture, pointing at all that cannot be carried over. This is often a way of figuring Claire-Solange's "mixed" parentage, as in the amusing scene when she sits down at the piano in the parlor to play Schumann's *Carnaval* and improvises away from the theme into "strange, nostalgic cadences, brief complaints, hoarse joys—*a tam-tam of sorrowful drunkenness*, whose syncopations tear the fevered soul: it is Ramadan, the African Carnival. Then the rhythm, starting to skip, creating a youthful gaiety, recalls a habanera" (55, my emphasis).

In not translating *tam-tam*, Edwards effectively pinpoints it as one of the "new vocables" of black transnationalism, where a certain percussive practice of involuntary memory and loss fails to carry over, to translate, or to textualize across boundaries of time and space. His choice respects precisely the powerful tension that posits this term's radical significance within black transnational discourse and European imperial history. Through her musical performance, the doudouesque Claire-Solange betrays a mixed cultural heritage where rhythm "comes to mark a certain inaccessibility, a certain part of an 'African' heritage that remains elusive and unconquered" (55). These are the conditions of possibility within which transnational black poets and thinkers bear "*tam-tams*" as material and mythological soundposts and sonic weapons in a larger field of percussion. If the imperial rhythm above sites the *tam-tam* in the contact zones of European conquest and expansion, negritude's negotiations of rhythm have to do with registering the quotidian blows of modern life in the contact zones of the imperial metropolis.

Of course, Fanon refused to get lost in the beat.

## THE PERCUSSIVE FIELD

Fanon's *Black Skin, White Masks* registers the trauma of race in repetition. It comes from "a series of defects" (xiv), "a series of affective disorders" (xii)," "a series of corrosive stereotypes" (108). Fanon's text constitutes a performance of the black Atlantic subject who tries to find himself but instead goes through a series of false breakthroughs and much-ado *ratés* leading nowhere. This is the temporal ambivalence of enthusiasm's fire that opens *Black Skin*: "Don't expect to see an explosion today. It's too early . . . or too late" (xi). Fanon's distance from the percussive "explosion" subtly critiques negritude's black scream. For Fanon, *le cri nègre* is a drunken moment of truth. Seemingly transcendental at the moment of its performance, the black scream cannot sustain its heat, it eventually loudly backfires (*raté*), if it does not break down altogether. Negritude's "enthusiasm" (or "zealousness" as Philcox translates it) is the arm of those who "heat the iron *to hammer it* immediately into a tool. We would like to heat the carcass of man and leave. Perhaps this would result in man's keeping the fire burning by self-combustion" (xiii, my emphasis). This enthusiasm, this percussive black beating of the iron, produces a burst of fire that emotionally strikes the subject only for a moment, only intermittently. Fanon's objective is to relocate that fire of beating from within.

Either way, the black subject receives a deathly pounding from representation, in encounters with the French language and in the field of speech. This is especially true in the quotidian life of the black Antillean subject in the imperial metropolis. Fanon most famously renders this dynamic in a scene depicting the black subject being called out by a white French child. "Look!" Sound and sight meet up as dominant culture sonically interpellates the black subject to see and hear its embodied presence from without. "The Negro is an animal, the Negro is bad, the Negro is wicked, the Negro is ugly; look, a Negro; the Negro is trembling, the Negro is trembling because he's cold, the cold that chills the bones, the lovely little boy is trembling because he thinks the Negro is trembling with rage, the little white boy runs to his mother's arms: 'Maman, the Negro's going to eat me'" (93). In Fanon's style, rather than the pulse of black authenticity, the rhythm of black subjectivity in the metropolis has to do with the endless fluid blows that beat the black subject into submission and marginalization. The "epidermalization" of subjective embodiment is a bruising hypostatization at the boundary line where the hammering from without and the explosive striking back from within meet (Mowitt).

The trembling skins of the Fanonian subject and the young white boy read like what percussionists refer to as sympathetic vibration, when a drum skin picks up another sound and resonates (vibrates) with it. We can critically hear sympathetic vibration in this scene as the fearful confusion of self/other boundaries and the seamless temporal and subjective skips in self-representation. Fanon critically locates and stages the fine line Mowitt explores between meaningful rhythm and "senseless beating," the latter which he describes as "the lack of apparent sense or meaning in the beating [. . .] that seems to spur a recursive escalation that, as hilarious as it may be, is also unmistakably violent" (2). Fanon's scene is an acceleration of senseless beating, erotically charged and violent; the Fanonian subject tries to laugh it off, but it remains full of implication, full of meaning. In other words, this senseless beating still interpellates the subject to embody a designated position in social order.

"Tiens"—"Hold on"—the young boys interpellates—"tiens" almost as in "prend ça," "take that!" A sonic blow delivers the specular beholding of the black body. And indeed this black subject does "hold" this vision, and that vision takes hold of the body, as the sympathetic vibration of his skin indicates. Later, still struggling "by the fire's light," when he can "see," Fanon performatively writes: "I [...] discover my livery for the first time. It is in fact ugly. I won't go on because who can tell me what beauty is?" (94). And the fire rises again: "I can feel that familiar rush of blood surge up from numerous dispersions of my being. I'm about to lose my temper" (94). Back to the pattern, the same trips to the fire, the same trembling skin, the same coldness awaiting the fire of the next strike. "The fire had died a long time ago, and once again the Negro is trembling" (94). The passage enacts Fanon's epidermalization of black skin, a visceral reaction, and visceral relationship and reaction to that reaction, hemming the black subject into symbolic and social space. A rhythmic interpellation in the daily speech of the imperial metropolitan contact zone sews up the subject in a black "body bag," to borrow Mowitt's provocative language.

The subject's scene of subjection becomes staged and specularized, a performance that draws an audience. "The circle was gradually getting smaller" (91). This specular formation of alienation closes in on the subject, choking expression, disorienting, nauseating. "The battlefield had been drawn up; I could enter the lists" (94). Fanon's work stylistically creates what, after Mowitt, we can call a *scene of beating*. If the boy is wrong to be afraid of the black subject's rage, his fear nevertheless produces that rage. The meaningless exchange, the simple reaction of an ignorant child in the city, has rhythmically accelerated into a violent scene. At the same time as this "senseless beating" figures the black subject it also imperially mints black value.

Fanon's language relates the black subject's mirror stage as also a sound stage, a scene of sound performance and struggle. In these scenes, battle is linguistic and sonic performance, alienation is less a loss of self than a public hammering of the self into its assigned subject position. As Mowitt writes concerning Louis Althusser, Fanon seems to importantly incorporate sound as a distinct modality "to account for the process whereby real people came to imagine themselves as holders, or perhaps bearers, of the positions opened for them by the historical unfolding of the mode of production" (Mowitt 44). Fanon's scene suggests that dynamics of sound function at multiple levels to interpellate the black colonial subject and instantiate the problematics of black corporeality in imperial modernity.

Interactions in social space are registered as a rhythm of slaps or blows: "my message was flung back at me like a slap in the face" (94); "Victory was playing cat and mouse; it was thumbing its nose at me. As the saying goes: now you see me now you don't" (99). His critical performance returns again in the train scene, repeatedly punctuated throughout with the exclamation "une honte!" ("disgraceful" or "shame"). The cat-and-mouse game of the black subject, the exchanged rhythms and sympathetic vibrations of daily encounters, the primal screaming explosions of revolt and authenticity but also the engagement with modes and productions of knowledge, they form together for Fanon a closed circuit of rhythmic violence.

This rhythm of *ratés*, outbursts, and psychological disorders is "out of place" temporally. The cat-and-mouse game of self/other knowledge and representation refers back to the imagery of Fanon's opening lines where he ambivalently places his work, and of a certain kind of revolt, as being out of time, too early or too late: "Two centuries ago, I was lost to humanity; I was a slave forever. And then along came a group of men and declared enough was enough. My tenacity did the rest; I was rescued from this civilizing deluge. I moved forward. Too late. Everything had been predicted, discovered, proved, and exploited. My shakey hands grasped at nothing; the resources had been exhausted. Too late!" (100). More than the problem of the overdetermined situation of black colonial subjectivity, Fanon's torn relation speaks in frustration about the practical use of any intellectual project for liquidating race as a legitimate category of truth. His concerns pose serious questions that still today can be used to interrogate the ability of the production of knowledge, whether in science or critical theory, to affect the everyday reality of race. In other words, is it still too early . . . or too late? Dominant discourse signals " 'You have come too late, much too late. There will always be a world—a white world—between you and us.' "

Fanon's excoriating critique of negritude discourse places it among the *ratés* of imperial modernity's percussive field. For Fanon, negritude's famed "black rhythm" represents another problematic blow in the imperial beating. "Understandably, confronted with this affective ankylosis of the white man, I finally made up my mind to shout out my blackness. Gradually, putting out pseudopodia in all directions, I secreted a race. And this race staggered under the weight of one basic element. *Rhythm!*" (101–102). Fanon's tone is dry enthusiasm. Negritude promises a break from the repetition, but what is this break in repeating? *Le rythme!* After quoting Léopold Sédar Senghor (the same passage that the famed scholar Christopher Chernoff would quote as inspiration many years later in his foundational ethnomusicological study *African Rhythm African Sensibilities*), the cutting irony continues. Fanon's style feigns excitement (or "enthusiasm") that symptomatically gets him stuck in this rhythm: "Did I read right? I reread it and redoubled my reading" [*Je relus à coups redoublés*" (99, my translation and emphasis)]. The repetition and beating only quickens its pace.

The emotional movement outlined above in the scene with the French child and the trips to the fire is triggered again, only in an inverted sense: "I began to blush with pride" (99). This time the enthusiasm of salvation mounts in the body, choking yet pushing out the screaming secretion of a race: "And now, let my voice ring out!" (102), Fanon exclaims, leading directly to a quote of Césaire's *Notebook*. This is not *un nègre*, Fanon writes, "but the Negro, alerting the prolific antennae of the world, standing in the spotlight of the world, spraying the world with his poetic power" (107). Fanon picks up the language of the (masculinist) imperial landscape, evoking this black soul operating an imaginative and symbolic transhumance of the sun. In Fanon's scene, "antennae" push up like plants being cultivated by heat of the black soul, watered with the desirous and abject secretion of a race.

Outside of his critical performance in *Black Skin*, Fanon distances himself from this *nausée*; but his sonographic stagings of black subjectivity and desire suggest an alternate way of understanding mythological and subjective violence of rhythm in New World colonial society and the French imperial metropolis.

## BLACK LABEL VAGABONDAGE

Léon-Gontran Damas poetically cuts a distinct beat in this percussive field with his unique representations of popular music. His entire oeuvre rhythmically stages the New World black subject's struggle with French imperial culture and history by figuring it as a percussive series of temporal breaks and corporeal seizures: from the invasion of slave drivers in Africa in his poem "Ils sont venus ce soir" (They Came That Night), to his portrayal of mulatto bourgeois society and assimilation in "Hoquet" (Hiccups), to the biting depictions of musico-choreographic complicity in "Nuit blanche" (Sleepless Night). The poetic subject of "Hoquet" laments:

> And in vain I've drunk seven swallows of water
> three to four times every twenty-four hours
> my childhood comes back to me in hiccups seizing my
>     instinct
> like a cop does a hoodlum[1]

Damas renders the treacherous lessons of colonial and imperial society as bitter sweet scenes in history that must be swallowed but that fail to stay down. The way he begins "Hoquet" starts it in the middle ("And"), locating it already within a stuck and broken repetition of speech that poetically crystallizes the Fanonian *raté*. As was the case in *Black Skin, White Masks*, the scene of black colonial embodiment and interpellation comes as a percussive hailing that blurs inside and outside boundaries. The "hiccups" of the past, colonial and racial trauma, keep "coming up," shaking the subject's relation to its body in a powerful colonial seizure.

Not only will the lessons of assimilation not stay down, like the "burps" at the dinner table in "Hoquet," or "all the shit bothering" the subject in "Pour sûr" ("For sure"), an iterative *raté* keeps coming up, staging the Damasian subject as the product and performance of an aesthetic of failure ("avoir beau"). In Damas' scenes of colonial subject formation, "the sonoric event of interpellation-qua-event is embodied in shock, or," as Mowitt contends is the case with Althusser, "in the beat of the hail or knock. The interpellative call strikes and moves the body, hailing it 'into position'" (Mowitt 58). This is the Damasian negotiation of the *raté*, a transcolonial and imperial poetic trajectory of black/self consumption in modernity that breaks up and breaks in on the speech sounds of embodied subject.

*Black-Label*'s scenes of musical and corporeal beating and repetition sound out the temporal and geographic *décalage* of the imperial metropolis, "MILES AND MILES AWAY / in Paris Paris Paris / Paris—Exil" (10).[2] Nostalgically echoing in and from the distance, *Black-Label* beats a rhythm of loss not unrelated to Lacascade's "*tam-tam* of sorrowful drunkenness." Just as Lacascade's "syncopations tear the fevered soul" (qtd in Edwards 55), Damas's black modernist epic percussively intones the colonial subject embodying historic syncopations of complicity and revolt. The poetic subject of *Black-Label* (again similar to *Claire-Solange*) negotiates colonial family drama—*métissage*, nostalgia, heteroglossia, and the problematics of loss—through hybrid musical forms and practices.

*Black-Label* carries a bittersweet memory of the *vogue nègre* from the interwar years in

PARIS-Center-of-the-World
at the mercy of AFRICA
at the mercy of its voice
at the mercy of its fever of its rhythm
of the dance floor the size of a handkerchief
of the invitation to travel on the wall
of the muted trumpet

DO YOU REMEMBER

If the Césairean subject fetishizes the apocalyptic fires next time that could spark a new beginning (in other words, if he rhythmically pushes the beat), and the Fanonian *raté* seems trapped in the black body bag (seated in imperial modernity's historic rhythmic pocket), the Damasian subject suffers from a rhythmic hangover, a time lag (playing behind the beat).

Hungover from the cosmopolitan tumult of the interwar years, the latter's "exotic" transnational encounters and intimacies risk becoming a lost memory. The biting refrain that dominates the first and the last of the poem's four long movements locates the New World subject within a rut of imperial exile and transnational melancholia:

BLACK-LABEL TO DRINK
no use in changing
Black-Label to drink
what good is changing

More of a Fanonian *raté* than a Césairean hero, this black postcolonial subject decidedly does not evolve; it is rather stuck in a rhythmic refrain whose alliterations, capitalizations, and repetitions register a bitter and bruising environment. Counterintuitively, this poetic subject drinks to remember more than to forget. Listening back through drunken rhythm, *Black-Label* hears the subject otherwise, locating the Damasian hero in a problematic percussive genealogy intimately related to French imperial history.

*Black-Label*'s title conspicuously launches this modernist trip under the sign of ambivalence. Named after a brand name product, the poem, and its refrain, plot a path of black alienation and self-consumption rather than one of self-realization or heroic transcendence. Pointedly, it is the English language/ whisky—not French/wine or Caribbean/rum—that kicks off and sustains this intoxicating trip. On one hand, the "label" highlights this trip's continued relations with a certain commodification of the New World black body. On the other, retranslating it back to the French, the "label" harks back to the demands of colonial bourgeois *étiquette* so often critiqued in Damas's work. The labeling interplay sets up the poem as a brand of aesthetic intoxication that has half swallowed and spit up rules of the colonial bourgeois cultural assimilation, but it also establishes "the black label" as the production and circulation of imperial history and value.

Establishing the link between colonial bourgeois culture and the imperial economies that consume black bodies and lands, Damas's poetic frequently plays with "ready-made" expressions in French, English, and Creole. In *Black-*

*Label*'s critique of the imperial economies of the black body, an increased use of English and Creole marks a shift in Damas's rhythmic poetics of language. *Black-Label* picks up the rhythmic critique nascent in *Pigments* but transforms it by rerouting its politics of authenticity and siting it as the scene where new economies and markets for consuming blackness emerge.[3] Accordingly, imperial discourse seamlessly transforms labels for blackness into advertising slogans, newspaper headlines, and popular entertainment.

But rather than disavow the label's rhythmic interpellation, as Fanon does, the Damasian hero rides out what Claude McKay's *Banjo* calls the "skin game" of French imperialism. *Black-Label*'s drunken bohemian vagabondage is decidedly closer to *Banjo*'s brand of intoxicating black nomadism than to Césaire's ascetic "nameless wandering" (*vagabondage sans nom*) in "Les Purs sangs" (The Thoroughbreds).

> I DRANK AWAY MY PAIN
> tonight like yesterday
> like so many
> other nights past
> where from dive to dive
> where from bar to bar
> where from glass to glass
> I drank away my pain. (14)

While Fanon would likely see Banjo and the beach boys as a bunch of *ratés*, the Damasian subject takes on a poetic tactic similar to Banjo and Ray's: regurgitating "all the shame drank" (*BL* 31) and nomadically moving along. If Johnnie Walker's Striding Man logo, created in 1908, was meant to symbolize "forward thinking" and "the pursuit of excellence," the Damasian vagabond's stumbling itinerary suggests the dark bodies whose displacement and alienation fuel "efficient" European advancement.

Deeper than the "hidden depths" that Johnnie Walker's "Black Label" brand is meant to represent, Damas dis-covers what Lindon Barrett calls "the other side of value." Like the unanswered ringing refrain "RING AND RING / ring my heart marinated in alcohol" that takes over the poem's second movement and reappears in the fourth (quoted below), the Damasian subject finds itself alone on the other side, both on the line and at the end of the line of this deep and transatlantic beating. To reconnect from the temporal and spatial distance, Damas's poetic concoctions of liquid percussivity flow through yet beyond the cultural and linguistic boundaries of the Hexagon. He imagines "the two welcome back rum *punches*" (emphasis in the original) that an uncle would prepare for him if he could return home. He seeks out connections while sipping his "Canadian *Club*" in the poem's famous third movement. Filled "with their cries / the nothingness of my nascent neon nights" (*BL* 25), framed together these punching, clubbing, and otherwise percussing memories, and the symbolism of the "liquid" and its depths, recall the violence of that other transatlantic trip, the Middle Passage.

These rhythmic liquid blows form "*désirs comprimés*" ("capsulated desires"). Condensed rather than erased, they harden in the liquid depths of a syncopated memory. Similar to the black pearls at the ocean's bottom referred to in the Haitian Jean Brierre's "New Black Soul," Damas's *désirs comprimés* come in the form of colonial sweets, Creole *mignardises*—forbidden appetites and bittersweet memories with doudouist overtones of complicity and betrayal. *Black-Label* gets at a negotiation of the consumption or indigestion of these bittersweet memories as historical representation and authentic culture become products for expropriation and global consumption.

Like Fanon's *raté*, the Damasian poetic subject navigates the rhythmic and desirous drinking in and "secretion" of a race. While Fanon's subject sees himself "in triple" in the urban imperial metropolis ("In the train, it was a question of being aware of my body, no longer in the third person, but in triple [. . .] instead of one seat, they left me two or three. I was no longer enjoying myself" 90), Damas' bohemian *raté* experiences disruptions in space, breakdowns that produce beating/ringing double visions and leave the poetic subject disoriented:

RING AND RING
ring my heart marinated in alcohol
that no one wanted to touch at the table yesterday
ring and ring
midnight full moon three
whose image is forever in ONE
WOMAN glimpsed on the Island of a thousand and one
    flowers (38)

Damas's critical rhythm, his drunk triple vision "implies a state of impaired, unreliable, or faulty perception" (Barrett 1) that locates the violent binarisms within constructs of black colonial value. The Damasian hero is not the voice of those without voice à la Césaire. Rather he calls home again and again but attempts to connect fail. The ringing goes right through his drunken heart in a rhythm of loss that flirts with the *doudou*'s posture of waiting.

*Black-Label*'s subject seeks out this beating and ringing; he "fills himself up with pain," and this pain becomes

> [...] suddenly
> at the very heart of man
> stronger and heavier and more sure and beautiful
> than the Tower dominating the City
> stretched out along the Seine (11)

This ringing and beating rhythm of black melancholia replaces the Eiffel Tower as the dominant point of orientation in Damas's city soundscape. Orienting itself in its intoxicating beating, the poetic subject drinks himself up. Like the repeated phrase "DO YOU REMEMBER" suggests, the punch-drunk poetic tactics seek to trigger a semi-voluntary series of memories that map out a transhistoric trajectory of line crossing and complicity.

While other negritude poets try to unearth an uncompromised site for black poetic expression, often imagining rhythm and "the *tam-tam*" as Afrocentric sites of authenticity, Damas complexly situates his beating poetic within the problematics of the French colonial family and the broader black Atlantic. Such genealogical rooting and routing scrambles binary oppositions of complicity and revolt, authenticity and assimilation.

Ultimately, the Damasian subject will come to recognize itself among "[t]hose who are born / those who grow up in Error / those who are raised in error" (15). This "error" is a *raté*, a failure, a break that forms a line of continuity. It captures the mislabeling, the expropriation, of the New World as well as a degrading labeling of black bodies. The poem amasses the *ratés* of the black label in order to retrace the insidious mechanisms of imperial value and black devaluation.

> Those who call each other
> savages
> dirty niggers
> *soubarous*
> *bois-mitan*
> *gros-sirop*
> *guinains*

*congos*

*moudongues*

*fandangues*

*nagues*

Those whose spine is weak

and whose back is beaten

and butt

kicked (16–17)

Damas's aggressive enumeration, forming its own rhythm and beat, creates not only a poetic corpus of self-loathing and self-negation but also a path. As the poem veers into Creole speech, the complicity of black labeling bludgeons. Denigrating the black body's "natural" country (versus city) manners (*"souba-rous"*), mocking the black body's otherness, darkness, and African past, evoking it as a beast of colonial production and cultural burden (*"gros sirop," "congo," "guinains"*), the poetic enumeration builds and beats a long poetic body on the page itself while it designates that corpus as a beating stick (*"moudongues"*). The subject cannot distance itself from the labels, insulting, breaking down, beating up and consuming black bodies in the European imperial machine.

The poetic *moi* locates itself within these colonial family genealogies of black labels. This lineage of alienation ("Those my memory / still finds in Exile") cannot be cut off, however painful ("STOP OR I'M HANGING UP"), for it traces

the bitter and rough and hard road

that leads

not

to CHRIST

but to DAMAS (12)

While Césaire creates an apocalyptic *fin du monde* in order to recover a primal *bombement* ("The Thoroughbreds") and Fanon distances himself from this screaming explosion of blackness, Damas skips and stumbles through the beat, for "It's less a matter of starting over / than continuing to be" (31). The black beats of negritude rarely portray a hero who has not faltered, yet Damas tactically follows through on this line of complicity in a distinct way, notably by drawing out the resonance between the musico-corporeal beatings of the past and those of popular culture of the interwar years, and playing them through to the postcolonial hangover after the riotous tumult.

Black Atlantic musical culture delivers a sonic beating to the subject, aligning it in dimensions of time as part of modernity's musical shock. While the striking trajectory of the *tam-tam* in Western musicology and ethnomusicology stages percussion as the music of the other, all music, in its engagements with rhythm and time, contains a percussive quality. As Mowitt writes

> in addition to music's interpellative dimension, there is the matter of music's irreducibly percussive character. Which means what? It means that beyond simply the beat effected by the rhythmic organization of any given piece of music, there is the duration and extension of the piece, the time and space of the performance, that breaks in on the subject in formation. The piece strikes us, catches our ear, regardless of whether it is scored for percussion instruments. We are, one might say, subject to its blows. (58)

In other words, music and the temporal and percussive associations that musicking activity puts into social play relay this imperial beating from the Old World to the New and back again.

From the black African primitivism of *Pigments* where "the *tam-tam* rolled from rhythm to rhythm the frenzy" ("They came that night"), *Black-Label* follows the rhythm of musical practices in the context of "the Error." Rhythmically retracing the transatlatic triangle, Damas drinks in a history of musical *compromission*—from "Those who to the sound of the hurdy-gurdy / started to dance under the overseer's eye / the overseer's whip," to Antillean bourgeois colonial society's "taste for sweet affectations / for niceties / for the pitch of nice skips / the chic of polite steps (*goût des mignardises / des politesses / le ton des entrechats / le chic des ronds-de-jambe*; BL 27). The path of musical *compromission* (leading to Damas, i.e., leading to the poetic subject's place in this history of loss) ends up in black Atlantic musicking in the heart of imperial Paris.

La CABANE CUBAINE
the uniform of the doorman with the red parasol
the stairs leading right to the brown dizziness
and throwing you wholeheartedly into the fever of the
    rhythm
the dance floor the size of a handkerchief
the invitation to travel on the walls
the champagne buckets with roses springing from them
the bitterness of the blues
the stomp
the maxixe

the evocation of islands
the danzon
the méringue
the Creole mazurka
the drum imposing silence
the speaker announcing MALHIA (48–49)

Damas's scene offers a fascinating polyglot depiction of the famous Cabane Cubaine where many Antillean performers played in the 1930s. The languages and genres ("drum" and "speaker" are in English in the original) evoke the transnational trajectory of black Atlantic practices during the interwar years.

The club was known in popular circles as an interracial, intercultural meeting place and had been characterized as such in popular culture. Ousmane Socé's *Mirages de Paris* and Brassaï's iconic photographs of the club circa 1932 illustrate the types of line-crossing taking place in Paris through the Antillean musical scenes. "It was in clubs and bals nègres that cultural and social mixing was no doubt the most marked," Décoret-Ahiha explains (76). The Cabane Cubaine evocation comes again in the most well-known (as it was published partially in Senghor's edited *Anthologie*) passage of *Black-Label*.[4]

—YOU WERE AT THE BAR
and me
    —among others—
right on the dance floor coated [*enduite*]
and polished [*patiné*] with steps
with stomps
with slows
with songs
with sons
with blues (57)

Stunningly, the Damasian subject cedes this crucial scene to "the Other" that marks his failure and loss, the woman's voice on the other side of the poetic subject's line-crossing encounter. Sonic and visual dynamics of social interpellation and taboo desire function together to trigger the continuation of a "cut film," a colonial/imperial romance narrative, briefly alluded to earlier in the poem.

Fascinated perhaps
suddenly your eyes

took on mine
but from you or me who were already
simply a single unsatisfied beautiful desire
I don't know anymore who came to the Other
while the band played
*Esclavo Soy*

*I don't know* anymore which one

And it was dizziness

Hanging to your steps
hanging to your eyes
hanging to your soul
I let myself go
to the rhythm of your drama (57–58)

A sonic-visual sync seals a poetic break, an intimate spontaneous encounter mapped onto pre-scripted histories. While the Damasian subject waits for the arrival of his Creole love from home, while he calls and the phone (dangerous arm) rings and rings in vain, "l'Autre" is immediately "hooked" (*accrochée*). The gaze that encounters "affronts," harking back to the Creole dictum quoted earlier in the poem: "Zié Békés brilé zié Nègues," which Damas follows with the translation (in French), "They say the white man will always keep an eye on the nigger" (17), but which more literally translated means "White men's eyes burn Nigger eyes." The saying speaks of the formal and informal rules forbidding certain types of eye contact across the racial and gender divide and indicates the violence of surveillance and enforcement of these rules. In short, with their eyes locked, and the band playing, a "line," socio-historic, discursive, and subjective has been crossed.

The song serves as the crucial framing of the scene. The reference to "*Esclavo soy*" ("I am a slave") relates the past beating of New World bodies to the contemporary musical culture, and once again does so outside of French national language and culture and inside transnational circuits of black Atlantic exchange and experience. Like the "punch," the "club," and the "drum" (all given in English in the original text), "*Esclavo soy*" triggers a drunken beat. A tumultuous rhythm ignites the encounter and gaze: it unites the two, enraptures them, compels them against one another; and it serves as the subjective site where the voice and desire of the other melds into the poetic subject's voice.

Damas refers to the popular song "Lamento Esclavo" (The Slave's Lament), which opens with the lines "Esclavo soy" (not to be confused with "La Complainte de l'esclave," also popular during this time and performed by some of the same groups). Here are the song's standard lyrics:

I'm a slave
I was born black
black is my color
and black is my luck.
Poor me
I go along suffering
this cruel pain until death

I'm a captured Lucumi
without freedom I can't live
Oh my dear Pancha let's dance
that Africans will one day be free
that blacks will be free[5]

Lucumi are an Afro-Cuban (Afro-Puerto Rican and Afro-Dominican) ethnic group likely of Yoruba descent; it's also the name of a Yoruba dialect used in Santeria. The singing subject's rhythmic lament of slavery and color ("black luck"), and its choreographic entreaty "that the 'congos' will one day be free," physically, subjectively, and spiritually resonates with *Black-Label*'s subjects, putting them into place for the chilling modern replay of an historic passion. The song intersects at multiple levels with the poetic trajectory of *Black-Label*, suggesting the ambivalent negotiation of suffering and separation manifest in dance culture, and that dancing to it must have stirred up ambivalent feelings for many people of color and of colonies.

The origins of "Lamento esclavo" carry an interesting split history of complicity and revolt. Now considered a traditional Cuban song, "Lamento esclavo" was composed by Eliseo Grenet in 1932. Grenet got his start playing piano for silent films before eventually starting up a jazz band in the 1920s. In the 1930s he set some of Nicolas Guillen's poems from *Motivos del son* to music. By 1932 he had to flee Cuba due to lyrics from another lament he composed: "Lamento cubano."[6] Grenet was one of the composers for *Princesse Tam Tam*. He is listed with last name only in the opening credits, along with Jacques Dallin, Walter Goehr, and Alain Romans. It's easy to imagine his creativity behind the film's climactic number in fact given his experience writing rumbas.

The song was popularized in the early to mid-twentieth century by groups like Don Barreto et Son Orchestre Cubain and Rico's Creole Band along with similar formations that performed formally or informally in venues across the black Atlantic. These pan-Caribbean groups performed at music halls and colonial balls, as well as numerous private events of course. Their work shows how clubs characterized as French West Indian or biguine clubs actually played a range of genres and featured musicians from all over the black Atlantic. Emilio "Don" Barreto was a Cuban expatriate who performed and recorded in France during the 1930s and 1940s, after having previously picked up Martinican musical styles, genres, and musicians during a stint in Martinique.[7] Barreto's recordings include biguine numbers (usually with the *beguine* spelling) such as "A si paré" (see the *Au Bal Antillais* recording listed in the discography) and "Biguine d'Amour," but they mostly featured Cuban *sones* like "Lamento esclavo." The *son* became popular in France in the late 1920s, marked especially by Rita Montaner's 1928 recording "El Manicero" for Columbia records. Rico's Creole Band similarly recorded numbers in French, French Creole ("Moin aime doudou moin"), and Spanish like "Alma de mujer."

These rhythms of popular culture, combined with exile and alienation in the imperial capital, trigger a deep rhythm that surges forth, overtaking and aligning the subject in scenes of imperial and colonial beating. Damas's almost ethnographic poetic scene pinpoints a Pan-American as well as colonial-imperial mixing that, when triggered by the music, creates uncanny and erotically charged resonance, sweeping the body away into pre-written scripts and choreographies (aka History). The syncronicity of the broken taboo, musical time, percussivity, and language serves as a disorienting *déclic*. The subject's encounter continues a history of line crossing whose violence screams from newspaper headings inserted into the intimate moment.

A NEGRO WAS
HUNG THIS MORNING
AT DAWN GUILTY
OF CROSSING THE LINE (58–59)

The rhythm of the poem, its stark juxtapositions of the white woman's voice and the white man's newspaper, and the rhythm of the musical relating, stages a deep moment of repetition, in short, a beat.

The dance floor's worn surface, "patinée de steps / de stomps," constitutes a site where authenticity and value have been tapped in, musically minted. Arjun Appadurai's discussion of value, temporality, and consumption is useful here.

The patina of objects takes on its full meaning only in a proper context, of both other objects and spaces for these assemblies of objects and persons who know how to indicate, through their bodily practices, their relationships to these objects [. . .]. When all these conditions are felicitous, then the transposition of temporality, the subtle shift of the patina from the object to its owner or neighbor, is successful, and the person (or family or social group) himself or herself takes on the invisible patina of reproduction well managed, of temporal continuity undisturbed. [. . .] Thus, the management of temporal rhythms is critical to the exploitation of patina. (75–76)

From this perspective, the musicality of the scene does more than stage the action: rather its assemblage of multiple black Atlantic people and musical expressions saturates the site with deep temporalities involved in the construction of value and with the relations of value between the people, objects, and sociocultural practices in the black Atlantic. With value musically minted into the floor boards, the conditions are ripe for "the transposition of temporality, the subtle shift of the patina from the object to its owner or neighbor," as Appadurai puts it; the question becomes how the subject will negotiate the "management of temporal rhythms" and their implications for his place in imperial value. Poetically moving to this rhythm of popular cultural and musical *compromission*, the Damasian hero arrives at a moment of historicity. The poem does not suggest a black "hero" with the power of history and "agency" à la Césaire. Instead it stages an embodied and desirous consumption of history in a moment of synchronicity and periodicity. *This* is the beat the poetic subject moves to, a historical dance. Rather than positing the subject as overdetermined by history, Damas shows it reliving history, corporeally and poetically registering history if not writing it.

The encounter embodies a repetition that shakes loose the hidden past of the subject, especially the broken, lost speech of a childhood *raté*, born with "a lazy rebellious tongue / a mouth / born sewn shut," (*BL* 75),[8] and without the Creole sweets called out by the woman merchant and longed for: "*pains doux / l'an-mou chinois / l'an-mou Cayen*" (*BL* 75), line-crossing love-sweets as part of authentic Creole expression. Prepared by an uncertain digestion of imperial and Antillean economies of self and other, Damas's poetic subject arrives at a "Batouque" of the heart. Rather than the mystified "tam-tam" so frequent quoted in negritude and doudouist discourse, Damas invokes the "tambour-ka" (78) making resonant what Mowitt calls the catachrestic nature of the drum, its intonement of black embodiment and time in the percussive fields of imperial modernity.

Still reeling even at the end of its epic journey (nowhere), the intoxicated black nomad within the landscapes and soundscapes of urban imperialism comes to midnight. The poem's climax seals the ambivalence of this special moment and place in time:

Midnight that could no longer accommodate
the power
ceaselessly awake
of bound up [*bandés*] taboos
from my Afro-Amerindian childhood (BL 84)[9]

The Damasian subject "arrives" at a state of self-awareness while erotically breaking free from anti/colonial taboos of the past. "Bandés," the poetic subject's erect stance openly taps into *désirs comprimés*, economies of colonial consumption and disavowal, as a site for continued transnational relations, however fraught with failure and loss they might be. These thunderous drums can be heard as a galloping *vidé*, a carnivalesque emptying out, marking the end of the Creole night more than the emergence of a pure African past. This poetic subject cannot completely swallow his loss, yet to elide loss is to continually spit up and drown on the discourse of bourgeois imperial society.

If Césaire's work represents the dominant beat of negritude, I suggest that further investigation of Damas's contributions to black rhythm and time can be considered part of an overlooked genealogy of negritude in the minor. Opposed to the high modernist tone of Césaire, and to the icy-hot response to the scream and the beat in Fanon, Damas engages in an "aesthetics of misery" (Mowitt) largely rejected and effaced in negritude and Fanonist discourse. While Césaire's subject begs to be "bound without remorse" to a "bitter fraternity" in the *Notebook*, stringing the body itself up into the negritudinal heavens, and while Fanon's subject finds itself on the spot, in a "circle [that] was gradually getting smaller" (*Black Skin* 91), the Damasian poetic subject rides out this rhythmic beating in *Black-Label* in search of a new critical postcolonial groove, a new poetic cut, within the history of black *ratés*. In short, the Damasian subject is still half lost in the rhythm of modernity, but his loss and losing represent a unique tactic that attempts to widen—if not break—the circle of black percussivity.

# five

## Le Poste Colonial

### Short-Wave Colonial Radio and Negritude's Poetic Technologies

But the beat must go on
—Friedrich A. Kittler, *Gramophone, Film, Typewriter*

When I switch on my radio and hear that black men are being lynched
in America, I say they have lied to us: Hitler isn't dead. When I switch
on my radio and hear that Jews are being insulted, persecuted, and
massacred, I say they have lied to us: Hitler isn't dead. And finally
when I switch on my radio and hear that in Africa forced labor has been
introduced and legalized, I say that truly they have lied to us: Hitler
isn't dead.
—Aimé Césaire, *Discours politiques*

Léona Gabriel's radio show career and the *speakerine*'s position as narrator of a certain musical family history in the film *Biguine* offer case studies of the ways in which French West Indian cultural agents took to the soundwaves to stage their own versions of New World colonial history and contemporary diasporic relations. Like the other soundposts critically listened to in this book (i.e., the *doudou*'s signature song, the biguine, the *tam-tam*, the black scream), radio technologies discursively and materially position self/other within a field of relations in space and time that is saturated with problems of race, gender, and colonial discourse. "In the force field of sonic Afro-modernity," as Alexander Weheliye writes, "sound technologies, as opposed to being exclusively determined or determining, form a relay point in the orbit between the apparatus and a plethora of cultural, economic, and political discourses" (48). Le Poste Colonial, France's first official colonial radio station, functions as just such a relay point, a literal and conceptual site where a range of ideas about French imperialism and black diasporic relations were debated, transferred, and translated.

At the same time as le Poste Colonial attempted to sonically inscribe a French imperial order on the world, black radical writers theorized the ways technologies of sound might impact community formation and offer new modes of diasporic intimacy and resistance against imperial hegemony. Césaire's comments in the epigraph above, and Fanon's relay of them in *Black Skin, White Masks,* serves as a critical example of the way the radio functioned as a critical relay point for negritude's critiques of colonial truth and racial ideology. Fanon's well-known account of transistor radio use during the Algerian revolution, in the essay "This Is the Voice of Algeria," is the classic, but not the only, example of how negritude thinkers explored the ways cultural agents might adopt and transform the imperial technological apparatus for and through anticolonial and national practices. Less attention has been paid to the poetic engagements and experiments with technology in negritude discourse. This chapter asks how le Poste Colonial reworked the conditions of possibility for colonially or anti-colonially speaking and hearing the world. It then asks how negritude discourse tapped into ideas about technology in its poetic experiments and theories about blackness and diasporic relations. Juxtaposing the discourse surrounding le Poste Colonial to representations of technology in Aimé Césaire's essays and poetry, especially focusing on his poem "Cristal automatique" (Automatic Crystal), the discussion below considers how sound technology mediates an imperial struggle over soundscapes but also enables a new poetics of transnational and diasporic relating.

## LE POSTE COLONIAL

Launched during the Exposition coloniale internationale in Paris, le Poste Colonial officially began in France on April 30, 1931.[1] The *"poste"* in France's Poste Colonial, refers to the machine itself, the *poste* is the physical apparatus. But Le Poste Colonial evokes also the meaning of *poste* as a relay point, a strategic if peripheral position in space. This latter definition makes sense especially considering the emergence of radio technology as a tool for locating geographic positions. Projecting to the world and beyond a sonic image of the French empire but also the "authentic" voice of France, le Poste Colonial marked the opening of a new discursive era of global relations. Just as the radio served as a "precious tool" during the First World War because "[s]hort wave radio relayed the trenches and the command posts, and the Eiffel Tower sent messages to ships through long wave radio" (Sudre 21), backers of le Poste called it an essential tool in France's strategic positioning within global relations of power and influence. Supported by colonial lobbyists at la Ligue maritime et colonial and l'Institut colonial français, backed by business interests, and run by la Fédération nationale de la radiodiffusion coloniale, the development of le Poste Colonial provided new material and discursive means for the French empire and its imperial others to *s'entendre*: to hear, understand, and project a hegemonic consensus of everyone's place in the world.

In his brief history of France's international radio presence, *Fréquence monde: Du Poste colonial à RFI* (1992), investigative reporter and documentary filmmaker Frédéric Brunnquell stages the arrival of the Poste as a sonic scene of imperial arrival.

> In the Côte d'Ivoire and in the bush in Bouaké, in Chad, in Oubangui-Chari, in Senegal in Saint-Louis like Dakar, in Indochina, but also in New Caledonia and in French Guiana, assembled around an old radio from the 1920s with two or three incandescent lights with bluish tints on top, the cafe owner and clientele, the settler and his family tend an ear to make out, through the squealing of the bad reception, a voice and some music that makes them weak with joy. Paris was buzzing to the rhythm of festivities at the Colonial Exposition and was thinking of its flock spread all over the world, contributing to the grandeur of the nation (Brunnquell 11).[2]

Brunnquell's scene of radio technology, especially focusing on the materially dated apparatus in the colonial setting, represents French imperial power as much as the "live" French voice itself. Effectively writing in what I have been calling "the genre of the imperial soundscape," what his image of French radio history brings to life is an ideological map of geopolitical relations. The "technological phenomenon," as Jacques Ellul explains, "[e]ssentially [. . .] takes what was previously tentative, unconscious, and spontaneous and brings it into the realm of clear, voluntary, and reasoned concepts" (20). The passage above, although ostensibly emphasizing a new mode of receiving the imperial word, actually scripts a multiple, if not panoramic, view of the imperial landscape. Despite their "peripheral" African, southeast Asian, southwest Pacific, and South American positions, despite (or even because of) the intermittent reception and the strident sounds of their dated radios, le Poste Colonial makes possible the passionate listening of the French empire. The colonial world is moved to tears, not exactly by the French voice, nor even by its own colonial music, but rather by this imperial soundscape: hearing Paris hearing the colonies. Paris "buzzing to the rhythm" of the Colonial Exposition provided irrefutable proof that the heart of France was beating for its distant "flocks" and beating *chez eux*, it marked global time in a sonic moment of imperial sympathetic vibration.

Speeches, interviews, review articles, and editorials in a range of periodicals, atlases, and trade magazines such as *L'Antenne*, *L'Annuaire de la Radiodiffusion Nationale* (1933 and 1935), *L'Intransigeant*, and *La Chronique coloniale* as well as in memoirs and historiographies such as Brunnquell's *Fréquence monde* offer numerous such examples of the ways in which discourse on radio technology triggered the imperial soundscape genre. They helped create sonic images of something difficult to picture: imperial harmony and hegemony despite colonial alterity and distance. "Radio broadcasting, victorious over time and distance," declared Julian Maigret, one of the pioneers behind le Poste Colonial,

> will finally come to break the horrible circle of solitude choking off our compatriots. From the depths of the most remote bush they will be able to see and to hear the daily life of Western civilization, with which they will remain in close communication. Under the veranda of his clay hut covered in straw, the settler in the tropics, surrounded by his family and his servants, will attend the grand ceremonies, the public events. French voices will tell him every day that he is no longer alone or forgotten, that the motherland still cares about the destiny of its distant sons. (qtd in Soulier-Valbert)

Maigret speaks in the soundscape genre in this interview published just days after the inauguration of le Poste Colonial. While he goes so far as to imagine that radio would make it possible both to see and hear ("voir et entendre") the daily life of the West, his description geographically ends up instead visualizing the scene of technological and sonic presence in the colonies.

The discourse surrounding le Poste Colonial's emergence situates it as "incontestably a historic date" in the French colonial mission, now possessing "new bases thanks to this instantaneous liaison across oceans. From now on, our compatriot overseas and the native himself, like the most modest inhabitant of the countryside, can hear the voice of the Motherland" ("La Radio-Diffusion" 199). While the technology of radio production, diffusion, and use may differ significantly from the writing-centered technologies of phono*graphy*, it nevertheless culturally serves as a locus of collective inscription. The symbolic impact of live radio broadcasts constitutes a type of history writing in the first half of the twentieth century, imprinting local and global moments into the collective memories of millions due to the medium of the address as much as its content. In other words, history not only happens on the radio, listening to the machine itself constituted an event in history. The radio's optic and textual inscriptions extend from its symbolic iconography of a dog staring head cocked while listening to the gramophone to the countless historiographies of Thomas Edison's experiments with sound technology.[3] Functioning through a series of *mises-en-abîme*, colonial and anticolonial discourse explored the ability to position the self and the other in the world by imagining the site of the other's listening, and thus the power of projection of the self's voice. Relay posts of sound technology represented a site for imagining the powerful re-membering and extension of imperial and anti-imperial senses.

On one hand, the radio's ability to penetrate into the "depths of the most remote bush" to relay the colonial position in space(/time) with France, reveals le Poste Colonial as simply—yet another—colonial outpost. (In other words, this isn't just your grandfather's *poste colonial*, it's also your great-grandfather's *poste colonial*.) On the other hand, the ideas of the interwar *sans-filistes* chart the technological and discursive terrain for the virtual culture that dominates postcolonial globalization today. Le Poste Colonial would later become Paris Ondes Courtes, then Paris-Mondial, and eventually Radio France Internationale, currently boasting 60 broadcasting hours per day in over a dozen languages via shortwave, FM, cable, Internet, and satellite, with 150 relay stations, and 40 million listeners worldwide.[4]

French colonization employed technologies of travel and warfare to rob land and liberty; French imperialism replaced land and liberty with hegemonic cartographies of social order. A new imperial packaging of time and space, le Poste Colonial's global network of sound marked the airwaves as a new (or neo)imperial site of relating the interests of capitalism and socioeconomic modernization to those of imperialism and French cultural dominance. The June 15–30, 1929, edition of the *Chronique* states that "France and its Colonies must have the same political outlook, the same economic unity. It's time that the voice of this country, with the City of Light as its capital, make itself heard in every corner of its conquered territories, and that the hearts of all populations of the world under the shelter of the French flag beat in unison" (196). The image of populations under the shelter of the French flag certainly calls to mind the rhetorical and performative dynamics employed in the Colonial Exposition. Le Poste syncs imperial politics of recognition and legitimation to modern techniques and technologies of knowing the other, ranging from social science discourse and colonial expositions to the emergence of the "exotic" entertainment industry. The *Chronique* describes the technological extension of the French voice to the farthest corners of the empire as a natural and necessary element in the development of French imperial unity and governance.

In its juxtaposition of colonial subjects with the latest technology, the Colonial Exposition provided the perfect discursive occasion for launching the radio. In fact, France showcased its most famous technological sign, which was also for a time a great *poste*, at the 1889 Universal Exposition: the Eiffel Tower. Gustave Eiffel's proposition to use the tower as a military *transmission sans fil* (TSF), or wireless, antenna reportedly saved his work from destruction.[5] Sound and writing machines such as the gramophone and the typewriter too made their first appearances to the general public via the venues of universal expositions, world fairs, and other exhibitions of "mechanical amusements" (Gitelman).

The Colonial Exposition's blend of technological showcasing and national spectacle exemplifies the way French imperial discourse temporally projected the Hexagon (as continental France is commonly called) into the (technological) future and cast the colonial subjects into the (technologically lacking) past. The following passage from *L'Antenne*, a radio enthusiast magazine, captures le Poste Colonial's momentous and shiny entry into the global fray over the airwaves: "By the time you read these lines le Poste Colonial will have made its joyous entrance into the domain of broadcasting. At Vincennes, in the Information City's studio, completely carpeted in blue velvet and visible to all thanks to its wonderful layout of immense windows, a series of reports on the Exposition will keep the whole universe abreast with this great colonial event [. . .] the microphone will stroll through colonial pavilions allowing for detailed description."[6] Writing before the actual launch of the station, the writer admires the scene more than the substance. Focusing on what the launch will have meant "when these lines (will) appear" rather than reporting on the launch itself, he highlights the way even the technologies of print press and daily newspapers will no longer be able to keep up with History the way the radio will. In other words, the language stylistically shows a fascination with the temporal *décalages* that the Poste will instantiate as a norm. Technology provided new modes for imperial witnessing, serving in its very materiality as "evidence" of the advanced superiority of French imperial order.

Le Poste Colonial was to provide, as Julien Maigret advances, consoling daily testimony that France cares about the colonial agent's future, that the Hexagon, continental France, remembers the colonial agent, that he is not alone. Maigret's and Brunnquell's scenes visually imagine the scene of colonialists abroad attending the official events of the home country, tending an ear while tending the imperial garden. The radio represents a break in colonial work, but, as manifested in the imperial soundscape, it introduces the voice of France into the break, creating a portrait of colonial domestic life and imperial leisure and aligning it with the imperial need for laborers and land. In this way, sound technology's ability to stretch across space and time collapses labor and leisure, making tending to colonial duties and imperial desires both part of the "colonial pact."[7] French imperialism relied on technology—and its spectacle—to produce efficiently and speedily an overwhelming mass of colonial "truths" in all aspects of life while demanding constant pledges of allegiance to *la France de 100 millions d'habitants.*

As early as February 1929, the official publications of le Poste Colonial's backers begin inscribing its meaning into a vision of ex/tending the imperial voice. *La Chronique colonial,* the official publication of L'Institut colonial français, declares that the plan for a radio will "spread the benefits of radio broadcasting to our far away possessions that, even more than our metropolitan countryside, have an imperious need to surmount the isolation multiplied by distance" (*La Chronique coloniale,* Feb. 15., 1929, 36). When the colonial radio is launched years later, the vision is the same. Alcide Delmont, a deputy from Martinique participating in a two-day conference held at the Exposition on the goals and direction of the new Poste, declares during the closing banquet that

> settlers who lived isolated in the deep bush will be comforted. The most backwards natives will understand our civilization's greatness. For this radio is an essential and marvelous tool. Every day we will reach the inhabitants of our overseas empire everywhere Pontoise broadcasts. Perhaps this very moment as I speak the dear friend I have over there in Fort-de-France joyously hears my voice. Those from Reunion, India, Saigon, African territories, now can hear French thought. (qtd in "Le Congrès au jour le jour" 352)

The radio will serve to broadcast and make audible "French thought," responding to geographic and psychological isolation. The *colon,* the settler farming the colonial garden, who, as Fanon writes in *The Wretched of the Earth,* lives steeped in an anti/colonial atmosphere of violence, especially feels the need for this psychological *recomfort.*[8] Again, like Brunnquell and Maigret, Delmont cannot resist imagining the possibility ("perhaps") of being simultaneously heard and physically present "everywhere," around the French imperial world, around "the entire universe" as *L'Antenne* put it. The "perhaps" is just as important as the "everywhere" because imagination plays as important a role in the discourse as does the technical realization. Delmont's speech, as is common on discourse on le Poste Colonial, posits the station as both an "essential" and a "miraculous" ("merveilleux") element of imperialism. Its essentialness represents it as a basic need for the colonial and imperial agent. Its miraculousness represents the god-like nature of the West: its imperious ability to be everywhere all the time.

Le Poste Colonial represents a material and a discursive outpost that aimed to mark, quantify, and explore imperial boundaries of difference. Thus technological "lack" in the colonies actually reflects less the absence of technology in the colonies than a view of colonized cultures and people as incapable of maintaining modern subject relations with it. That which is "essential" or basic for the imperial agent represents that which is "miraculous" and unattainable for the colonized. At the same time, this lack is rendered within ideas about temporality. Whether the Exposition Coloniale Internationale, the Citroën-sponsored motorized Croisière noire, or Belgian comic strip adventurer Tintin's adventures to the corners of the earth, imperial spectacle consistently juxtaposes ultramodern technology with indigenous others, representing imperialism as a foray into the exotic world of the technological future as much as an adventure into the exotic world of the colonial past.

## NEW SPEAKING MEN

Implementing new technologies for imperial missions requires recruiting a new generation of imperial and colonial agents to operate them. Even as the Exposition put African school children learning French on display, it specifically targeted French children from their earliest ages in an effort to plant seeds for the future of colonial service in the field.[9] According to Jean-Noël Jeanneney, in *L'Echo du siècle, Dictionnaire historique de la radio et de la télévision en France*, "The first associations of passionate amateurs fed their hunger for short wave radio with the most improbable exoticisms. The image—Belgian—of Tintin in the beginning of *The Blue Lotus* working his transistor radio at the maharaja's to pick up a Chinese message in Morse code, marked for some time the cultural imaginary. Such that this new media is marked from its birth with a constant tension between two forces: centripetal and centrifugal" (529).

Not everyone possesses the unadulterated "juvenile" nostalgia many express for yesterday's imperial cartoons and adventure comic book heroes (like Johnny Quest and Tintin). Despite the fact that radio ostensibly derived its power and authenticity through its sonic presence, it participated in and even precipitates the fundamental scripting of imperial relations. Internationally documented in the local specialized press of amateur technicians, spectacularly staged for the world by the state, fantastically imagined in the world of children's books, the radio was "marked" by the meanings of its domestic/imperial split.

From far away, Tintin finds the mysterious other he has been tracking in radiophonic space. He intercepts the other's seemingly indecipherable message and pinpoints the other's position in space. Tintin is a new European colonial

# LE LOTUS BLEU

# 藍蓮花

### DES NOUVELLES DE TINTIN

On se souvient de la lutte sans merci que le jeune reporter Tintin avait engagée contre une puissante bande internationale de trafiquants de stupéfiants.

Nos lecteurs n'ont certes pas oublié que le jeune globe-trotter avait réussi, après de multiples aventures, à faire mettre sous les verrous les principaux affiliés de la bande, à l'exception de leur chef qui, à la suite d'une chute dans un précipice, avait trouvé la mort.

Rappelons à cet effet que ce personnage mystérieux n'a jamais pu être identifié et que son corps, d'ailleurs, n'a jamais été retrouvé.

Nous apprenons aujourd'hui que le sympathique reporter et son inséparable Milou sont toujours les hôtes du Maharadjah de Rawhajpoutalah, chez qui ils goûtent un repos bien mérité.

Image from Hergé, *Le Lotus Bleu*, published in English as *The Blue Lotus*.

communication man; through the latest, futuristic technology, he controls the flow of information, appears and disappears into the imperial terrain, all the while slipping through the fingers of his American multinational and imperial nemeses. When the covert group that Tintin has been investigating captures him, they also seize control of the transmission of information and put it to the service of multinational business, the super rich, and an international opium cartel. The group launches a disinformation campaign that seamlessly jumps from an emergency phone along a remote stretch of railroad, to the telephone lines, to the telegraph, to the radio, to the printed press, to political speeches, and finally culminates in military action, all in the span of about a dozen small picture frames.

The power of the radio comes from a discursive synchronicity that extends beyond its production of temporal simultaneity. Not only does communication technology synchronize time, the speed of transmission accelerates the events themselves, ultimately surpassing them, creating them. As the 1935 *Annuaire de la Radiodiffusion Nationale* puts it, the colonial radio in particular represented "the virtual suppression of distance and time" ("La Radio-diffusion coloniale.— Le problème général" 315). The new *poste colonial* speed of sound presages the dynamics of postmodernity in its frightful ability to upset traditional terms of keeping time and writing History.

In the Caribbean, where *l'écriture du registre* constitutes the birth of textual culture (Confiant et al.), the shift to new sound and writing technologies—as well as the new modes of legitimacy that discursively situated these shifts with relation to previous forms of authority—must have completely revolution- ized the administration of the French Antilles. The advent of new technolo- gies of writing/reading and sounding/hearing created anxieties about shifts in the meaning of French overseas territories as that country's imperialism transitioned into new modes of recording, storing, and transmitting imperial knowledge and authority. Managing and manipulating these technologies cre- ated divisions of labor that followed racial but also geographic and gender lines. "Just as the 'reading machine'—phonograph described in the U.S. Copyright Act of 1909 provoked (not wholly unpleasant or unprofitable) anxieties about the racial identity and the mimetic remoteness of performers, mystified in the mass market," Lisa Gitelman writes, "the new 'writing machine'—typewriter similarly involved some defining anxieties about intention, gender, and other conditions of authorship" (188). The division of labor that Gitelman points out suggests an important avenue for investigating the engendering of imperial ad- ministration. Just as the colonial family work of the *Antillaise* revolves around textiles: *madras* and *foulard* (the Antillean *doudou*), sheets and linens (the Antillean *blanchisseuse*), and the fabric seamstress, modern imperialism stages her as the always crucial keeper of state documentation (the Antillean *fonctionnaire*).

For, despite the historic and systemic denial of black literacy, *being black is a lot of paperwork*. If imperialism transformed colonized cultures into objects for technological instruments to scrutinize, document, and classify (if not to destroy), it transformed "the indigenous man into an instrument of production" (42), as Aimé Césaire argues in *Discourse on Colonialism*, "colonization = thingification" (18–19). French colonialism and imperialism transformed colonial subjects into writing machines: transcribers and translators (Paulette, Jane, and Andrée Nardal), ethnographers (Léon-Gontran Damas, Zora Neale Hurston) and administrators (René Maran), tour guide writers (Suzanne Roussy Césaire), and, ultimately, recording artists (Ernest Léardée and Alexandre Stellio). Most of all it designated colonial peoples to be bearers of the trace of French writing; from the *dictées* and history lessons of school to the identity papers and the linguistic requirements of citizenship. Writing might be antithetical to colonial "primitives" and slaves in the French imperial imagination; but in the end, the proper way to document French others—still the stuff of postcolonial debate today—is truly too much work. Or at least too much work for people. The technology of colonial posts had to create media for transmitting authenticity and authority that bridged the sonic and the textual while controlling passage between the two.

The symbolic constellation of speaking and hearing positions works to sonically map the French imperial family into place. A letter from "Dr. Gargin in Fort-de-France (*Martinique*): It's so beautiful to hear France! . . . Paris! . . . It brings tears of joy. All our souls tremble with hope and raise to France the cries of a lost child who has found his mother" ("Le Poste 'Radio-Colonial' de Pontoise" 332). The familial metaphor, in addition to reinforcing imperial patriarchies of order and authority, represents the infantalization of colonial sound and posits the imperial moment as a type of birth. Just as the folk song "Adieu madras, adieu foulard" recalls the balance of duty and desire (as well as force and consent) in Antillean-French relations, Dr. Gargin's letter places a maternal duty on the empire to respond to its colonial infants' tearful cries.

In radio journals and trade magazines, the backers of *Le Poste*, who struggled for years to get the state as well as private interests to invest in this new imperial venture, often published such letters from the colonies testifying to the joy the colonial radio brought to its imperial subjects. "These examples could be multiplied. They testify to the success obtained both in the technical field and—if you will—in the psychological field by the launch of the colonial broadcasting station" ("Le Poste 'Radio-Colonial' de Pontoise" 330). These citations, dating from 1935, demonstrate that the station's leading proponents continued to feel the need to justify its existence even after its launch. Like much of modern technological achievement, le Poste required a collaboration of government resources and private initiatives, U.S. style capitalism and imperial style infrastructure and investment. At the same time as these testimonials appealed to the government and the French citizen, they also advertised to big business and potential investors.

## LE TON SPEAKER

The history of learning to speak on the radio demonstrates the very constructed nature of radiophonic speech, especially within a national context of anxiety about increasing regional and non-Hexagonal sound. Among the "new" men and women created by technologies of imperialism, the radio produces new communication men and women, professionalized in the person of the radio personality—the *"speaker"* as it is called in French—and the experimenting amateur *sans-filistes*, the wireless radio enthusiasts. Marcel Laporte was French national radio's first *speaker*. Nicknamed "Radiolo," this pioneering radio comedian became the voice of Radiola, a private station owned by Société Française de Radiophonie (SFR) and launched by the engineer and entrepreneur Emile Girardeau. In *Les Mémoires de Radiolo*, Laporte describes his experiments in search of the proper radio diction for Radiola (renamed early on Radio Paris), a station broadcast from the Eiffel Tower in the 1920s. Radio Paris offered its first *journal parlé*—"spoken newspaper"—and its first live news reports in France in 1923. As Benedict Anderson contends for print media, the radio even more powerfully provided a space for relaying ideas about nationhood and offered opportunities to emotionally invest in the imagined community of Hexagonal.

But while le Poste's backers offered images of the French colonial family to imagine extending that emotional investment to overseas France as well as the French empire, the very question of which French voices were authentic and legitimate within the Hexagon was a subject of debate and anxiety. The misappropriated English terminology *le speaker* exemplified this tension. René Sudre, in *Le Huitième art: Mission de la radio* (1945), lamented the use of English for this important new position: "Is our language so impoverished that it is impossible to adapt an existing word to a new usage?" (105). Sudre's work represents an important intervention considering his intellectual and career itineraries and their postwar destinations at the French Ministry of Information and the For-

eign Ministry. A professor at the Ecole de Hautes Etudes en Sciences Sociales
(1931–40), Sudre contributed research to the *Revue metaphysique* (1926–1930)
and worked with *Radiodiffusion française* (1926–1940). His work—some of which
sought connections between the parapsychological (including telepathy and
techniques of automatic writing) and radio waves—may seem new age experimental. When it came to the rules of language and speech, however, Sudre was
a stickler. "It's stupid to say that radio is the reflection of life with the good and
bad. Radio is an institution with an immense power of suggestion. It radiates, in
every sense of the word, the French spirit. Its rays must be pure" (104). Sudre,
among many others, weighed the radio's role as a "school teacher of French"
(104) and its power to instatiate "legitimate" French against a more democratic
view of the ways it might more "authentically" transfer French speech and taste
with all its "faulty pronunciation due to local speech" (69), its poor choice of
programming (116), and its vulgarized knowledge (111).

In the quote below, Sudre treats language as the material essence of France;
its slowness and centrality represent timelessness and legitimizing authenticity instead of backwardness or geographic limitation. Sudre gives lip service to
the local authenticity and authority of regional speech, but he insists on "sub-
mitting these initiatives to national unity" (69). "If there's no such thing as a
French race, there is a French nation, and language is precisely the expression
of its existence. Language can and should slowly evolve. But just as written language is officially protected by the Academy," Sudre continues, "spoken language usage should be protected by this enterprise of universal verbal publication that is the radio, and the Minister of Public Instruction should zealously
oversee it" (69). Sudre calls for radio technology to realize its institutional role
as a unifying, codifying force through language. By positing language (and other
sounds) as the essence of Frenchness, imperial discourse attempts to divert the
question of race, to pretend that assimilation is possible while systematically
racially encoding the meaning of sound to construct and conserve its purity.

In contrast, many French critics argued that this conservation and codifica-
tion of speech endangered the vitality of French as a living language. For example Roland Dhordain's radio history, *Le Roman de la radio: De la T.S.F. aux radios
libres*, lamented "the general presentation tone," which, for him was "the most
detestable: what one calls 'the speaker tone' [*le ton speaker*] where the declama-
tory and the pedantic, the solemn and sinister, compete against one another.
If Radio-Paris is happy," he sardonically explained, "Paris-P.T.T., an official
station, is frankly sad" (42). One must sit through enormous amounts of military music "with, as a reward: Madame Segond-Weber and other 'ladies' of the

'Théâtre Français' on the microphone whispering verses or howling out trage-
dies" (42). Dhordain's critique can be read more broadly as the tension between
the egalitarian and exclusionary potential of the technologically enabled French
voice as it comes up against the gendered, raced, and classed dynamics of cultural exclusion in France and the colonies. Hearing le Poste Colonial and its discourse this way repositions it as a site of dissonance as much as harmony. The
debate concerning the meaning of French radio on the national and international scene replays a representational paradox inherent in the legacy of the Enlightenment, pitting "political egalitarianism" against "the desire to 'enlighten
people's thinking'" (Cowans 148). Historian Jon Cowans's work demonstrates
the way choosing a path for radio development and programming amounted to
the crystallization of a crisis of authority and legitimation, which was intimately
connected with the sociocultural and political aftermath of the Occupation,
starting with postwar purges of the radio industry. The work above suggests this
need to solidify the authority and legitimacy of the French voice also has to do
with French imperialism and the way black and colonial sound was making an
impact in Hexagon's field of sound.

As I discuss in the first chapter, Fanon's account of the colonial subject as an
automatic language failure has to do with the way French imperialism posits its
speech as the essential yet unattainable criteria for becoming, assimilating, or
at least passing as French. This imperialist racial logic manifested itself on the
national scene as well. Anxiety over proper expression, pointing up the multiple
formations of French speech and linguistic practices, puts pressure on imperial
claims about the authentic power of French voice through sound technology, a
pressure which the postcolonial critic can "hear" and sound out as a loud *raté*
resonating through its discourse of hegemony.

## LES CRIS ET L'ÉCRIT: CÉSAIRE'S EPHEMEROMATERIAL
## DÉCALAGE AND AUTOMATICITY

The quote of Césaire in Fanon's *Black Skin*, which I refer to in the epigraph of
this chapter, imagines the type of technological detouring that Fanon would
later find manifest in the Algerian context. The radio, rather than proving the
power of French imperial technology, continued to testify to Europe's moral
defeat. Césaire's reference in 1945 could not ring more resonantly considering the importance of radio technology during the wars as well as the collaboration of radio industry professionals with the Germans during the Occupation (see Cowans). His emphasis on the turn of the radio dial suggests the
physical and intellectual connection with technology that imperial discourse

paints as impossible. In the hands and ears of the anti-colonial agent, the radio, if heard correctly ("véritablement"), offers counter-testimony to dominant histories.

In his epic *Cahier d'un retour au pays natal* (Notebook of the Return to My Native Land), Césaire claims as his own

> those who invented neither powder nor compass
> those who could harness neither steam nor electricity
> those who explored neither the seas nor the sky but know
> in its most minute corners the land of suffering

The tactical move, a promise of unconditional love and categorical refusal of imperial values, demonstrates the extent to which technology serves as a symbol for European superiority and colonial lack.

But in the *Discours sur le colonialisme*, Césaire responds to those who would cast his poetic apology of African cultures and systems of exchange as a position that risks understating, or even disavowing, the concrete, material needs for building a postcolonial world. Césaire retorts, "it seems that in certain circles they pretend to have discovered in me an 'enemy of Europe' and a prophet of the return to the pre-European past. For my part, I search in vain for the place where I could have expressed such views; where I ever preached a *return* of any kind; where I ever claimed that there could be a *return*" (45, his emphasis). Césaire's insistence on return invokes his monumental *cri nègre*, the "Notebook of a Return." His tactic is to deconstruct any seeming incommensurability between a "systematic defense of societies destroyed by imperialism" (44) and the call for Europe to fulfill its (belated) colonial promise: the technological and industrial retooling and renewal of French West Indian social and cultural infrastructures. In the context of his scathing critique of French colonialism and racism, Césaire's language both provokes and denounces a tendency to collapse different types of "returns," the first one in space (return to a native land) and the other in time (return to precolonial Africa) but also in material means (return to a "pre-technological" authenticity).

When Césaire sounds the theme of Europe's moral defeat, his alternate listening tactics form a scorching denunciation of French imperialism as fascist ideology. Césaire's rhetoric turns to a *discours du procès*—a discursive staging of judgment, a "hearing" involving critical interrogation and witnessing. The proof of the radio and its anti/colonial testimony foreshadow the relationship between new techniques of listening, on one hand, and voicing an anti-imperial politics and ethics of recognition, on the other. "What is serious is that 'Europe' is morally, spiritually indefensible. And today the indictment is brought [*proféré*] against it not by the European masses alone, but on a world scale, by tens and tens of millions of men who, from the depths of slavery, set themselves up as judges" (32). The act of accusation is "proffered," an action-message carried forth in a new collective (and highly gendered) way. Césaire posits authentic language as a performative speech act. His work attempts to respond to oppression and terror by breaking the representational ground of silence and discovering alternate tactics of hearing and listening to suffering in the world.

The *Cahier* inscribes *le cri nègre* as a poetic listening tactic as much as a poetic speaking one.

> I hear coming up from the hold the enchained curses, the gasps of the dying, the noise of someone thrown into the sea . . . the baying of a woman in labor . . . the scrape of fingernails seeking throats . . . the flouts of the whip . . . the seethings of vermin amid the wariness. (61, 63)[10]

The scream's power and authenticity comes from its resonance with sounds heard. The poetic chains of *ma négritude* cry out the subject's mark of a "personalised enregistration of time and a diachronic understanding of language" (Gilroy 203). This act itself represents Césaire's *cri*, clearing out discursive space for grievance yet affectively binding the subject. The *cri* constitutes a demand that the counter-testimonies of history be heard physically, legally, and affectively. As the points of suspension mark the poetic beat, the poem situates its poetic subject as the time/space for a deathly identification of and with others in the dark. The sounds of the dead and dying are chained curses, both material and continuous in their testimony to "the distinctive rapport with the presence of death which derives from slavery and a related ontological state," as Paul Gilroy writes: "the condition of being in pain" (Gilroy 203). Césaire's black scream sets up the ethical hearing of history's sounds in the present.

Crystallized between *les cris* (the screams) and *l'écrit* (the written), Césaire's poetic participates in what black studies critic Alexander Weheliye calls *ephemeromaterialities*.[11] "This interplay between the ephemerality of music [along with sonic culture] (and/or the apparatus) and the materiality of the audio technologies/practices (and/or music) provides the central, nonsublatable tension at the core of sonic Afro-modernity" (Weheliye 7). As an instance of ephemeromateriality, *le cri* is a sonico-material corpus where loss/absence and materiality/presence encounter each other in the embodiment of black diasporic subjectivity. At the same time *le cri* is a poetic experiment attempting to

construct alternate ways of hearing/sounding/understanding subjective relations of historic suffering.

As Césaire's poem "Le cristal automatique" shows, even as this exploration of poetic form serves as a means of interrogating conventional communication and facilitating negritude's "sacred duty" of transmission (Rosello), it
also highlights the radical indeterminacy and profound loss that marks "Afro-
modernity."

> hullo hullo one more night stop guessing it's me the cave man there are cicadas
> which deafen both their life and their death there also is the green water of la-
> goons even drowned I will never be that color to think of you I left all my words at
> the pawn shop a river of sleds of women bathing in the course of the day blonde
> as bread and the alcohol of your breasts hullo hullo I would like to be on the clear
> other side of the earth the tips of your breasts have the color and the taste of that
> earth hullo hullo one more night there is rain and its gravedigger fingers there is
> rain putting its foot in its mouth on the roofs the rain ate the sun with chopsticks
> hullo hullo the enlargement of the crystal that's you . . . that is you oh absent one
> in the wind an earthworm bathing beauty when day breaks it is you who will
> dawn your riverine eyes on the stirred enamel of the islands and in my mind it is
> you the dazzling maguey of an undertow of eagles under the banyan (123)

The cave falls into the French surrealists' exploration of the *abîme*s, holes, gaps,
and cracks in the urban landscape for hidden histories that will trigger a resurgence of revolutionary truth. Surrealist poetics have a predilection for the
indeterminate and in-between spaces of the Parisian urban space, plotting itineraries through "passages, as if in these corridors hidden from the day no one
was allowed to stop more than a moment" (Aragon 20), they end up "always in
a cavern" (Breton, *L'Amour fou*, 16). The darkness and cavernous stereophon-
ics that constitute this site require an alternate mode of "connecting" with the
other "on the clear other side of the earth."

Who is the cave man, "l'homme des cavernes," whose speech cuts through
the darkness in "Le cristal"? No point in searching ("Pas la peine de chercher")
—the poetic voice obliquely approaches the question of identification, immediately posed and seemingly swept aside as the poem's central problematic. The
cave functions to situate the philosophical aporia of black modernity, it also
situates the subject's voice as emergent from a hauntingly lost location. Ultimately this voice sounds out a break and stages it as a scene of black sound listening and writing.

"Could 'cristal' then be a figure for *écriture*? Both contain a hidden *cri*" (Scharfman 68, her emphasis). Ronnie Leah Scharfman's question points up the fact that *le cri* is more than a poetic figure within the work of negritude and more than a metaphor for the ideological positions of its poets. *Le cri* itself refigures the idea of writing and disrupts its technologies of meaning and communicating. The "hullo hullo" in the poem functions as a sort of microphone check, pointing up the experimental nature of the poetic form itself. At the same time it calls attention to the apparatus of connection, amplification, and inscription. The echoing interpellation ("hullo hullo") sounds out the urgency and also the fragility of the poetic technology.

The Césairean poetic resonates with Breton's idea that surrealist writers serve as "the deaf receptacles of so many echoes, the modest *recording machines* [*appareils enregistreurs*] that aren't hypnotized by the design they sketch" (*Les Manifestes* 39, his emphasis). For Breton, surrealist writing represents a convergence of hearing and writing, a form of dictation.[12] Césaire's poem too reads like the product of a mixed mode of automatic dictation not unlike other automatic writing machines. Césaire refuses to cede the technology of writing and the French language, but, having "left all my words at the pawn shop," the poetic subject taps into an alternate sounding and inscription of (French) speech and language value.

Rather than consisting of unedited dictation, Césaire reworks surrealist techniques of "automatic writing" through a poetic of fragments. This poetic resides in and in-between various versions of poems as they appear in differing editions (such as Césaire's cuts from his poem "Batéké" in the 1946 edition of *Les armes miraculeuses* to form the "new" poem "Mythologie" in the 1971 edition). These versions and edits might then be heard in Césaire's poetic as so many "sessions," or "takes" of an ideal recording, an impossible (en)registration of a lost totality.[13] In other words, they are also themselves performances, different riffs on the script, calling attention to the technological demands of writing on the body, and pointing up the materiality of the text on the body.

Given its layout on the page, one cannot help but view the poem itself as a material block of text, an "unrelieved typographical density" (Arnold 112). The orality of the apparent poetic telephone-like conversation runs to the limits of the page in a way that refuses sublimation of the poem's extra-oral materiality. The monodialogic fragmented nature of the communication, forged from surrealist poetics of automaticity, produces a form of materiality out of the dark for the subject to hold on to. This dynamic departs decidedly from the interpellations of race Fanon stages in *Black Skin*, where the black subject "holds on to" ("Tiens!") an embodiment of subjectivity triggered by the sonic "look"

("Regarde!") of the French imperial stage. Césaire's poem instead defers the reification of identity, when he declines the call of direct identification and visualization in favor of a more opaque sounding of self and self-other relations. Here, in "the enlargement of the crystal that's you . . . that's you oh absent one," the subject posits its self as the site for the poetic transformation of lack, absence, and faulty connection into crystalline material presence.

In sum, "Automatic Crystal" produces a block of corporeal materiality. Its automaticity, a flickering intimate connection, becomes an extraphenomenal materialization rather than only a fleeting moment. "Automatic Crystal" functions as a stylus, a sharp (temporal and spatial) point of exploration, making resonant a history of loss. As a technology of sound inscription, Césaire's text destabilizes, like other sound technologies, the requirements of presence and present time that form the basis of traditional modes of communication and thus of identity and identification as traditionally conceived.

As a *poste colonial*, another technological sonic post for hearing and situating oneself and others, "Automatic Crystal" is a subjective and poetic (en)registering of black voice, in short another tool of recording. Then again the poem itself has a materiality independent of its voice from beyond. The poem may be a tool of recording yet it also materially constitutes that recording itself. "Automatic Crystal" picks up a voice from beyond and, while refusing to render visually its speaking subject, the poem leaves itself, its body, as the posting site of writing, the material apparatus of the inscription. What first fails to fully appear, through flickering connections with the other in the dark, slowly stages the production of a material connection.

As black studies critic Frederick Moten asks of Amiri Baraka's "BLACK DADA NIHILISMUS": "Where is the poem?" (96). Understanding the poem as fragmented materially and temporally, as practically existing both pre- and post-performance, resituates the importance of "the fragment" in Césaire's poetic technology. Césaire's work requires we pay attention to what has been "recorded out" of his poetic corpus. These cut bits are the outtakes left on the studio floor, the waste, excess, scrap, and other remainders of the creative process. They complicate even further "the relations between versions of or variations on the poem, manifestations of the eye and ear that raise the too deep question of the ontological status of the poem itself" (Moten 90). Yet Césaire's work in many ways specifically aims to point up the remains; the waste of the Martinican city Fort-de-France, the remains of the dismembered subject, the diseases wasting black bodies, the excessiveness of blackness, the rubbish of colonial cultural production. Césaire's work cites the violence of being edited out of History, revisiting and reliving (or performing) the act of marginalization, the cutting out gesture of modernity's exclusions.

In "Le cristal automatique," Césaire's poetics of modernity, and his fragmented recording of a lost totality, come together as the search for a lost essential female other. In this poetic, scenes of intimacy, even failed, fragmented, overheard ones, serve in their rhythmic cutting and reconnecting as a tactic of relation. In other words, "Automatic Crystal" materializes poetic recording as a form of intimate relations, an erotically and maternally charged connection. Again the search for the lost female other relates to, but significantly differs from, that of dominant surrealist praxis. While Breton's *Nadja* and *L'Amour fou* explore the possible alignment between desiring an elusive woman and desiring an elusive subject/social revolution, the stakes of intimacy carry a distinct resonance in the black diaspora. Considering the long history of relations between the *doudou*'s sweet-talk and that other island sweet (sugar), exploring the loss and re-possession of the woman gets at the torn imperial economies within black Atlantic systems of symbolic exchange.

As a recording sound post, the poetic subject does not fully inhabit a single position of enunciation in this intimate dialog. Split between female listening and male speaking, the *poste* (over)hears and (over)writes. Where the speaking stops, and where listening cannot register itself as such, the *poste* marks the break—". . ."—a political economy of its (almost) silent noise not only records lost time, and the break, the missing woman, but it is itself the scene of the subject's "presencing," its turning over its self, as the soundtexting machine. The material fragment of this sacred transmission, the recording subject medium that is the poem, leaves only its materiality, its supplemental black (male) body of text, as the trace of this missing woman, a *supplément* still providing a trail back to her.

This automaticity is still a beat, a *syncope*. Even in its minor technological modes of reappropriation, this automaticity represents a tyrannical and violent ravishment. Those who charge that it was the French language that cannibalized Césaire, and not the reverse as negritude discourse famously claims, miss that Césaire's poetic pointedly offers up the black body, both in materiality and representation, for a violent beating, a drowning, a consumption to death.[14] Only, as I have been contending, this corporeal loss often falls back on the woman; she is the sacred medium, and the black radical aesthetic provides scenes of her male (re)possession. Put differently, Jean-Paul Sartre's striking label of negritude as a genre of *tam-tam* corresponds to his inscription of negritude under the mythological title of his essay, "Black Orpheus." While

Fanon condemns the way Sartre stages negritude as the weak beat (syncopation) of relation, he fails critique the loss of the black woman in the gendering of negritude rhythm Sartre describes. "She" is staged as absent both before and after the mythology of black beats as well as in the Fanonist critique of rhythm.

Given its status as poetic production and poetic product, how does time figure into this alternate mode of subject formation and diasporic connection? In other words, again as Mowitt asks in his study of the black radical aesthetic, when is the poem? Asking where and when the poem is points up this engendered mediacy and gets back at Fanon's critically ambivalent "too early . . . too late" temporal performance. The writing subject functions as a "medium," picking up and marking messages from an other space and time. This scene reproduces the figure of the third, as the writing subject signals itself as the relay between the speech of the male poetic *je* (I) and the (lost) listening female *tu* (you). As a *poste colonial*, both belated (a voice from the past) and projecting a future (a unity of listening), the writing subject does not listen, as would the woman/group, but rather *hears*. As a sound inscribing machine rather than an ear, the *poste colonial* subject records everything. There is a material objectification here that veers from the colonialist *thingification* Césaire denounces in the *Discourse on Colonialism*, and from the *affective tetanization* Fanon cites in *Black Skin* that risks making man a machine. As a medium that hears and records everything, rather than subjectively demarcating sound, the subject authentically "arrives" by locating its self as object/ivity: proffered material evidence, recorder and record of history.

The poetic cuts of the time and space of relation in Césaire's poem exemplify the types of *décalage* that Brent Edwards writes about as constitutive of black diasporic models. Edwards explains:

> The verb *caler* means "to prop up or wedge something" (as when one leg on a table is uneven). So *décalage* in its etymological sense refers to the removal of such an added prop or wedge. *Décalage* indicates the reestablishment of a prior unevenness or diversity; it alludes to the taking away of something that was added in the first place, something artificial, a stone or piece of wood that served to fill some gap or to rectify some imbalance. [. . .] In this sense, *décalage* is proper to the structure of a diasporic "racial" formation, and its return in the form of disarticulation—the points of misunderstanding, bad faith, unhappy translation—must be considered a necessary haunting. (Edwards 65)

Césaire's "crystal" exemplifies the supplemental "stone" that, counterintuitively, must be removed and cut in order to articulate, even if only through the fractal relations of writing, black diasporic relations. In resonance with *décal-age* discourse, "Automatic Crystal" is the stone that refracts as it intercepts and transmits. Read this way, Césaire's poetic apparatus creates both a transcription and a translation of the other's speech and its position in time and space. Rather than sweeping "points of misunderstanding, bad faith, unhappy translation" under the rug, this poetic confronts the reader with the remainder, the traces, simultaneously testifying to connection and rupture within the points of enunciation that articulate the meaning of diasporic identity.

Césaire's experiment, which engages with the trope of the woman's loss and the space of *decalage* in all writing, gets at the psychoanalytical and deconstructive tensions and economies that circulate in the *décalage* of the black diaspora. Césaire's "Automatic Crystal" is the material remainder of an utterance that is no more and that ultimately cannot be firmly situated in time and space because we lack all of the pieces to put the whole back together. In that way we can think of this fragment as a deathly remainder; what's in the language is there no more. Césaire only proffers this symbolic remainder that still testifies to what has always already been absent.

Edwards's language evokes these deconstructive and psychoanalytic economies even if he does not fully express them:

> If a discourse of diaspora articulates difference, then one must consider the status of that difference—not just linguistic difference but, more broadly, the trace or the residue, perhaps, of what resists translation or what sometimes cannot help refusing translation across the boundaries of language, class, gender, sexuality, religion, the nation-state. Whenever the African diaspora is articulated (just as when black transnational projects are deferred, aborted, or declined) these social forces leave subtle but indelible effects. Such an unevenness or differentiation marks a constitutive *décalage* in the very weave of the culture. (Edwards)

Just as the text is the material remainder of the sacred ephemeral connection, its language offers leftover linguistic bits from a deeper symbolic exchange across a deathly border, one where both the "authentic" original and the "faithful" translation remain unavailable. In a sense, negritude's scream sounds out *décalage*; it transmits an utterance *décalé*, playing with temporal and spatial tension in the sound and text relay. The text constitutes less a body of meaning and more a material object (like supplemental stone, the crystal) whose sacred (or precious) worth comes from the residual aura remaining after the oblique encounter through the abyss.

The *décalage* within articulations of black diasporic relations that Edwards discusses above must be related this *décalage* of desire and speech that Fanon calls *raté*, a breakdown in black subjectivity. The "Automatic Crystal" mediates the poetic subject's desire "to be on the clear other side of the earth the tips of your breasts have the color and the taste of that earth." What Césaire removes from the text, the feminine intimate other on the other side of the line, situates this slippage and loss as residing in desire as much as in language. The poetic crystal makes possible a type of recovery of intimacy, even as it is suggestive of the gendered value of loss and of the supplementality of text within projects of black internationalism and diasporic expression. The crystal cuts through but does not completely illuminate the abyss, representing the break of diaspora but also the breaking up of institutions of language and speech that le Poste *Colonial* sought to standardize.

Both *le ton speaker* ("radio voice" or "radio diction") in French radio and the cavernous voice of Césaire's poetic apparatus project a decidedly patriarchal and masculinist embodiment of technological sound. Césaire's sonic post and the historic Poste Colonial both amplify male voices and their anti/colonial agendas of domination in space and time. One attempts to standardize while the other disrupts standardization of language and speech, but in both cases this takes place at the expense of the female voice, even as work by Léona Gabriel-Soïme shows how women were able to reappropriate these technologies. While le Poste Colonial sought to eliminate *décalage* through simultaneous material and ideological presence in different geographic and cultural times and spaces, Césaire's poetic apparatus exploits and widens the gap, as its subject's voice cannot be referentially situated in time and space. The poem's juxtaposition of the automatic and the primitive problematizes temporal projections of a technologically ultramodern *Metropole* and a lost, primitive African past.

Césaire's automatic crystal is otomatic (Derrida); it locates and loses itself and its value in the ear of the other. Whereas Edwards thinks through *décalage* largely in terms of textual translation, this otomaticity gets at the problematic loops of speech and self-inscription. *Décalage* must then turn on speech acts (and musicking acts) as much as written texts, and it must take place within the subject as much as without. Césaire turns Fanon's *discours raté* against itself; because it is through failed speech that Césaire locates the conditions for the possibility of a radical poetic intervention. That radical intervention consists in an alternate networking of desire. Pushing the *raté* back on language, logos, and writing, Césaire's work suggests the way these technologies fail to articulate the black diaspora, requiring the construction of an alternate apparatus for the body, ultimately serving as an alternate configuration of the body itself.

# conclusion

## Notes from the Sound Field

O my body, always make me a man who questions!
—Frantz Fanon, *Black Skin, White Masks*

Desire *beats* at the heart of New World soundtexts. But if rhythm is a series of continuities and ruptures in time, when is the break the end and when is it just the missing moment inherent in the beating? Given the cross-rhythms of mythology manifest in the *tam-tam*, the *doudou*, *le cri noir*, *le poste colonial*, the *raté*—when are the aesthetic and intellectual breaks of the black diaspora, like those between Fanonist discourse and negritude, or between negritude and doudouism, when are they definitive ruptures and when are they just other modes of continuity and engagement? In both instances, the beat sounds itself as part of "the essential drama of black life" (Moten) in the Americas and beyond. The beating of drums, the beating of a poetic, the beating of desire, and the beating of black and colonial people, all have a long history of relations. These beats always carry the potential to be heard as a call and response to one another, for even a cold turn of the shoulder can read like just another step in the cultural dance—depending on one's vantage point.

Fanon's quote above, speaking in apostrophe to the body, points toward the way the doubleness of blackness offers a critical posture of the "dis-covery of black value" as much as posing an insuperable problem. Fanon's performative embodiment of black colonial subjectivity, the inscription of the materiality of the body and its paradoxical doubled nature and inscrutability within imperial economies of value, sounds out a broken relation between *le cri noir* and *le doux parler chantant des îles*. But, if the firm emotional stance of negritude writers dialectically takes on the *doudou*, their move is generative of the masculinist dynamic of critique in the genealogy of black radical discourse. For, while the doudouist mythology crystallized in "Adieu madras" sets up her loss, the song's own ethnomusicological history suggests the ways Creole women built foundational soundtext blocks across boundaries of race and social standing at the very core of Antillean artistic production.

The problem of black (black/white) desire often plays itself out in rhythm(s), making the dance floor an essential site where ideas about encounters with the other imaginatively and literally take place. But the syncopations of anti/colonial desire also mark time in the rhythm of the city, its public places and means of transport, its racial and colonial humiliations, and crucially in its transnational and transcolonial dynamics of travel. Both the *nègre fondamental* and the *doudou* negotiate this specular terrain, and both come up short, so to speak. Both are *ratés*—subject to sonic failures that sound out slips in the colonial machine and its productions of value.

The 2006 compilation *Au Temps des colonies* (In the Colonial Times)—originally entitled *Au Bon Temps des colonies* (In the *Good* Colonial Times, my emphasis) before online protests sparked a title change—demonstrates the continued imperial resonance between bad French, *petit-nègre*, Creole, and "exotic" music in the French cultural imagination. For its cover art *Au Temps des colonies* reappropriates the infamous *Y a bon Banania* publicity image with the stereotypical smiling Senegalese soldier, while covering the crate he sits on with classic colonial song tracks like "Biguine à Bango." Even today nostalgic colonial music typifies the way the imperial hearing of black sound and speech thrusts an entire repertoire of colonial mythology onto the speaking and singing subject. This colonial voice, designated *baragouin* (gibberish) by the earliest colonialist agents and travel writers, then considered a patois *doux chant des îles* (sweet song of the islands), gains musical recognition and (ephemeral) legitimacy before and instead of other types of social and cultural recognition. As the Nardals suggest, a certain temporal warp and juxtaposition serve as the valuable basis for this consumption of history. The confusion in and over language in biguine music accounts for part of the economy of desire in so-called doudouist musical creation.

Antillean musical performance in France, like other "colonial" musics, must negotiate the imperialist staging of the black Atlantic, as is the case today. At the same time, the coincidence of black performance in Jazz Age Paris with advances in sound recording technology (as well as radio broadcasting) means that *chanson coloniale*, whether "authentic" or "inauthentic," resonates through the recorded history of French songs. The "new records" column of the journal *Dépêche africaine*, for example, notes Josephine Baker's releases were recorded "in French with the amusing English accent that, on the phonograph, is one of the elements of its success" (4, signed P.F.).

Similar dynamics of threatening presence and textual absence function within the lucrative and esteemed history of French national cinema as well. The latter remains haunted by the absence of black subjects within (and it remains fearful of the latter's atavistic resurgence). Why haunting? The fetishized specularity of the black body fueled the emergence of French sound era cinema via the popularity of black Atlantic live performance. If French popular film in the 1930s thought of itself as staged recordings of live performances, how must the boisterous popularity of black Montmartre have informed that cinematic vision? Critical histories of French national cinema tend to focus on the stage while "overlooking" the black performing subjects, si(gh)ting them as the disparate blank ornaments of the French cinematic scenic self. This black invisibility at the heart of French film, the violent and even deathly return of the black subject to its place off stage, fails to eradicate its presence from the constitution of French filmic value.

The cultural commentary of the time by French author Georges Marie Goursat reveals the discursive resonance in the French imperial imagination between black linguistic performance and black musical performance. Goursat, who wrote under the pseudonym Sem, published an account of black performance in Paris equating the history of relating on the dance floor to French linguistic history of relating with black colonial populations. "These mixed couples speak clearly through their expressive dance, albeit in petit-nègre, so that it is superfluous and dangerous to dwell on it" Sem concludes. Sem's description, as Brent Hayes Edwards notes, runs on a lack of recognition of the differences between petit-nègre, patois, and Creole. "In fact, *petit nègre* is one of the strangest legacies of World War I," Edwards explains, "it was a simplified, deformed version of French that the military codified and deliberately *taught* to African soldiers as they came to fight in Europe, as a means both to infantilize them and to control their modes of interaction with their mainly white French commanding officers" (52, emphasis in the original). Biguine musicking, categorized as petit-nègre when in fact its lyrics are in Creole (if not in French), underlines the musical disconnect operating within the cultural life of the biguine in France as well as the linguistic one with which the imperialist ear heard this music. Misreading the body language of the interracial dance as *petit-nègre*, observers (mis)read the power relating within the dialog of the dance.

Translation, as Edwards shows, lies at the heart of any project of transnationalism, and the negritude women played a crucial role in this aspect of black radical activity. In the bilingual *La Revue du monde noir*, the translator, usually writing in direct discourse, interrupts Gisèle Dubouillé's chronicle on the "A si paré" recording by Stellio's orchestra:

Of course, "Odéon" competes in this rush for the new music: Stellio's band takes once more advantage of the resources of its Director's supple and dexterous clarinet, in *A si paré*, (Sorry. But any attempt at a translation would lead to disaster. It would take nothing less than a treatise on Martinican philology and a great deal on the psychology of the girls over there. Cf. After you've gone with Sophie Tucker) and *Soigné i ba moin* (Take care of him for me). (56)

The translations of French to English often varied in journals. The translators seem to take into account the possible cultural outsider status of Anglophone readers, but the lengthy parenthetical comment above exceptionally pinpoints a lack of understanding of the colonial history of French Antillean connections and their unique manifestations in language and music.

Sem's description demonstrates the very limited authority of Creole language, inaudible in affluent social circles, misunderstood even within the space of the Bal Nègre. Fanon points out that social identification and order function through French linguistic legitimacy even on the islands. This dynamic produces an ironically ambivalent situation for the biguine; if performance in Creole was required for authentic *biguining*, band leaders had to have mastered the French language both to conduct business relationships and to speak to the audience, especially in France, but even before as well. Mavounzy's description gives the juxtaposition of the diction of speech and the "diction" of the clarinet style in the context of Alexandre Kindou, whose playing but also his "gentillesse et sa *correction linguistique*" made him a favorite in Point-à-Pitre (Mavounzy 32; my emphasis).

Fanon's description of the Antillean practicing for hours the perfect French "r," "striving to become diction" (*Black Skin* 16) reveals assimilation to be an (unsuccessful) social performance requiring the shedding of speech. Biguine lives between a discursive rock and a hard place; while the Antillean radical tradition (understandably) refuses the genre's Creole voice, the imperial scene erases the genre's Creole specificity, commodifies it, and incorporates it into an imperial economy of pleasures and purchases. The continued imperial currency of black Antillean music and colonial speech as effeminate and infantile in the French imagination gives an idea of why many radical poets found writing their poems in Creole unthinkable. Fanon screams frustration with the way the black subject, positioned through speech and diction, is constantly made to find its self on stage in France, but the Antillean musical subject can only flee the position of the stage at professional and financial detriment. While the negritude women critiqued the expropriation of the biguine, their *cercle d'amis* demonstrates a sympathy for these musical genres and their hybrid forms and practices that testify to histories of the types of intimate exchanges official colonial discourse forbade.

This book suggests the ways negritude—both as a critical movement of black international dialog and as a mythological construct of literary criticism—engages in dynamics of naming (titles), writing (authorship), sound/text conversion (*le cri*), and colonial family romance, that ultimately effects a genealogical erasure of the *doudou* in Antillean cultural history. Such erasure extends into a line of writers and thinkers critical to the movement yet whose participation has been continually discounted. Among these are the many women writers and performers around the interwar years. The Nardal sisters and Susanne Césaire are now receiving more scholarly attention. Still waiting for proper recognition in this cultural moment are the women of the French West Indian musical scene in France such as Nelly Lungla, Léona Gabriel, Lola Martin, and Moune de Rivel. The groundbreaking sounds these cultural pioneers and practitioners forged affected both sides of the Atlantic.

The *tumulte noir* during the Third Republic laid the French discursive framework for black New World culture practices and consumption in France for the future. I would argue that we can trace perhaps the most dominant cultural dynamics in the "blacking and beuring" of the Hexagon today back to this noisy scene. In dominant discourse, the drum, *le ka*, still represents authentic (i.e., black) local music and the biguine, its doudouist relative. In today's popular Antillean parlance, the *doudou* might be called a "Bounty"—like the candy bar: chocolate on the outside, white on the inside—a member of the black community filled up and consumed in dominant white culture. In contrast, my argument has been that the *tam-tam*'s mythology of primal sonic authenticity and virile masculinity mints black value on the other side of the doudouist coin. Does not the rhythmic echo, *doudou tam-tam*, reveal rather uncoincidentally a gendered and racialized system of speech and musicality circulating in structures of colonial family romance?

Posited as elemental speech, onomatopoeic and infantile, material and at the cusp of the possibility of articulation, the two strike at primal scenes of black colonial embodiment and inscription. As such they point toward the shared rhythm of desire and separation, the violently shared and shorn soundtext dynamics of inclusion and exclusion that mark the black New World. Built on dreams of exclusion and inclusion, the *doudou* and the *tam-tam* are both anti/colonialist speech acts, they manifest the ambivalence of colonial desire where linguistic signs of relation and of intimate entanglement become sonic posts of misrecognition and authenticity.

The soundscape serves as an imaginative site of cultural re-membership for the black Francophone Atlantic, staging a long-standing negotiation of loss and recovery that points up histories of displacement and discontinuity all the while stubbornly enabling the transfigurative processes—also known as healing—that make speaking pain to power or to pleasure possible. Is culture anything other than such forms of collective healing? In this light, the discursive transformations of hybridity into essentialism do not constitute logical paradoxes of culture. On the contrary, such imaginative and emotional transformations are themselves really the stuff of authenticity. The latter notion is deconstructed in much poststructuralist and postcolonial discourse, yet how does one imagine the function of culture without it?

The surprising absence of the *doudou*'s song in postcolonial criticism, in addition to reflecting the latter's methodological privileging of textual paradigms, results from the way her ethical ambivalence cannot be easily reappropriated for demands for anticolonial narratives of heroic subversion. At the same time, the context of the *doudou*'s production reveals the colonial coauthorship of "the victim's discourse," which conservatives within and without the academy cite as constitutive of the politically correct agendas of postcolonial and ethnic based studies as well as identity politics more generally.

Herein lies an integral part of the doudouist problematic, one certainly not absent in the Fanon's work: the analysis of the *doudou* inevitably takes the form of an interrogation where the ethical and aesthetic sanctions of black radicalism resonate with colonial paradigms of authority and power. Crudely put, this *bête noire* has been on trial by patriarchy since the early days of Father Labat, and negritude's scream contributes to that virulent grilling. The so-called doudouist horizontal relations in the Caribbean have become symbolically designated as a song and dance of the woman's loss, while vertical modes of resistance in negritude get tagged as authentic man-to-man combat. The problematic gender dynamics facing the representation of black pain and pleasure make negritude's critique of the *doudou* aesthetic resonant with her colonialist designation, since the *Code noir*, as the site of conflicted ethical decisions concerning the true, the good, and the beautiful. Considering this gendered *discours du procès* that lies at the heart of transnationalism and its discontents, my objective has been to transform the poststructuralist transnational utopia into another type of *non-lieu*, a deconstruction of the grounds for accusation, rather than a defense or prosecution of the representational voice.

While negritude's scream seeks to operate poetic aggression by sounding the psychic distance between the colonial subject and the Hexagon, the *doudou*'s demands will only be heard if her condition of pain sounds beautiful and thus resonates beyond the trauma of separation and interrogation. Self representation for the *doudou* is a melancholic mode of otobiography. If the *doudou*'s song and dance relates her pathetic beauty, doudouism's hegemonic power play represents the willing submission of that beauty to the discourse of the master. But the *doudou*'s lament is her performance of seduction and the sound of her survival. Her song suggests that the colonizer cannot be heartless, that even relations of overt force must also rely on types of complicity, that macro-level ruptures are often only hearable, rendered meaningful, through mirco-level structures of continuity.

Léon-Gontran Damas's work, especially his epic *Black-Label*, situates a new critical relation with doudouism that extends what I call the minor genealogy of negritude. By focusing on rhythmic melancholy, itineraries of loss, and practices of line crossing, Damas rediscovers continuity amid the traumatic compromises exacted on blacks in colonial culture and imperial life. The question of "black labels" has everything to do with the possibilities of naming and beating, signing and singing, blackness in the twentieth and twenty-first centuries. Damas uses language and desire to work out questions dealing with the commodification and exploitation of black vernacular culture, specifically New World and Creole selling out. In this poetry, as in Josephine Baker's performances, and other mythologies born in the dark of the City of Light, "love is for sale," but, paradoxically, extricating the two involves a risky surgery, a cutting up of the sociolinguistic and psychic makeup of the black modern subject. Damas uses references to popular culture to get at the way blacks adopted and adapted many musical and cultural traditions to navigate the jolting rhythms of black modernity. His work offers critical portrayals of quotidian life and black popular culture that critique the high modernism of dominant negritude poetics.

Listening in to popular music's ephemeral yet iterative productions of sociocultural structures of feeling, knowing, and relating, one hears an aural past that differs from high culture's ideological dogmas and retroactive histories of canonization. This ephemeral quality lends it a lively flexibility such that aural culture, fueled through popular networks of circulation, often offers a more timely and flexible feel for popular ideas and attitudes toward race and French imperialism than the literary figures of postcolonial criticism. While the stakes of the colonial text negotiate forms of authority backed, for example, by the legal contracts of History that situate the state and the citizen, the stakes of colonizing the soundscape often have to do with generating popular legitimacy for discursive shifts and new understandings of the letter of the law. The latter functions through constructions of time to regulate the boundaries of European imperialism. At the same time, temporal tensions revealed in anti-colonial and negritude discourse point up important differences in the way thinkers articulated ideas about revolutionary activity, thought, and subjectivity. Musical culture and imperial soundscapes serve as crucial sites for the ideologies of time underlying anti/colonial and transnational discourse.

Musical discourse and practice raises problems for postcolonial studies seeking to assign positions to others in the complicity/resistance binary. What happens to the notions of authorship and accountability based on textual paradigms when taken to the field of sound? Who is "responsible" for Josephine Baker's song and dance in *Princesse Tam Tam*? The cultural practitioners and projects in this book struggle over the definition of authentic sound and tap into new modes of its creation, recording, reproduction, and circulation in order to negotiate the transnational and transcolonial terms of authorship, ownership, and authority in the New World. Heard in concert, their tyrannical dictaphonics, ambivalent sweet-talk, and jagged cuts in avant-garde literature, radical thought, and popular music constitute a wide cultural debate about the inscription of authenticity, minor transnational exchange, and imperial globalizations into the body of French West Indian history.

Authenticity is a dream; it isn't just a "false construct." It's a crucial cultural and community project that is wholly worthwhile despite our postmodern and poststructuralist theoretical schemes that seek to foreclose on it. Why? Precisely if such project amounts to dealing with the deep histories of imperial and racial violence that constitute the terrain where black Atlantic musical practices take up meaning, then access to authenticity means constructing the conditions of possibility for claims of legitimation rooted not in exclusionary fantasies of purity, nor in romantic narratives of pure agency, but rather in critically oriented, self-aware cultural practices that plant stakes every day in history.

# Notes

## CHAPTER 1: "Adieu Madras, Adieu Foulard"

1. I use Richard Philcox's translations for all of Fanon's works unless otherwise indicated.

2. There are many lyrical variants to the song. This version comes from Léona Gabriel-Soïme's *Ça! C'est la Martinique!* All translations are my own unless otherwise indicated.

3. See Liauzu and Liauzu, *Quand on chantait les colonies.*

4. See Boulanger et al., *La Musique antillaise en France.* See also the extensive liner notes by Jean-Pierre Meunier in the three-volume set *Biguine* (see discography).

5. Fanon's virulent and masculinist attack of Capécia goes so far as to conflate the representation of the *doudou* with the writer herself, positioning her and her text as failures. Some critics try to return the favor by citing Fanon's own marriage to a white woman as proof of his critical hypocrisy.

6. See Jacques Derrida's *Otobiographies: L'enseignement de Nietzsche et la politique du nom propre.* My analysis builds from Derridean deconstruction of the proper name, the signature, the text, and "the ear of the other."

7. John Mowitt also notes this translation error. For his reading, see *Drumming, Beating, Striking.* It is interesting to note the way in which Markmann's translation of Frantz Fanon's *Black Skin White Masks* failed to render Fanon's original language—that is, his musical externalization of what Fanon depicts as an aural, internal penetration—demonstrates the sexually rhythmic and violent confusion of self/other boundaries in anti/colonial discourses. Markmann's "battered down by tom-toms" naturally picks up on the racialization of rhythm and time and the fetishization of the drum/skin inherent in this mode of violent contestation, a theme I explore in the context of negritude in chapter 4, building from Mowitt's work.

8. Léon-Gontran Damas, "Hoquet" (Hiccups), in *Pigments—Névralgies.*

9. See "Diction."

10. See Mernissi, *Scheherazade Goes West.*

11. See Gilman's *Difference and Pathology.*

12. "Lisette quitté la plaine" is attributed to Duvivier de la Mahautière.

13. "Le Départ du Jean-Bart."

> Adieu, Foulards, adieu, Madras!
> Adieu, grains d'or, adieu, coliçons!
> Doudou a moué, li qu'a pati
> Hélas! hélas! c'est pour toujou.

Adieu, *Jean-Bart*, li qu'a pati
Emportant la joie, l'espérance et la vie!
Doudou pleuré, coeur gros comm' ça
P'tits aspirants qu'a plus vini!

Adieu, Lucie, adieu, Amélie!
Vous, p'tit Nana, vous grossé Julie!
Adieu, Matisma, pleure Rosella,
Adieu, Cocotte, adieu, Doudou!

Bonjou, missié le gouverneur,
Mi vini fai you p'tit pétition:
Doudou à moué li qu'a pati,
Vous pas baillé z'embarcation.

Ma chère enfant, il est trop tard;
Les connaissements sont déjà signés,
Le beau navire est sur sa bouée,
Bientôt il va appareiller.

Déjà à bord tout le monde est rentré,
Les voiles sont larguées et tribord brassé
Pilote est à bord, tout le monde est paré
Et les tangons sont déjà rentrés.

Quand moué vini pour badiné li,
Quand moué vini pour caressé li,
Li pas vélé Cocotte, li pas vélé Doudou
Li pas vélé che zami moué.

Les filles du Hâve sont bien intigantes
Li qu'a baillé leur coeur pour agent,
Tandis que nous à la Martinique
Nous qu'a baillé li pour rien du tout.

14. The discourse of the "tragic mulatta," which often centers on the woman of color's proximity to founding fathers of national and nationalist dreams, continues to serves as the site linking wide-ranging contemporary anxieties about the "purity" of founding texts and cultures. Witness, as Eve Raimon astutely does in *The Tragic Mulatta Revisited*, the return of debates in the American context about Thomas Jefferson's relations with Sally Hemings.

15. See work by minor writers like Drasta Houël (*Cruautés et tendresses: Vieilles moeurs coloniales françaises*), Thérèse Herpin (*Cristalline Boisnoir*), and Albert Bérard (*Juana, fille des tropiques*).

16. The *Principe de l'exclusif* was the official commercial exchange policy imposed on the French colonies, dictating all exports and imports go first go through the imperial *métropole*.

### CHAPTER 2: "To Begin the Biguine"

1. My translation.

2. I am using Ellen Conroy Kennedy's translation, found in her collection of translations *The Negritude Poets*, for Damas's "Hoquet" and my own for his poems "Trêve" and *Black-Label*.

3. Some of the early biguine recordings in France have been rereleased more recently through Frémeaux & Associés, many with excellent liner notes by Jean Meunier. See the discography for titles.

4. "'COMME ELLE ETAIT BELLE . . . MA MARTINIQUE!' Avec ses 'commères' (en France, ce sont des tantes). De l'homme, ils n'ont que le sexe. Nos commères, 'COUCOUNE,' 'CHERUBIN,' 'FERNAND,' 'ETIENNE,' tous vendeurs au marché. Rois de la bonne humeur. Mais aux prises avec quelqu'un, en colère, aucun rapide ne coulait avec plus de fracas, de précipitation, que le fleuve de paroles violentes et désordonnées qu'ils lançaient, les ponctuant parfois d'une forme d'humour qui n'était certes pas à la portée de n'importe qui. Ils avaient la spécialité, au temps du carnaval, de se déguiser en femme et s'occupaient de la vente de chansons."

5. "SAINT-PIERRE comme subissant un pressentiment, signe avant-coureur du malheur! SAINT-PIERRE, en ce carnaval de 1900, se dépêche de vivre, de danser, tandis que la 'PELEE' majestueuse et grave, pareille à une belle femme au sourire de 'SPHINX,' se dresse de son air tranquille et semble dire à SAINT-PIERRE étalé à ses pieds, dans toute sa splendeur: 'DEVINE OU JE TE DEVORE.'"

6. Sharpley-Whiting, *Negritude Women*, 45–46.

### CHAPTER 3: La Baker

1. My emphasis. All transcriptions and translations are my own unless otherwise noted.

2. The translations are from subtitles to the film. I place my minor changes and additions in brackets.

3. This may be what prompts Jules Rosette to read the film as a spoof on French colonial cinema. "Deux amours" pits the sad plot of anonymous failure against the exciting trajectory of unheard of success, singing over the violence on her that the text enacts. Differently put, it sets up the endless *mise en abyme* of performativity and authenticity, their shared mark of Joséphine's signature.

4. I discuss this ambivalence in the term "tam-tam" at length in chapter 4.

### CHAPTER 4: Negritude Drum Circles

1. My translation.

2. The translations of *Black-Label* are my own.

3. In "Pour ou contre l'assimilation," a critical essay against departmentalization, Damas explicitly takes up the question of the circulation of colonial and metropolitan products and labeling with respect U.S. economies of circulation. He pinpoints the circulation of wine and alcohol as a crucial economic sector being targeted by the metropole. The fundamental question Damas poses in the piece echoes *Black-Label*: "On revient toujours à la même question: qu'aura-t-il de changé?"

4. See Boittin's *Colonial Metropolis*.

5. These lyrics represent the version recorded by Rico's Creole Band. I got help in my transcription from Ana Lucia Araujo's fascinatingly similar account of the reaction to this

song while dancing to it. See Araujo, *Public Memory of Slavery*. Here are the lyrics in Spanish: "Esclavo soy negro nací, negro es mi color y negra es mi suerte, pobre de mi sufriendo voy este cruel dolor hasta la muerte. Soy Lucumí cautivo, sin la libertad no vivo. Ay mi negra Pancha vamos a bailar, que les congos libres algún día serán, que los negros libres serán." (I'm a slave I was born black, black is my color and black is my luck, woe is me I suffer this cruel pain until death. I'm a captured Lucumi, without freedom I can't live. Oh my négresse Pancha let's go dance that one day the Congos will be free, that one day the Negros will be free.)

6. See Orovio, *Cuban music from A to Z*.

7. "Le guitariste cubain Emilio 'Don' Barreto aura dans son orchestre le batteur martiniquais Robert Mommarché en 1936 et 1937 puis le saxophoniste guadeloupéen Édouard Pajaniandy de 1946 à 1950." (http://www.lameca.org/dossiers/biguine_paris/biguine04.htm)

8. "une langue paresseuse et rebelle / d'une bouche / cousu née" (*Black Label* 75).

9. "Minuit dont ne saurait désormais s'accomoder / la puissance / sans cesse en éveil / des tabous bien bandés / de mon enfance afro-amérindienne" (*BL* 84).

### CHAPTER 5:  Le Poste Colonial

1. Duval, *Histoire de la radio en France*.

2. All translations from journals and studies of French radio are mine.

3. See Gitelman, *Scripts, Grooves, and Writing Machines*. For another reading of the way radio technology and the radio waves constituted a new means of writing history, see Ian Baucom's essay about "the midnight hour of August 15, 1947, the hour at which India gained its independence" (17). "[A]t that very moment," Baucom writes, "Jawaharlal Nehru chose to inaugurate the moment of independence—the moment that was, for him, the birth of the postcolonial—with a radio address in which he called the scattered subjects of the subcontinent to gather themselves around the unifying cadences of his broadcast voice" (17). Baucom's analysis reflects the way radiophonic moments constituted historiography even as they sped up the historical event(s).

4. See the official website of Radio France International, www.rfi.fr/pressefr/articles/072/article_30.asp.

5. According to "Paris sur les Ondes: L'Histoire de la télévision et la radio dans la capitale." Oct. 2004–Feb. 2005. An Exposition organized by the Marie de Paris and the Institute National de l'Audiovisuel for INA's thirtieth anniversary.

6. "Les radio-reportages à l'Exposition coloniale," 76.

7. The expression *pacte colonial* "was created later, in a period where it was desired people believe that the colonial regime was the result of a pact," Charles André Julien emphasizes, "in other words, an agreement freely consented to implying reciprocal obligations, when in fact it was imposed by the French on its colonies the latter which protested its application" (13, my translation). See my discussion of "Colonial Family Romance" in chapter 1.

8. "Les colons, les agriculteurs surtout, isolés dans leur fermes, sont les premiers à s'alarmer. Ils réclament des mesures extraordinaire" (Fanon, *Les Damnés*, 70).

9. For more on the Exposition, see my "Imagining Métissage."

10. The English is from Clayton Eshleman and Annette Smith's translation in Aimé Césaire, *Aimé Césaire: The Collected Poetry*.

11. I borrow the term "ephemeromateriality" from Weheliye, *Phonographies*.

12. "Surréalisme, n. m. Automatisme psychique pur par lequel on se propose d'exprimer, soit verbalement, soit par écrit, soit de toute autre manière, le fonctionnement réel de la pen-

sée. Dictée de la pensée, en l'absence de tout contrôle exercé par la raison, en dehors de toute préoccupation esthétique ou morale" (Breton, *Manifeste du surréalisme*, 36).

13. "But it's wrong to speak here of the poem as if it were the function of relation, of some determined mode of interaction between elements—rather, we might want to think of the poem as the entire field or saturation, flood or plain, within which the page, the sound and meaning, the live, the original, the recording, the score exist as icons or singular aspects of a totality that is, itself, iconic of totality as such" (Moten 97).

14. I plant the *poste colonial* in the "fertile soil" of "various metaphors of continuation, inheritance, influence, posterity" as well as Mireille Rosello's concern about sacred transmission, "filiation and [. . .] legacy" (Rosello 77). As for "using Césaire's work and Cesairian pre-existing mythologies as a vast repertoire of material that we could all use to justify and corroborate any coherent narrative about the fictional figure that we constantly re-invent for different purposes" (Rosello 77), I see in Césaire's poetic an offering up of the body (the text) for the reader's critical incisors, even a violent force feeding, for ritual consumption.

# Bibliography

## Books and Periodicals

Adorno, Theodor, and Max Horkheimer. "The Culture Industry: Enlightenment as Mass Deception." *Dialectic of Enlightenment*. New York: Continuum, 1986.

Agawu, Kofi. "The Invention of 'African Rhythm.'" Music Anthropologies and Music Histories. *Journal of the American Musicological Society* 48.3 (Autumn 1995): 380–395.

Alloula, Maleck. *The Colonial Harem*. Trans. Myrna Godzich and Wlad Godzich. Minneapolis: University of Minnesota Press, 1986.

Amiot, Jean Joseph Marie et al. *Mémoires concernant l'histoire, les sciences et les arts et les moeurs etc. des Chinois par les missionnaires de Pékin*. Paris: Chez Nyon l'aîné, 1779.

Antoine, Régis. *Rayonnants écrivains de la Caraïbe*. Paris: Maisonneuve & Larose, 1998.

———. *Les Écrivains français et les Antilles: Des Premiers pères blancs aux surréalistes noirs*. Paris: G. P. Maisonneuve et Larose, 1978.

Appadurai, Arjun. *Modernity at Large: Cultural Dimensions of Globalization*. 1st ed. Minneapolis: University of Minnesota Press, 1996.

Apter, Emily. "Theorizing *Francophonie*." *Comparative Literature Studies* 42.4 (2005): 297–311.

———. " 'Je ne crois pas beaucoup à la littérature comparée': Universal Poetics and Postcolonial Comparatism." *Comparative Literature in an Age of Globalization*. Ed. Haun Saussy. Baltimore: Johns Hopkins University Press, 2006.

Aragon, Louis. *Le Paysan de Paris*. Paris: Gallimard, 1926.

Araujo, Ana. *Public Memory of Slavery: Victims and Perpetrators in the South Atlantic*. Amherst, NY: Cambria Press, 2010.

Archer-Straw, Petrine. *Negrophilia: Avant-Garde Paris and Black Culture in the 1920s*. New York: Thames & Hudson, 2000.

Baker, Jean-Claude. *Josephine: The Hungry Heart*. 1st ed. New York: Random House, 1993.

Baker, Josephine, et al. *Josephine*. 1st ed. New York: Harper & Row, 1977.

Barrett, Lindon. *Blackness and Value: Seeing Double*. Cambridge: Cambridge University Press, 2009.

Barz, Gregory, and Timothy J. Cooley, eds. *Shadows in the Field: New Perspectives for Fieldwork in Ethnomusicology*. 2nd ed. Oxford: Oxford University Press, 2008.

Baucom, Ian. "Frantz Fanon's Radio: Solidarity, Diaspora, and the Tactics of Listening." *Contemporary Literature* 42.1 (2001): 15–49.

Benjamin, Walter. "The Work of Art in the Age of Mechanical Reproduction." *Illuminations*. Trans. Harry Zohn. New York: Schocken Books, 1969.

Benoit, Édouard. "Biguine: Popular Music of Guadeloupe, 1940–1960." *Zouk: World Music in the West Indies*. Ed. Jocelyne Guilbault. Chicago Studies in Ethnomusicology. Chicago: University of Chicago Press, 1993.

Bérard, Albert. *Juana, fille des tropiques*. Paris: Baudinière, 1932.

Berliner, Brett. *Ambivalent Desire: The Exotic Black Other in Jazz-Age France*. Amherst: University of Massachusetts Press, 2002.

Bermingham, Ronald. "Le Cri de la nature et la nature du cri: Étude d'une coupure épistémologique." *Études sur les discours de Rousseau / Studies on Rousseau's Discourses*. Ed. Jean Terrasse. Ottawa: Association nord-américaine des études Jean-Jacques Rousseau / North American Association for the Study of Jean-Jacques Rousseau, 1988.

Berrian, Brenda F. *Awakening Spaces: French Caribbean Popular Songs, Music, and Culture*. Chicago Studies in Ethnomusicology. Chicago: University of Chicago Press, 2000.

Blainville, Charles Henri de. *Histoire générale, critique et philologique de la musique*. 1767. Geneva, Switzerland: Minkoff Reprints, 1972.

Blaise, Antoine Andraud, et al. *Dictionnaire du commerce et des marchandises*. Paris: Publ. sous la direction de m. Guillaumin, 1852.

Blake, Jody. *Le Tumulte Noir: Modernist Art and Popular Entertainment in Jazz-Age Paris, 1900–1930*. University Park, PA: Pennsylvania State University, 1999.

Boittin, Jennifer. "In Black and White: Gender, Race Relations, and the Nardal Sisters in Interwar Paris." *French Colonial History* 6 (2005): 119–136.

———. *Colonial Metropolis: The Urban Grounds of Anti-Imperialism and Feminism in Interwar Paris*. Lincoln: University of Nebraska Press, 2010.

Bost, Suzanne. *Mulattas and Mestizas: Representing Mixed Identities in the Americas 1850–2000*. Athens: University of Georgia Press, 2005.

Bouche, Pierre Bertrand. *Sept Ans en Afrique Occidentale: La Côte des esclaves et le Dahomey*. Paris: E. Plon Nourrit, 1885.

Boulanger, Alain, et al., *La Musique antillaise en France: Discographie 1929–1959 / French-Caribbean Music in France: A Discography 1929–1959*. Basse-Terre, Guadeloupe: AFAS LAMECA, Conseil Général de la Guadeloupe, 2008.

Breton, André. *L'Amour fou*. Paris: Gallimard, 1976.

———. *Manifeste du surréalisme*. 1924. Paris: Folio, 1985.

———. *Nadja*. Paris: Gallimard, 1972.

Brunnquell, Frédéric. *Fréquence monde: Du Poste Colonial à RFI*. Paris: Hachette, 1992.

Césaire, Aimé. *Aimé Césaire, The Collected Poetry*. Trans. Clayton Eshleman and Annette Smith. Berkeley: University of California Press, 1983.

———. *Les Armes miraculeuses*. Paris: Gallimard, 1946.

———. *Cahier d'un retour au pays natal*. Paris: Présence africaine, 1983.

———. *Discourse on Colonialism*. Trans. Joan Pinkham. New York: Monthly Review Press, 2000.

———. "Poetry and Knowledge." *Refusal of the Shadow: Surrealism and the Caribbean*. Ed Michael Richardson et al. New York: Verso, 1996.

Chanvallon, Thibaut de. *Voyage à la Martinique*. Paris: CI. J.B. Blanche, 1763.

Cheng, Anne Anlin. *The Melancholy of Race: Psychoanalysis, Assimilation and Hidden Grief*. Oxford: Oxford University Press, 2001.

Chernoff Christopher. *African Rhythm African Sensibilities: Aesthetics and Social Action in African Musical Idioms*. Chicago: University of Chicago Press, 1981.

Clément, Catherine. *La Syncope: Philosophie du ravissement*. Paris: B. Grasset, 1990.

Clifford, James. *The Predicament of Culture: Twentieth-Century Ethnography, Literature, and Art*. Cambridge, MA: Harvard University Press, 1988.

Colin, Paul et al. *Josephine Baker and La Revue Nègre: Paul Colin's Lithographs of Le Tumulte Noir in Paris, 1927*. New York: Abrams, 1998.

Colomb, Louis Casimir. *La musique*. Paris: Hachette, 1878.

Condé, Maryse. "Order, Disorder, Freedom, and the West Indian Writer." *Yale French Studies* 97.50 (2000): 151–165.

———. "Propos sur l'identité culturelle." *Négritude: Traditions et développement*. Ed. Guy Michaud. Paris: PUF, 1978.

Confiant, Raphaël, and Patrick Chamoiseau. *Lettres créoles: Tracées antillaises et continentales de la littérature, Haïti, Guadeloupe, Martinique, Guyane (1635–1975)*. Paris: Gallimard, 1999.

"Le Congrès au jour le jour." *L'Antenne* May 31, 1931.

Corre, Armand. *Nos Créoles*. Paris: Alber Savine, 1890.

Dalton, Karen C. C., and Henry Louis Gates. "Josephine Baker and Paul Colin: African American Dance Seen through Parisian Eyes." *Critical Inquiry* 24.4 (1998): 903–934.

Damas, Léon-Gontran. *Black-Label: Poèmes*. Paris: Gallimard, 1956.

———. *Pigments—Névralgies*. 1937. definitive ed. Paris: Présence Africaine, 2003.

Dash, Michael. *The Other America: Caribbean Literature in a New World Context*. Charlottesville: University of Virginia Press, 1998.

Décoret-Ahiha, Anne. *Les Danses exotiques en France 1880–1940*. Paris: Centre national de la danse, 2004.

Derrida, Jacques. *Otobiographies: L'enseignement de Nietzsche et la politique du nom propre*. Paris: Editions Galilée, 1984.

Dhordain, Roland. *Le Roman de la radio: De la T.S.F. aux radios libres*. Paris: La Table ronde, 1983.

"Diction," *Le Trésor de la langue française informatisé*, Dec. 1, 2005. Available at http://atilf.atilf.fr/tlf.htm.

Diderot, Denis, Jean Le Rond d'Alembert, and Pierre Mouchon. *Encyclopédie: Ou Dictionnaire raisonné des sciences, des arts et des métiers, par une sociéte de gens de lettres*. 3rd ed. Paris: A'Livourne, 1751.

Dower, John. *Embracing Defeat: Japan in the Wake of World War II*. New York: Norton and The New Press, 1999.

Dubouillé, Gisèle. "Nouveaux Disques de musique nègre. / New Records of Negro Music." *La Revue du monde noir / The Review of the Black World. Collection complète. No 1 à 6*. Paris: Jean Michel Place, 1992.

Du Tertre, Jean Baptiste. *Histoire générale des Antilles habitées par les François*. Paris: T. Iolly, 1667–1671.

Duval, René. *Histoire de la radio en France*. Paris: Alain Moreau, 1979.

Edwards, Brent Hayes. *The Practice of Diaspora: Literature, Translation, and the Rise of Black Internationalism*. Cambridge, MA: Harvard University Press, 2003.

Ellul, Jacques. *The Technological Society*. Trans. John Wilkinson. New York: Vintage, 1967.

Ezra, Elizabeth. *The Colonial Unconscious: Race and Culture in Interwar France*. Ithaca: Cornell University Press, 2000.

Fabre, Michel. *From Harlem to Paris: Black American Writers in France 1840–1980*. Urbana: University of Illinois Press, 1991.

Fanon, Frantz. *L'An V de la révolution algérienne*. Paris: La Découverte, 2001.

———. *Black Skin, White Masks*. Trans. Charles Lam Markmann. New York: Grove Weidenfeld, 1991.

———. *Black Skin, White Masks*. Trans. Richard Philcox. New York: Grove Press, 2008.

———. *Les Damnés de la terre*. Paris: Découverte/Poche, 2002.

———. *A Dying Colonialism*. Trans. Haakon Chevalier. New York: Grove Press, 1994.

———. *Peau noire, masques blancs*. Paris: Editions du Seuil, 1952.

———. *Pour la révolution africaine: Ecrits politiques*. Paris: La Découverte, 2001.

———. *Toward the African Revolution*. Trans. Haakon Chevalier. New York: Grove Press, 1994.

———. *The Wretched of the Earth*. Trans. Richard Philcox. New York: Grove Press, 2004.

Flavia-Léopold, Emmanuel. *Adieu foulards, adieu madras: Chants pour la terre créole*. Paris: Littré, 1948.

Gabriel-Soïme, Léona. *Ça! C'est la Martinique!* Paris: La Productrice, 1966.

Garraway, Doris. "Race, Reproduction, and Family Romance in Moreau de Saint-Méry's *Description . . . de la partie française de l'isle Saint-Domingue*." *Eighteenth-Century Studies* 38.2 (2005): 227–246.

Gilman, Sander. *Difference and Pathology: Stereotypes of Sexuality, Race, and Madness*. Ithaca, NY: Cornell University Press, 1985.

Gilroy, Paul. *The Black Atlantic: Modernity and Double Consciousness*. Cambridge, MA: Harvard University Press, 1993.

Gitelman, Lisa. *Scripts, Grooves, and Writing Machines: Representing Technology in the Edison Era*. Stanford, CA: Stanford University Press, 1999.

Glover, Kaiama. "Introduction: Why Josephine Baker?" *The Scholar and Feminist Online*. http://www.barnard.edu/sfonline/baker/index.htm. Special double issue *Josephine Baker: A Century in the Spotlight*. Guest ed. Kaiama Glover. 6.1–6.2 (Fall 2007 / Spring 2008).

Goddard, Chris. *Jazz Away from Home*. New York: Paddington Books, 1979.

Guilbault, Jocelyne. *Zouk: World Music in the West Indies*. Chicago Studies in Ethnomusicology. Chicago: University of Chicago Press, 1993.

Guilbault, Jocelyne, and Line Grenier. "Créolité and Francophonie in Music: Socio-Cultural Repositioning Where It Matters." *Cultural Studies* 11.2 (1997): 207–234.

Haney, Lynn. *Naked at the Feat: A Biography of Josephine Baker*. London: Robson, 1981.

Hartman, Saidiya. *Scenes of Subjection: Terror, Slavery, and Self-Making in Nineteenth-Century America*. Oxford: Oxford University Press, 1997.

Hazael-Massieux, Marie-Christine. *Chansons des Antilles: Comptines, formulettes*. Paris: L'Harmattan, 1996.

Head, Matthew. "Birdsong and the Origins of Music." *Journal of the Royal Musical Association* 122.1 (1997): 1–23.

Hearn, Lafcadio. *American Writings: Some Chinese Ghosts, Chita, Two Years in the French West Indies, Youma, Selected Journalism and Letters*. New York: The Library of America, 2009.

Herpen, Thérèse. *Cristalline Boisnoir: Ou, Les dangers du bal Loulou*. Paris: Plon, 1929.

Hill, Edwin C., Jr. "Imagining Métissage: The Politics and Practice of Métissage in the French Colonial Exposition and Ousmane Socé's *Mirages de Paris*." *Social Identities: Journal for the Study of Race, Nation and Culture* 8.4 (2002): 619–645.

Houël, Drasta. *Cruautés et tendresses: Vieilles mœurs coloniales françaises*. Paris: Payot, 1925.

Hughes, Langston. "The Negro Artist and the Racial Mountain." Reprinted in Patton, Venetria K., and Maureen Honey. *Double-Take: A Revisionist Harlem Renaissance Anthology*. New Brunswick: Rutgers University Press, 2001.

Irving, David. " 'For Whom the Bell Tolls': Listening and Its Implications." *Journal of the Royal Musical Association* 135.1 (2010): 19–24.

Jackson, Jeffrey. *Making Jazz French: Music and Modern Life in Interwar Paris.* Durham: Duke University Press, 2003.

Jallier, Maurice, and Yollen Lossen. *Musique aux Antilles: Mizik bô kay.* Paris: Editions Caribéennes, 1985.

Jeanneney, Jean-Noël, ed. *L'Echo du siècle: Dictionnaire historique de la radio et de la télévision en France.* Paris: Hachette, 1999.

Jefferson, Margo. "The Intelligent Body and Erotic Soul of Josephine Baker." *The Scholar and Feminist Online.* http://www.barnard.edu/sfonline/baker/index.htm. Special double issue *Josephine Baker: A Century in the Spotlight.* Guest ed. Kaiama Glover. 6.1–6.2 (Fall 2007/ Spring 2008).

Jenson, Deborah. "Mimetic Mastery and Colonial Mimicry in the First Franco-Antillean Creole Anthology." *The Yale Journal of Criticism* 17.1 (Spring 2004): 83–106.

Johnson, Sara. "*Cinquillo* Consciousness: The Formation of a Pan-Caribbean Musical Aesthetic." *Music, Writing, and Cultural Unity in the Caribbean.* Ed. Timothy J. Reiss. Trenton, NJ: Africa World Press, 2005.

Jules-Rosette, Bennetta. *Josephine Baker in Art and Life: The Icon and the Image.* Urbana: University of Illinois Press, 2007.

Julien, Charles-André. Preface. *Toussaint Louverture: La Révolution française et le problème colonial.* By Aimé Césaire. Paris: Présence Africaine, 1981.

Kamuf, Peggy. *Signature Pieces: On the Institution of Authorship.* Ithaca, NY: Cornell University Press, 1988.

Kelman, Ari. "Rethinking the Soundscape: A Critical Genealogy of a Key Term in Sound Studies." *Senses and Society* 5.2 (2010): 212–234.

Kennedy, Ellen Conroy, ed. *The Negritude Poets: An Anthology of Translations from the French.* New York: Thunder's Mouth Press, 1989.

Kesteloot, Lilyan. *Les écrivains noirs de langue française: Naissance d'une littérature.* Brussels: Université libre de Bruxelles, Instutut de sociologie, 1971.

Kittler, Friedrich A. *Gramophone, Film, Typewriter.* Writing Science. Stanford, CA: Stanford University Press, 1999.

Labat, Jean Baptiste. *Nouveau voyage aux isles de l'Amérique.* La Haye, France: P. Husson, 1724.

Lacascade, Suzanne. *Claire-Solange, âme africaine. Roman. suivi de trois bel-airs des Antilles.* Paris: Eugène Figuière, 1924.

Lahille, Abel. *Mes Impressions sur l'Afrique Occidentale Française: Étude documentaire au pays du tam-tam.* Paris: Alcide Picard, 1908.

Léardée, Ernest, Jean Pierre Meunier, and Brigitte Léardée. *La biguine de l'oncle Ben's: Ernest Léardée raconte.* Paris: Editions caribéennes, 1989.

Le Page, Adrien. "Guadeloupe." *Guadeloupe, Guyane, Martinique, Saint-Pierre et Miquelon.* Ed. Commissariat Générale de l'Exposition Coloniale Internationale. Paris: Société d'Editions Géographiques, Maritimes et Coloniales, 1931.

Liauzu, Claude, and Josette Liauzu. *Quand on chantait les colonies: Colonisation et culture populaire de 1830 à nos jours.* Ed. Claude Liauzu. Paris: Editions Syllepse, 2002.

Macey, David. *Frantz Fanon: A Life.* London: Granta Books, 2000.

Marable, Manning. *How Capitalism Underdeveloped Black America: Problems in Race, Political Economy, and Society.* London: Pluto Press, 2000.

Maran, René. *Un Homme pareil aux autres: Roman*. Paris: Éditions A. Michel, 1962.

Mavounzy, Marcel Susan. *Cinquante ans de musique et de culture en Guadeloupe: Mémoires, 1928–1978*. Paris: Présence africaine, 2002.

May, Gita. "Beauty in Context." *A New History of French Literature*. Ed. Denis Hollier. Cambridge, MA: Harvard University Press, 1989.

McCarren, Felicia. "The Use-Value of 'Josephine Baker.'" *The Scholar and Feminist Online*. http://www.barnard.edu/sfonlinxwe/baker/index.htm. Special double issue *Josephine Baker: A Century in the Spotlight*. Guest ed. Kaiama Glover. 6.1–6.2 (Fall 2007 / Spring 2008).

McClary, Susan. *Feminine Endings: Music, Gender, and Sexuality*. Minneapolis: University of Minnesota Press, 1991.

Ménil, René, et al. *Légitime défense*. Paris: Éditions Jean-Michel Place, 1979.

Mernissi, Fatima. *Scheherazade Goes West*. New York: Washington Square Press, 2001.

Meunier, Jean-Pierre, and Brigitte Léardée. *La Biguine de l'Oncle Ben's: Ernest Léardée raconte*. Paris: Editions Caribéennes, 1989.

Moten, Fred. *In the Break: The Aesthetics of the Black Radical Tradition*. Minneapolis: University of Minnesota Press, 2003.

Mowitt, John. *Percussion: Drumming, Beating, Striking*. Durham: Duke University Press, 2002.

Nardal, Andrée. "Etude sur la biguine Créole." *La Revue du Monde Noir* 2 (Dec. 1931): 51–53.

Nardal, Paulette. "Eveil de la conscience de race chez les étudiants noirs." *La Revue du Monde Noir* 6 (Apr. 1932): 25–31.

Negrit, Frédéric. *Musique et immigration dans la société antillaise en France métropolitaine de 1960 à nos jours*. Paris: L'Harmattan, 2004.

Nesbitt, Nick. "Caribbean Literature in French." *Cambridge History of African and Caribbean Literature*. Cambridge: Cambridge University Press, 2008.

Orovio, Helio. *Cuban music from A to Z*. Durham, NC: Duke University Press, 2004.

Pagès, François Xavier. *Voyages autour du monde, et vers les deux poles, par terre et par mer: Pendant les années 1767, 1768, 1769, 1770, 1771, 1773, 1774 & 1776*. Paris: Moutard, 1782.

Perse, Saint-John. *Saint-John Perse: Oeuvres Complètes*. Paris: Nouvelle éd. Gallimard, 1972.

Poizat, Michel. *L'Opéra ou le Cri de l'ange: Essai sur la jouissance de l'amateur d'opéra*. Paris: Editions A.M. Métailié, 1986.

"Le Poste 'Radio-Colonial' de Pontoise." *Annuaire de la Radiodiffusion Nationale*, 1935.

Pratt, Mary Louise. *Imperial Eyes: Travel Writing and Transculturation*. Oxford: Routledge, 1992.

Radano, Ronald Michael. *Lying up a Nation: Race and Black Music*. Chicago: University of Chicago Press, 2003.

Radano, Ronald Michael, and Philip Vilas Bohlman. *Music and the Racial Imagination*. Chicago: University of Chicago Press, 2000.

"La Radio." *La Chronique coloniale*, Dec. 30, 1931.

"La Radio-diffusion aux colonies." *La Chronique coloniale*, Feb. 15, 1929.

"La Radio-diffusion coloniale: Déclarations de M Guernier, Ministre des Postes, Télégraphes et Téléphones." *La Chronique coloniale* May 30, 1931.

"Les Radio-reportages à l'exposition coloniale." *L'Antenne* 424 (May 10, 1931).

Raimon, Eve Allegra. *The Tragic Mulatta Revisited: Race and Nationalism in Nineteenth-Century Antislavery Fiction*. Rutgers, NJ: Rutgers University Press, 2004.

*La Revue du monde noir / The Review of the Black World. Collection complète. No 1 à 6*. Paris: Jean Michel Place, 1992.

Rose, Phyllis. *Jazz Cleopatra: Josephine Baker in Her Time*. 1st ed. New York: Doubleday, 1989.

Rosello, Mireille. "The 'Césaire Effect,' or How to Cultivate One's Nation." *Research in African Literatures* 32.1 (2001).

Rosemain, Jacqueline. *Jazz et biguine: Les Musiques noires du Nouveau-Monde*. Paris: L'Harmattan, 1993.

———. *La Musique dans la société antillaise 1635–1902 Martinique Guadeloupe*. Paris: L'Harmattan, 1986.

Ross, Kristen. *Fast Cars, Clean Bodies: Decolonization and the Reordering of French Culture*. Cambridge, MA: MIT Press, 1995.

Rousseau, Jean-Jacques. *Collected Writings of Rousseau*. Trans. John T. Scott. Hanover, NH: University Press of New England, 1998.

———. *Dictionnaire de musique*. Paris: Chez la veuve Duchesne, 1768.

———. *Écrits sur la musique*. Paris: Editions Stock, 1979.

Ruscio, Alain. *Amours coloniales: Aventures et fantasmes exotiques de Claire de Duras à Georges Simenon: Romans et nouvelles*. Brussels: Éditions Complexe, 1996.

———. *Que la France était belle au temps des colonies . . . Anthologie de chansons coloniales et exotiques*. Paris: Maisonneuve et Larose, 2001.

Sahib. *La frégate l'Incomprise: Voyage autour du monde à la plume*. Paris: L. Vanier, 1882.

Sartre, Jean-Paul. "Orphée Noir." *Anthologie de la nouvelle poésie nègre et malgache de langue française*. Ed. Léopold Sédar Senghor. 6th ed. Paris: Quadrige/PUF, 1948.

———. Preface. *Les Damnés de la terre*. Paris: Découverte/Poche, 2002.

Schafer, R. Murray. *The Soundscape: Our Sonic Environment and the Tuning of the World*. Rochester, VT: Destiny, 1993.

Scharfman, Ronnie Leah. *Engagement and the Language of the Subject in the Poetry of Aimé Césaire*. Gainesville: University Press of Florida, 1980.

Schmouchkovitch, Michel. "La fonction du désir dans l'origine des langues selon Rousseau." *Musique et langage chez Rousseau*. Ed. Claude Dauphin. Oxford: Voltaire Foundation, 2004.

Sem, "Bars et cabarets de Paris." *L'Illustration*. Dec. 7, 1928.

Scott, John. "Rousseau and the Melodious Language of Freedom." *The Journal of Politics* 59.3 (1997): 803–829.

Senghor, Léopold Sédar. *Ce que je crois: Négritude, francité et civilisation de l'universel*. Paris: B. Grasset, 1988.

———. "Ce que l'homme noir apporte." *L'homme de couleur*. Ed. Jean Verdier. Paris: Librairie Plon, 1939.

Shack, William A. *Harlem in Montmartre: A Paris Jazz Story between the Great Wars*. Berkeley: University of California Press, 2001.

Sharpley-Whiting, T. Denean. *Negritude Women*. Minneapolis: University of Minnesota Press, 2002.

Shohat, Ella, and Robert Stam. *Unthinking Eurocentrism: Multiculturalism and the Media*. New York: Routledge, 1994. Berkeley: University of California Press, 2001.

Simon, Julia. "Music and the Performance of Community in Rousseau." *Musique et langage chez Rousseau*. Ed. Claude Dauphin. Oxford: Voltaire Foundation, 2004.

Sonnerat, Pierre. *Voyage aux Indes orientales et à la Chine: Fait par ordre du roi, depuis 1774 jusqu'en 1781*. Paris: Published by author, 1782.

Soulier-Valbert, F. "Ondes coloniales: Le Poste de Pontoise—Interview de Julien Maigret." *L'Antenne* May 10, 1931.

Stovall, Tyler Edward. *Paris Noir: African Americans in the City of Light*. Boston: Houghton Mifflin, 1996.

Sudre, René. *Le Huitième art: Mission de la radio*. Paris: René Julliard, 1945.

Thomas, Downing. *Music and the Origins of Language: Theories from the French Enlightenment*. Cambridge: Cambridge University Press, 1995.

Tirolien, Guy. *Balles d'or, poèmes*. Paris: Présence africaine, 1960.

Todorov, Tzvetan. *On Human Diversity: Nationalism, Racism, and Exoticism in French Thought*. Cambridge, MA: Harvard University Press, 1993.

Toumson, Roger. *La Transgression des couleurs: Littérature et langage des Antilles XVIIIè, XIXè, XXè siècles*. vol. 2. Paris: Éditions Caribéennes, 1989.

*Trésor de la Langue Française informatisé*, Paris: Centre national de la recherche scientifique, 2013.

Tudesq, André Jean, in collaboration with Serge Nédelec. *Journaux et radios en Afrique aux XIXe et XXe siècles*. Paris: Groupe de recherche et d'échanges technologiques, 1998.

Uri, Alex, and Françoise Uri. *Musiques & musiciens de la Guadeloupe: Le Chant de Karukéra*. Paris: Con brio, 1991.

Ventura, Michael. *Shadow Dancing in the U.S.A.* New York: Tarcher, 1985.

Verba, Cynthia. *Music and the French Enlightenment: Reconstruction of a Dialogue, 1750–1764*. Oxford: Clarendon Press, 1993.

Vercel, Roger. *L'Ile des revenants*. Paris: Editions Albin Michel, 1954.

Vergès, Françoise. *Monsters and Revolutionaries: Colonial Family Romance and Métissage*. Durham, NC: Duke University Press, 1999.

Weheliye, Alexander G. *Phonographies: Grooves in Sonic Afro-Modernity*. Durham, NC: Duke University Press, 2005.

Wilks, Jennifer. *Race, Gender, and Comparative Black Modernism: Suzanne Lacascade, Marita Bonner, Suzanne Césaire, Dorothy West*. Baton Rouge: Louisiana State University Press, 2008.

Young, Robert. *Colonial Desire: Hybridity in Theory, Culture, and Race*. New York: Routledge, 1995.

## Discography
### Artists

Alpha, Jenny. *Jenny Alpha et l'Orchestre Sylvio Siobud*. Paris: Pathé, 1953.

Baker, Josephine. *Centenary Tribute: Songs From 1930–1953*. London: Sepia Recordings, 2006.

———. *Fabulous Josephine Baker*. New York: RCA, 1995.

———. *J'ai deux amours*. New York: Arkadia Entertainment, 1997.

Barreto, Don. *Don Barreto et son Orchestre*. Paris: Pathé, 1946.

Boislaville, Loulou. "Biguine nous—Biguine" and "Grande robe et ti pantalon—Biguine." Loulou Boilavillet with Marie Freton et son orchestra "Concerto." Fort-de-France, Martinique: Madinina, 1957.

Castendet, Sam. "Les adieu d'une Créole." *Sam Castendet et son orchestre integral 1950: Festival Biguine*. Vincennes: Frémeaux & Associés, 1950.

Gabriel, Léona. "Solange—Biguine" and "Maman Corine—Biguine." Accompanied by Stellio et son Orchestre Créole. Paris: Polydor, 1934.

Grenet, Eliseo. "Lamento esclavo—Canto negro." *Sexteto Habañero 1926–1948*. England: Harlequin, 1996.

La Viny, Gérard. "Adieu foulards, adieiu madras." *Gérard la Viny, Les bélaisières et les Doudous de la Grande Terre, Fête Créole aux Antilles*. Paris: Arion, 1976.

Léardée, Ernest. *Orchestre E. Léardée du célèbre Bal Colonial de la rue Blomet*. Paris: Salabert, 1930.

Lirvat, Al. *Biguine Wabap*. Paris: Disques Déesse, 1970.

Orchestre du Groupe Folklorique Martinique. "Adieu foulards, adieu Madras." Fort-de-France, Martinique: RTF 1953.

Rico's Creole Band de la Coupole. *Rico's Creole Band*. Paris: Harlequin, 1934.

Salvador, Henri. "Adieu foulards, adieu madras." *Le Loup, la biche et le chevalier*. Vincennes, France: Frémeaux & Associés, 1946–1950.

Stellio, Alexandre. *L'Orchestre Stellio de l'Exposition Coloniale, Paris 1931*. Paris: Polydor, 1931.

———. *L'Orchestre du bal Antillais, sous la direction de M. Stellio*. Paris: Odéon, 1930.

## Compilations

*Au Bal Antillais: Franco-Creole Biguines from Martinique, Early Recordings of Caribbean Dance Music*. El Cerrito, CA: Arhoolie Records, 1992.

*Biguine*, vol 1: *Biguine, valse et mazurka créoles*. Vincennes: Fremeaux & Associés, 2003.

*Biguine*, vol. 2: *Biguine, valse et mazurka créoles*. Vincennes: Fremeaux & Associés, 2003.

*Biguine*, vol. 3: *Biguine, valse et mazurka créoles*. Vincennes: Fremeaux & Associés, 2005.

*Biguine à La Canne à Sucre: Intégrale antillaise musique monde 1946–1949*. Vincennes: Fremeaux & Associés, 1996.

## Filmography

*Biguine: La fabuleuse histoire d'une ville et de sa musique*. Dir. Guy Deslauriers. Screenplay by Patrick Chamoiseau. Perf. Nicole Dogué, Micheline Mona, Max Télèphe. Kréol Productions, France, 2004.

*Princesse Tam Tam*. Dir. Edmond T. Gréville. Perf. Josephine Baker, Albert Préjean, Robert Arnoux, Germaine Aussey, and Georges Péclet. Kino Video, France, 1935.

*Zouzou*. Dir. Marc Allégret. Perf. Josephine Baker, Jean Gabin, Yvette Lebon, Illa Meery, Pierre Larquey. Kino Video, France, 1934.

# Index

"Adieu 'Adieu Foulards'" (Tirolien), 47

"Adieu madras, adieu foulard," 17, 20–21, 24, 31, 133, 146; alienation in, 25; authenticity of, 24; authorship of, 44; composition of, 40–41; contexts for, variety of, 41; Corre's study of, 41–43; as cultural statement about origins, 45–46; Hearn's transcription of, 36–37, 39–40; improvisation and, 40–42; linguistic dimension of, 43; linking the Antilles to France, 22; melody of, 21–22; as movement toward France, 25; musicality of, 33; positioned at the border, 73; recordings of, 22; rejected by negritude in the major, 22; representation in, of desire, 46; Sahib's version of, 43; sentimentality of, 24; signaling arrival, 32; as sound sample, 42; soundtext of, 33; symbolizing themes in Fanon's work, 24; text of, 20–21; textual variants of, 22; voices in, 40

Africa, 87, 89, 103–4, 109–10, 115–16, 119, 145; women of, 86–88. See also African diaspora; Princesse Tam Tam

African diaspora, 78, 119, 124, 143–45; Brent Hayes Edwards on, 104–5, 144–45, 148

African rhythm, myth of, 98

African Rhythm African Sensibilities (Chernoff), 108

Afro-modernity, 139

Agawu, Kofi, 98, 99

alienation, 28, 107, 111, 115

Alloula, Malek, 33, 86

Althusser, Louis, 107, 110

Amiot, Jean Joseph Marie, 99–100

L'Amour fou (Breton), 142

Anderson, Benedict, 134

Annuaire de la Radiodiffusion Nationale (1935), 132

Anthologie de la nouvelle poésie nègre et malgache de langue française, 97

anthologies, power of, 97

anticonquest discourse, 4, 10

Antilles: in colonial travel texts, 4–11; expatriates and, 64–72, 106, 117, 147; and language, 148–49; race-mixing in, 37; and typewriter, 132–33; "whitening" of, 23; women of, 42, 49, 68–69. See also beguine; doudou; tragic mulatta; individual artists and poets, places, and songs

Antoine, Régis, 24

Apanon, Léon, 57

Appadurai, Arjun, 120–21

Armelin, Mademoiselle, 22

Arnoux, Robert, 80

assimilation, 149

Attuly, Finotte, 67

aural culture, timeliness of, 152

Aussey, Germaine, 78

Au Temps des colonies, 147

authenticity, 153

"Automatic Crystal" (Césaire). See "Le cristal automatique" (Césaire)

automaticity, 142

automatic writing, 140

Awakening Spaces (Berrian), 52

Baartmann, Sarah, 33

Baker, Josephine, 2, 14, 18; choreography of, 76, 96; compared with Frederick Douglass, 76; condemnation of, 74–75; double disqualification of, 75; as doudou, 77; fascination with, 71–72; as a first, 74–76; life stories of, real and imagined, 76; in Princesse Tam Tam, 77–96; recordings of, 147; sound corpus of, 77

Balles d'or (Tirolien), 47

Banguio, Maurice, 67

*Banjo* (McKay), 112

Baraka, Amiri, 141

Barreto, Emilio "Don," 120

Barrett, Lindon, 12, 14, 18, 112

beat, as part of black life, 146

Belisario, Isaac Mendes, 70

Benoit, Édouard, 49

Berrian, Brenda, 17, 50, 52, 53, 61, 62

biguine, 17–18; anxieties in, 53; becoming an institution, 66, 68–69; break and continuity in, 63; celebrating Saint-Pierre, 54–63; characterized as petit-nègre, 148; clubs, 120; criticism of, 50; doudouism of, 72; emergence of, as musical style, 57–59; excluded from black radical thought and imperial discourse, 72; gender dynamics in, 51; and hypersexualization of dances, 69; imperial consumption of, 67–69; language confusion in and over, 147; loss in, 51, 64; moving to Paris, 63, 66–68; musical influences on, 49–50; nostalgia in, 54, 64; origins of, 49; politics of mixing in, 51, 72; positioned at the border, 73; recordings of "Adieu," 22; rivaling official French discourse, 59; and satire, 58–59, 70; signifying on, by other genres, 68–69

*Biguine: La fabuleuse histoire d'une ville et de sa musique* (dir. Deslauriers), 54–63, 66, 123

birds, 8–9; sounds of, different meanings for, 13

black Antillean speech, French imperialism and, 26

black bodies: degrading labeling of, 114; sounding of, *raté* and, 28

"BLACK DADA NIHILISMUS" (Baraka), 141

*Black-Label* (Damas), 18, 98, 110–22, 152

blackness: consumerization of, 112, 113; doubleness of, 146; linked to sound and fungibility, 26–27; 71–72

*Blackness and Value: Seeing Double* (Barrett), 14

black performance: in France, 1–2; linguistic and musical, discursive resonance in, 147

black poetry, in France, 2

black scream, 15, 105; rallying cry for the coming revolution, 47. See also *le cri nègre*

*Black Skin, White Masks* (Fanon), 17, 23–24, 28–29, 30, 98, 105–10, 122, 124, 136, 140–41, 143

black sound, 14–15

black subject: and Damas, 109–22; and Fanon, 106–9; as hysteric, 29

black subjectivity, rhythm of, 106

black transnationalism, 105

black/white desire, problem of, 147

*Blue Lotus, The* (Hergé), 130, 131

Boislaville, Loulou, 50

Bost, Suzanne, 34

Bouche, Pierre Bertrand, 103, 104

Bouillé, Marquis de, 17

Brassaï, 68, 117

Breton, André, 140, 142

Brierre, Jean, 113

Brunnquell, Frédéric, 125, 126, 128, 129

Cabane Cubaine, 67, 116–17

*Ça! C'est la Martinique!* (Gabriel-Soïme), 51–56, 59, 61, 67–68

*Cahier d'un retour au pays natal*, 72, 109, 122, 137–38

Capécia, Mayotte, 23

carnival songs, 55, 59

*casinos*, 58, 71

Castendet, Sam, 22, 57, 67

Césaire, Aimé, 15, 18, 19, 28, 62, 72, 109, 112, 113, 115, 121–24, 133, 136–37; denouncing French imperialism as fascism, 137; poetic apparatus of, in "Automatic Crystal," 142–45; representations of technology in works of, 124; on return, 137

Césaire, Susanne, 150

Chamoiseau, Patrick, 55

*chanson coloniale*, 44, 66, 68–69, 147

*chanson de cocotte* tradition, 17

Chanvalon, Jean Baptiste Thibault de, 3, 7

Charlery, Robert, 66, 67

Châteaubriand, René de, 7, 13

Cheng, Anne, 26

Chernoff, Christopher, 108

China, musical culture of, 100

*Claire-Solange, âme africaine* (Lacascade), 104, 110

Claisse, Robert, 66

clarinet, 57, 70

*cocottes*, 36

Collat, Victor, 66

Colonial Exposition (Exposition colonial internationale; Paris 1931), 19, 52, 65–67, 69, 124, 129; blending technological showcase and national spectacle, 128; rhetorical and performative dynamics of, 127

colonial music, 69

colonial service, planting seeds for, 130

colonial subjects, formation of, 11, 29

colonization: materialism of, condemned, 7; subjects of, requiring paperwork, 133 color, women of. *See* women of color

Comedian Harmonists, 87

commodification, 27

comparative musicology, 100

conversion disorder, 29

Coppet, Honoré, 57

Corre, Armand, 41–42

Coursat, Georges, 68

Cowans, Jon, 136

Créol's Band, 67

Creole: language, 43, 149; women, as teller of secrets, 10

*le cri nègre*, 18, 29, 47, 105; demanding hearing for history's counter-testimonies, 138; as ephemeromateriality, 138–39; as poetic listening tactic, 138; refiguring idea of writing, 140. *See also* black scream

"Le cristal automatique" (Césaire), 19, 139–45

Croisière noire, 130

Cullen, Countee, 97–98

cymbals, Western production of, 101

d'Alembert, Jean Le Rond, 102

Dallin, Jacques, 119

Damas, Léon-Gontran, 18, 30, 48–49, 98, 109–22, 133, 152

dance, 2, 9, 41–42, 48–49, 69–70, 119–21. *See also* beguine; Baker, Josephine

Dash, Michael, 2

*décalage*, 77, 110, 128, 143–45

Décoret-Ahiha, Anne, 66, 68, 117

*Défense, La*, 59

Delmont, Alcide, 129

Delouche, Eugène, 57, 67

"Le Départ du Jean Bart" (Sahib), 43–44, 155–56n14

Derrida, Jacques, 18

*Description topographique . . . de l'isle Saint-Domingue* (Moreau), 36

*désirs comprimés*, 113, 122

Deslauriers, Guy, 54, 55

Dhordain, Roland, 135–36

diction, 30–31

Diderot, Denis, 102

*Discourse on Colonialism* (Césaire), 28, 133, 137, 143

Dogué, Nicole, 55

Don Barreto et Son Orchestre Cubain, 120

*doudou*, 16–17, 20–21; as anti/colonialist speech act, 150; associated with Antillean *da* (nurse-maid), 33; as Bounty, 150; Creole meaning of, 32; demands of, 151; dilemma of, 77, 93; double rejection of, 23; embodying France's New World Colonies, 22–23; flirting with African and European boundaries, 42; French meaning of, 32–33; genealogical erasure of, in Antillean cultural history, 150; Hearn's study of, 36–39; Josephine Baker and mythology of, 18, 71–72; maternity of, 33; mythology of, roots of, 37; negritude's critique of, 151; performing narrative of manifest destiny, 95; presenting possibility of interracial love, 24, 33–34; representing relations in colonial family dream, 33; self-representation of, 151–52; significance of term, 22; situation of, 44–45; song of, absent in postcolonial criticism, 151; structural situation of, echoed in *Princesse Tam Tam*, 80; value of, 96

doudouism, 17, 20, 22–23, 50–51, 70, 72; horizontal relations of, in the Caribbean, 151; mythology of, 146; poetics of, 49

*doudouiste*, 22

Douglas, Louis, 2

Douglass, Frederick, 76

drum, 56–57, 61, 106, 116–18; catachrestic nature of, 121; membranophone (skin), 99, 103–4. See also *Princesse Tam Tam*; *tam-tam*; tom-tom

Dubouillé, Gisèle, 148

Du Tertre, Jean Baptiste, 2–3, 4–7; on birdsong, 9; pity of, for blacks, 10

ear, fetishization of, 26

*L'Echo du siècle, Dictionnaire historique de la radio et de la télévision en France* (Jeanneney), 130

Edison, Thomas, 126

Edwards, Brent Hayes, 18, 97, 104–5, 143–45, 148

Eiffel, Gustave, 127–28

Eiffel Tower, 127–28

electronic revolution, imperialist advances of, 13–14

Ellul, Jacques, 125

embodiment, subjective, 106

*Encyclopédie ou dictionnaire raisonné des sciences, des arts et des métiers* (Diderot and d'Alembert), 102

"En exil" (P. Nardal), 51, 64–65, 69

Enlightenment, legacy of, 136

epidermalization, 106, 107

eretheism, 26

ethnographies, 2–3; fetishism of, 38

ethnomusicology, 100

"Etude sur la biguine créole" (A. Nardal), 51, 69

"L'Eveil de la conscience de race chez les étudiants noirs" (P. Nardal), 65–66

Exposition Internationale Coloniale. *See* Colonial Exposition

Fanon, Frantz, 17, 20, 23, 98, 105–9, 115, 122, 124, 129, 136, 140–43, 149; on "Adieu," 23–32; analytical stance of, 45; critiquing the *doudou*, 22; disavowing Gabriel's description of gay culture, 54; hybrid writing voice of, 25; intertextual dialogs in, 30; pointing toward doubleness of blackness, 146; on *ratés*, 79 (see also *ratés*); themes of, 24

la Fédération nationale de la radiodiffusion coloniale, 124

Fétis, François-Joseph, 100

film, 117, 119, 125; black invisibility in, 148; French colonial, African inspiration for, 80, 81–82; sound in, 69. *See also individual artists and films*

Flavia-Léopold, Emmanuel, 23, 47

Fludd, Robert, 13

forests: force of, 7–8; secret horrors of, 7

fragmentation, 83

France: "Adieu" as movement toward, 25; authoritative voices for, 134–35; black Atlantic performance in, 1–2; exotic entertainment in, 62, 64, 66–67, 69, 78; imperialism of, and shortwave radio, 19 (*see also* le Poste Colonial); language as material essence of, 135, 136; Occupation in, 136

*La frégate l'Incomprise: Voyage autour du monde à la plume* (Sahib), 43

French-Antillean imperial relations, "Adieu" and, 21

French imperial power: familial feeing for, 133; radio technology representing, 125–26; relying on technology, 128–29

French language: Antilleans practicing, 30, 149; colonial subject's relationship with, 30–31; conservation vs. vitality of, 135; proper, valued for band leaders, 61–62

French national cinema, black invisibility in, 147–48

*French-Set Girls* (Belisario), 70

*Fréquence monde: Du Poste colonial à RFI* (Brunnquell), 125, 126

Gabriel (Gabriel-Soïme), Leona, 21, 22, 51–55, 59, 61, 67–68, 72, 123, 145, 150

Garraway, Doris, 37

gender, imperial dynamics of, 69

Gilroy, Paul, 138

Girardeau, Emile, 134

Gitelman, Lisa, 132–33

Glissant, Edouard, 63

global relations, new discursive era of, 124

Glover, Kaiama, 75

Goddard, Chris, 74

Goehr, Walter, 119

Gossec, François-Joseph, 100

Goursat, Georges Marie (Sem), 148–49

Gramsci, Antonio, 77

Gratiant, Gilbert, 52

Grenet, Eliseo, 119

Guadeloupe, mapped with sound, 5–6

Guillen, Nicolas, 119

Hall, Adelaide, 74

*Harlem in Montmartre* (Shack), 74

Harlem Renaissance, discourse of, 97

Hartman, Saidiya, 27

healing, culture and, 151

hearing double, 14

Hearn, Lafcadio, 3, 7–9, 17, 24, 52; anticipating islands' soundscapes, 10; describing speech and musical cultures, 10–11; interested in Creole cultures and populations, 11; on Labat, 9–10; on Saint-Pierre, 37; study of *doudou*, 36–39; transcribing "Adieu," 36–37, 39–40; transnational trajectory of, 37

Hexagon, the (France), 66, 80, 128, 134

*Histoire générale des Antilles habitées par les François* (Du Tertre), 4–5

History, movement of, 89

"Hoquet" (Damas), 30, 109–10

Hughes, Langston, 97–98

*Le Huitième art: Mission de la radio* (Sudre), 134

human sound, imperial history and, 10

Hurston, Zora Neale, 133

hybridity, transformed into essentialism, 151

hypercorrection, 31

*Idylles, ou essais de poésie créole* (anon.), 34–35, 36

*Imperial Eyes: Travel Writing and Transculturation* (Pratt), 3–4

imperial gaze, limitations of, 6

imperialism, 13; technologies of, creating new men and women, 134 imperial mapping project: birdsong's function in, 9; margins of, 8; violence of, 14

imperial pleasure industry, 69

l'Institut colonial français, 124, 129

"J'ai deux amours," 88

jazz, 49–51, 61, 66, 68–69, 74. *See also individual artists*

Jeanneney, Jean-Noël, 130

Jefferson, Margo, 76

Jenson, Deborah, 34–35

Johnson, Sara, 63, 70

Joyau, Auguste, 52

Kamuf, Peggy, 82

Kelman, Ari, 12, 14

Kesteloot, Lilyan, 23

Kindou, Alexandre, 57, 149

Labat, Jean-Baptiste, 3, 9–11

Lacascade, Suzanne, 23, 104, 110

Lahille, Abel, 104

"Lamento Esclavo," 118–20

language: authentic, as performative speech act, 138; as material essence of France, 135. *See also* Creole language; French language

Laporte, Marcel, 134

Laviny, Gérard, 72

Léardée, Ernest, 57, 63, 66, 67, 68, 133

*Légitime Défense* (Ménil et al.), 23

Léro, Etienne, 22

Lévy-Bruhl, Lucien, 70

la Ligue maritime et colonial, 124

Lirvat, Al, 49–50

"Lisette quitte la plaine," 35–36

listening, new techniques of, 137–38

Lock, Alain, 70

Lucumi, 119

Lungla, Nelly, 21, 150

Macey, David, 45

Mademoiselle Estrella. *See* Gabriel, Leona

Maigret, Julien, 126, 128, 129

Maran, René, 133

*Marche funèbre* (Gossec), 100

"Marie-Clémence," 59–61

Markmann, Charles Lam, 155n8

Martin, Lola, 150

Martinique, 7

Mavounzy, Marcel Susan, 149

McClary, Susan, 155n6

McKay, Claude, 58, 112

*Mémoires concernant l'histoire . . . des Chinois par les missionnaires de Pékin*, 99–100

*Les Mémoires de Radiolo* (Laporte), 134

Ménil, René, 22

Mernissi, Fatima, 33

*Mes Impressions sur L'Afrique Occidentale Française: Etude documentaire au pays du Tam-tam* (Lahille), 104

*métissage*, aesthetic of, 73

*métisse* figure, 23, 34, 37

Middle Passage, 113

Mirabeau, Honoré Gabriel Comte de, 100

*Mirages de Paris* (Soce), 117

misery, aesthetics of, 122

modernity: poetics of, 142; sonic profile of, 13–14

modern world: encroaching on sonic environment, 12–13; sounds of, 13

Mona, Micheline, 55, 58–59, 62

Montaner, Rita, 120

Morand, Paul, 70–71

Moreau de Saint-Méry, Médéric Louis Elie, 3, 36–38, 69

Moten, Frederick, 14, 18, 141

*Motivos del son* (Guillen), 119

mountains, immeasurability of, indicated by sound, 5

Mount Pelée, eruption of, 37, 62–63

Mowitt, John, 18, 98, 104, 106, 107, 110, 116, 121, 122, 143

mulatta, tragic. *See* tragic mulatta

*Mulattas and Mestizas: Representing Mixed Identities in the Americas 1850–2000* (Bost), 34

musical difference, 100

musical instruments, signaling cultural positions, 57

musicality, black vs. textual, 85

*Nadja* (Breton), 142

Nardal, Andrée, 49, 51, 68–70, 72–73, 133, 147, 150

Nardal, Jane, 49, 51, 69–73, 75, 133, 147, 150

Nardal, Paulette, 49, 51, 64–66, 69, 72–73, 133, 147, 150

negritude: discourse of, Fanon's critique of, 108; dominant beat of, 122; dynamics of, 150; enthusiasm, of, 105–6; as genre of *tam-tam*, 142; minor genealogy of, 152; poetics of, 52, 97–98; and women, 73

negritude in the major, 16, 22, 49, 72

negritude in the minor, 16, 23, 49, 122

"New Black Soul" (Brierre), 113

*New Negro, The* (Lock), 70

New World: landscapes of, gendered depiction of, 10; regenerative power of, 8; soundscapes in, 4; space and value in, qualification of, 6; as testament to ancient world, 9

*Nos Créoles* (Corre), 41–43

*Notebook of the Return to My Native Land* (Césaire). See *Cahier d'un retour au pays natal* (Césaire)

*Notes historiques* (Moreau), 36

"Nuit Blanche" (Damas), 48

Orchestre de la Boule Blanche, 22

Orphélien, Crémas, 66, 67

other/ness, 3; female, 33; French imperial hierarchy of, 81; percussion of, 98

"Pantins exotiques" (J. Nardal), 51, 70–71

parapsychology, radio waves and, 135

Paris: Jazz Age in, 51; musical scene in, 66–68

Paris-Mondial, 127

Paris Ondes Courtes, 127

Paris-P.T.T., 135

patina, 121

*Peau noire, masques blancs* (Fanon). See *Black Skin, White Masks* (Fanon)

percussive field, 98

Perse, Saint-John, 81

*Le Petit Larousse illustré*, 32–33

petit-nègre, 147, 148

Philcox, Richard, 106

phonograph, anxiety about, 132

*Pigments*, 116

*Pigments-Névralages* (Damas), 48, 112, 116

plantation cultures, domestic and cultural relations on, 36

poetics, 13, 16, 22, 34–35, 63, 97–99; and landscape, 52; and Jean-Paul Sartre, 97; regionalist, 49; of relation, 63, and time, 143

poetry, 13, 15–16, 109. *See also* negritude; *individual poets and works*

postcards, medium of, 86

le Poste Colonial, 19, 123; amplifying male voices, 145; beginnings of, 124–25, 128; as colonial outpost, 127; exploring boundaries of difference, 129–30; historic place of, in French colonial mission, 126; imperialism of, 129; introducing the voice of France, 128; justifying the existence of, 134; as site of dissonance, 136; vision of, for extending the imperial voice, 129

postmodernity: dynamics of, radio preceding, 132; soundscapes of, 12

Pound, Ezra, 13

*Practice of Diaspora, The* (Edwards), 104–5

Pratt, Mary Louise, 3–4, 5, 10, 15

Préjean, Albert, 78

*Princesse Tam Tam* (dir. Gréville), 18, 77, 119; disorder depicted in, 90; musical transformations in, 83–84; narrative loop in, 92–94; plot of, 78–96; soundscape of, 79, 85, 87, 91; soundtrack of, 78, 80, 83, 86–88; textuality in, 95

queer culture, 54

race, 17, 23–25, 27–29, 45, 65, 108–9, 113, 105; theories on, 38. See also *doudou*; negritude; women of color

*Race, Gender, and Comparative Black Modernism* (Williams), 23

race-mixing, 33–34, 37

race stories, 82

radio: domestic/imperial split of, 130; joy of, for imperial subjects, 133–34; offering countertestimony to dominant histories, 137; personality, 134; power of, 132, 135; presenting colonial and anticolonial discourse, 126–27; as relay point for negritude critiques, 124; scripting imperial relations, 130; speaking on, learning about, 134; speed of, 132; testifying to Europe's moral defeat, 136; transistor, in the Algerian revolution, 124. See also *speaker/ine*; *individual radio stations*

Radio France Internationale, 127

Radiola, 134

Radiolo. *See* Laporte, Marcel

Radio Martinique, 52

Radio Paris, 134

Rameau, Jean-Philippe, 100

*raté*, 14–15, 28–30, 114; announcing failure of culture, 30; in *Princesse Tam Tam*, 79

"Rêves," 86, 88

*La Revue du monde noir*, 148–49

*La Revue musicale*, 100

*Revue nègre*, 1–2

Rezard-Devouves, Jean, 66

Rico's Creole Band, 120

Rivel, Moune de, 150

Rock, Robert, 67

*Le Roman de la radio: De la T.S.F. aux radios libres* (Dhordain), 135–36

Romans, Alain, 119

Rose, Phyllis, 85

Rosemain, Jacqueline, 69–70

Rosette, Jules, 81

rue Blomet, 66, 67, 71

Ruscio, Alain, 44

Sahib, 43–44

Saint-Hilaire, Archange, 66

Saint-Pierre (Martinique), 37, 54–63

Salavina, 52

Salvador, Henri, 22

*sans-filistes* (wireless radio enthusiasts), 134

Sartre, Jean-Paul, 15, 97, 142–43

Schafer, Murray, 10, 12–14

Scharfman, Ronnie Leah, 140

schizophonia, 14

seeing-man, 3–4, 5

Segond-Weber (Madame), 135–36

Sem. *See* Goursat, Georges Marie

Senghor, Léopold Sédar, 108

Services de propagande de la résidence générale, 80

*Seven Years in West Africa* (Bouche), 103

Shack, William, 74

Shohat, Ella, 95

silence, 7–8

skin, 25, 47, 58; porous nature of, 26. See also *Black Skin, White Masks*; drum; race; race-mixing

skin game, 58, 86, 112

slave, fungibility of, 27

Smith, Bessie, 74

Socé, Ousmane, 117

Société Française de Radiophonie (SFR), 134

Sonnerat, Pierre, 101–2

soundposts, 123

sounds: extinction of, 12–13; loss of, 15; marginalization of, 3; pleasure from, purity of, 7. *See also* soundscapes

*Soundscape, The: Our Sonic Environment and the Tuning of the World* (Schafer), 12–13

soundscapes, 12; challenging botany's classifications, 9; colonizing of, 152; composition of, 14; demise of, linked to modern machines, 14; friction of, 11–12; imperialism and, 7, 13, 124, 155; in the New World, 4; marking borders, 7; as site of cultural re-membership, 150–51

sound technology, affecting community formation, 123–24

soundtext, 11

"Sous le ciel de l'Afrique," 86–88

*speaker/ine* (radio personality), 66, 67, 123, 134

Spengler, Oswald, 13

Stam, Robert, 95

Stellio, Alexandre, 57, 57, 66, 67, 133, 148

Sudre, René, 134–35

surrealism, 139–40

sympathetic vibration, 106–7

taboo love, 68

*tam-tam*, 18, 103; as anti/colonialist speech act, 150; as black label, in French imperial discourse, 98; definitions of, 99, 101–4; fetishization of, 103–4; historic trajectory of, 98–99; imperial rhythm of, 99; in Indian culture, 101–2; musical value ascribed to, 100–104; as mythological soundposts, 105; mythology of, 150; natural historians' take on, 102–3; negritude as genre of, 142; power of, 99; representing music of the other, 116

Télèphe, Max, 55, 58–59

Thaly, Daniel, 23

thingification, 28, 143

Tintin, 130–32

Tirolien, Guy, 47

tom-tom: definition of, 99; in Harlem Renaissance discourse, 97–98

*le ton speake* (radio voice, radio diction), 145

tourism, biguine as aspect of, 68

tragic mulatta, 17, 23, 26, 33–34, 39, 41, 42, 61, 70, 156n15. See also *beguine*; *individual songs*

translation, significance of, 148–49

travel narratives, 2–3, 103; *doudou* stereotype in, 53; naturalizing imperial expansion, 4–5; providing information for capitalist investment, 5; role in, of island speech and musical practices, 10; sound in, 4

*Trésor de la Langue Française informatisé*, 1

"Trêve" (Damas), 48–49

Tricentennial Celebration (1935), 22

*tumulte noir*, 1–2, 150

*Two Years in the French Indies* (Hearn), 36–37

typewriter, anxieties about, 132

*Ultruisque Cosmi Historia* (Fludd), 13

Universal Exposition (Paris 1889), 127–28

Valvert, Felix, 67

Vergès, Françoise, 33

*Voyage aux Indes orientales et à la Chine* (Sonnerat), 101

Waters, Ethel, 74

Weheliye, Alexander, 123, 138

wilderness, 7–8

Wilks, Jennifer, 23

women of color: Creole as spoken by, 43; experience during Paris's interwar years, 73; in French imperial discourse, 33, 34

world music, 69

World Soundscape Project, 12

*Wretched of the Earth, The* (Fanon), 129

writing, documenting colonial subjects with, 133

*Y a bon Banania*, 25, 26, 27, 98, 147

Zelier, Bernard, 66